FOR Dummies

BESTSELLING
BOOK SERIES

Gifts from the Kitch[en]
For Dummies®

W9-DCV-764

Food Gifts That Like to Hang Out Together

Like pastrami on rye or apple pie with a slice of cheese, some foods just naturally go together. Use this list of soul mates as your guide to some great combinations — and check "Recipes at a Glance" for the page numbers.

- Jumbo Pretzels / Tangy Apricot Mustard
- Cornmeal Toasting Bread / Rhubarb Fig Conserve
- Pineapple Ginger Scones / Flavored Sugar / Strawberry Pineapple Jam
- Bloody Mary Mix / Curried Cashews / Marinated Olives
- Savory Walnut Pepper Digestives / Smoked Salmon Spread
- Waffle Mix / Blueberry Orange Waffle Topper / Nut Butter
- Cream Cheese Brown Sugar Pound Cake / Pear Cranberry Compote
- Buttermilk Streusel Coffee Cake / Hot Chocolate Mix
- Basic Brownies/ Hot Chocolate Sauce (supply your own ice cream)
- Mulled Cider Mix / Bountiful Fruitcake
- Oat and Ale Bread / Red Pepper Hummus
- Pâté 101 / Sweet Onion Marmalade
- U.S. Senate Bean Soup Mix / Chili Cheddar Muffin Loaf
- *Party six-pack*: Curried Cashews / South of Somewhere Salsa / Baked Cheese Balls/ Layered Goat Cheese Mold / Marinated Olives / BBQ Almonds

Larder List for Last-Minute Gifts

You can make many food gifts from on-hand ingredients if you keep the pantry stocked with the following items (in addition to staples like sugar, flour, butter, and eggs):

- Cheeses — Parmesan, cheddar
- Nuts — walnuts, pecans, and almonds are most useful
- Instant espresso coffee
- Raisins and other dried fruits, including dried pineapple
- Candied ginger
- Balsamic vinegar

- Light corn syrup
- Sugar cubes
- Cream of tartar
- Cornmeal
- Gelatin
- Cornstarch

For many more details on a well-stocked pantry, see Chapter 2.

Gifts from the Kitchen For Dummies®

Three Reminders about Gift-giving Etiquette

- **The recipient of your food gift is not obliged to serve it immediately.** Your splendid creation may not fit the menu or the moment, but that does not make it any less thoughtful.

- **When taking food to a large gathering, put a gift tag on your contribution.** A thoughtful host will want to know who brought what.

- **If you don't know the food preferences or food allergies of a gift recipient, you may want to include the ingredients on the label.** See Chapter 13 for some label ideas.

365 Good Reasons to Make a Gift from Your Kitchen

Every day is a good day to make a food gift for *someone*. But if you're having trouble getting started, here are some special dates around the year:

- **Chinese New Year (sometime between January 21 and February 19):** Fortune Cookies (Chapter 7)

- **Groundhog Day (February 2):** Baked Olive-Stuffed Cheese Balls (Chapter 12)

- **Valentine's Day (February 14):** White Chocolate Coeur a la Crème with Fresh Strawberry Sauce (Chapter 5)

- **National Pets Day (February 20):** Dog/Cat Cookies (Chapter 7)

- **Mother's Day (the second Sunday in May):** English Ginger Scones (Chapter 11) and Orange Rhubarb Jam (Chapter 9)

- **Flag Day (June 14):** U.S. Senate Bean Soup Mix (Chapter 13)

- **National Pickle Day (July 5):** Hot Diggity Dog Relish (Chapter 9)

- **Leif Ericson Day (October 9):** Smoked Salmon Spread (Chapter 12)

- **Columbus Day (October 12):** Cannoli Orange Pie (Chapter 10)

- **Kwanzaa (December 26 through January 1):** Benne Sesame Candy (Chapter 6)

For Dummies: Bestselling Book Series for Beginners

Gifts from the Kitchen

FOR

DUMMIES®

Gifts from the Kitchen

FOR

DUMMIES®

by Andrea B. Swenson

Wiley Publishing, Inc.

Gifts from the Kitchen For Dummies®

Published by
Wiley Publishing, Inc.
909 Third Avenue
New York, NY 10022
www.wiley.com

Copyright © 2002 by Wiley Publishing, Inc., Indianapolis, Indiana

Published by Wiley Publishing, Inc., Indianapolis, Indiana

Published simultaneously in Canada

For general information on our other products and services or to obtain technical support, please contact our Customer Care Department within the U.S. at 800-762-2974, outside the U.S. at 317-572-3993, or fax 317-572-4002.

Wiley also publishes its books in a variety of electronic formats. Some content that appears in print may not be available in electronic books.

Library of Congress Cataloging-in-Publication Data:

Library of Congress Control Number: 2002110294

ISBN: 0-7645-5452-2

Manufactured in the United States of America

10 9 8 7 6 5 4 3 2 1

1B/QZ/QZ/QS/IN

Wiley Publishing, Inc. is a trademark of Wiley Publishing, Inc.

About the Author

Andrea B. Swenson has been a food stylist, recipe developer, and consultant in New York City for 24 years. Her work has lured you to buy Wendy's hamburgers, snatch Aunt Jemima Pancake mix off the shelf, and rip open a bag of Pepperidge Farm cookies. She has cooked and arranged every imaginable food for most of the major food companies and such magazines as *Food and Wine, McCall's, Woman's Day, Newsweek, Prevention, Playboy, Chocolatier,* and *Bon Appetit.* She has been a guest lecturer at The New School for Social Research. Andrea enjoyed nationwide acclaim when a feature article about her appeared in *Life* magazine and when she was headlined in a special segment on *Good Morning America.*

Andrea Swenson and Java.

Dedication

To Farmor. Tack så mycket.

Author's Acknowledgments

Less than halfway through this book, I knew that I couldn't wait to write this page. If it takes a village to raise a child, it takes a family and friends to write a book. So here is my "gift" to everyone who was part this endeavor.

To Grace Freedson, my agent, for your total confidence.

To the dedicated and crackerjack staff at the Dummies group, from Erin Connell who launched me; to Pamela Mourouzis, Tina Sims, Christine Beck, Elizabeth Kuball, Emily Nolan, the recipe tester; to the marketing and publicity departments; and especially to Norm Crampton, for his delicious humor and sense of style.

To the talented photography team: David Bishop, photographer; Brett Kurzweil, food stylist; and Randi Barritt, prop stylist.

To all the food boards and councils that tirelessly answered my questions. And to Gert Trani, the wonderful head librarian at the CIA (Culinary Institute of America!).

To Elizabeth Fassberg and Karen Hatt for sharing all their food knowledge.

To all my friends who generously offered me their kitchens when mine was under construction. And especially to Barbara Thanhauser who could not find enough ways to help me.

To Elsie and Seymour, my in-laws, for their infectious cheerfulness and for introducing me to mandelbrot.

To Daddy for your loving words and support from afar (it did work out after all!).

To Tom, who "crafted" kind words.

To Rob and George, my ever-willing tasters.

To Lori, who helped keep my "mental hygiene."

To Rhona, who showed me how to "speak the speech."

But most of all, to Jeff, my husband, who questioned, tasted, challenged, provoked, listened, proofed, comforted, washed, dried, encouraged, schlepped . . . and prevented me from being twee.

Thank you one and all.

Publisher's Acknowledgments

We're proud of this book; please send us your comments through our Dummies online registration form located at www.dummies.com/register/.

Some of the people who helped bring this book to market include the following:

Acquisitions, Editorial, and Media Development

Project Editor: Norm Crampton

Acquisitions Editor: Pam Mourouzis

Senior Copy Editor: Tina Sims

Technical Editor: Lori Fox

Recipe Tester: Emily Nolan

Illustrator: Elizabeth Kurtzman

Photographer: David Bishop

Food Stylist: Brett Kurzweil

Prop Stylist: Randi Barritt

Photography Art Director: Michele Laseau

Editorial Manager: Christine Beck

Editorial Assistant: Melissa Bennett

Cover Photos: David Bishop

Author Photo: Jeffrey A. Silverbush

Production

Project Coordinator: Maridee Ennis

Layout and Graphics: Joyce Haughey, Barry Offringa, Brent Savage, Jacque Schneider, Julie Trippetti, Jeremey Unger, Erin Zeltner

Proofreaders: Andy Hollandbeck, Susan Moritz, Angel Perez, Carl W. Pierce, Linda Quigley, Charles Spencer, TECHBOOKS Production Services

Indexer: TECHBOOKS Production Services

Publishing and Editorial for Consumer Dummies

Diane Graves Steele, Vice President and Publisher, Consumer Dummies

Joyce Pepple, Acquisitions Director, Consumer Dummies

Kristin A. Cocks, Product Development Director, Consumer Dummies

Michael Spring, Vice President and Publisher, Travel

Brice Gosnell, Publishing Director, Travel

Suzanne Jannetta, Editorial Director, Travel

Publishing for Technology Dummies

Andy Cummings, Vice President and Publisher, Dummies Technology/General User

Composition Services

Gerry Fahey, Executive Director of Production Services

Debbie Stailey, Director of Composition Services

Contents at a Glance

Recipes at a Glance

Table of Contents

· ·

Introduction

●●

*N*ine catalogs (at least nine) came to your doorstep today. Forty-one TV commercials urged you to buy everything from an overcooked meat product to the mechanical miracle of your dreams. And yes, "You have mail!" — most of it electronic litter. The 21st century has perfected the message of *getting*. So maybe it's time to remember a much older and nobler impulse, *giving*. *Gifts from the Kitchen For Dummies* is written in that spirit. It's about giving a little of yourself to others.

Perhaps cooking is such an alien notion that you think a gift from the kitchen is a coupon to a fast food chain. If so, this book can start you off with a few easy recipes. On the other hand, if you make your famous, time-consuming, caramel-dipped Croquembouche only at Christmas, then this book can offer scrumptious, quick recipes for gifts at any time of year. And for everyone, the book contains suggestions on how to creatively package food gifts — to make them intriguing and enticing.

So read on and discover how easy it is to make someone else feel special at any time of the year. They'll think you're pretty special, too!

How to Use This Book

The holidays (capital H) were over before you had the last roasting pan cleaned. You really wanted to give homemade food gifts this year, but you never found the time. Take heart: Flip through this book, and you'll find that there are more "holidays" than you ever dreamed of — all good reasons to give food gifts. You find recipes — some easy, some more involved — for candies, chocolate, condiments, mixes, sauces, cakes, and lots of other treats. I even tell you how to coordinate delectable food gifts with imaginative holidays.

Each chapter focuses on a different kind of food gift and gives you everything you need to get through the recipes. You can delve into the chapters and pull away exactly what you want, like plucking some morsels of Cranberry-Walnut Monkey Bread in Chapter 11. Some of you may need good, basic guidance to get started, and others may be able to hopscotch around the recipes right away. No matter what your cooking level, each chapter has a tasty tidbit for you.

How This Book is Organized

This book is divided into six parts. You can scan the parts in this section for a look at what each section has in store. If you're just looking for recipes to whet your appetite, check out "Recipes at a Glance," in the front of the book.

Part 1: Getting Started: The Why, What, When, and How

This part begins with sort of a pep rally. If you need reasons for giving, I provide them here; and if you already like doing nice things for other people, you'll appreciate knowing about the giving opportunities of the lesser-known holidays. Chapter 1 also includes a list of ingredients to keep on hand for last-minute gifts. And if you're feeling particularly ambitious, there's even a list of recipes that like to be given together.

Part I also helps you to stock the pantry and outfit the kitchen, in Chapters 2 and 3, respectively. The basic cooking techniques I provide in Chapter 4 are optional if you're an experienced cook but reassuring if you're not. You can find a number of technique tips plus kitchen safety information in this chapter, too.

Part II: Magnificent Mouthfuls

What better recipes to start with than chocolate? Chapter 5 contains selections for lovers of dark chocolate, milk chocolate, and white chocolate, shaped into candy, cakes, and sauces. Moving on to more sweets (yum), Chapter 6 has candies in all forms and flavors. You can whip up Easy Alabaster Mints, Piña Colada Candies, and even "Sushi" (not the fishy kind). Chapter 7 discusses how to roll out cookies and beat egg whites, but mostly it's chock-full of recipes like Lemon-Cardamom Shortbread and Eggnog Cookies, and tempting morsels like Savory Walnut-Pepper Digestives. Even Fido gets a cookie in this chapter.

Part III: Over the Top: Flavorful Sauces and Spreads

You can make a good dish even better with all the tempting toppers in this part. Chapter 8 has sauces like Chimicurri Steak Sauce and Happy Hubby Steak Sauce — great over poultry or meat. The Flavored Butters open up intriguing taste possibilities with your choice of herbs or spices. Chapter 9 is a great place to find gifts for every palate. Brimming with information about organic vegetables and selecting oils and vinegars, it has a condiment for every occasion. Recipes range from Grainy Apricot Mustard to Rhubarb-Fig Conserve to Sweet Onion Marmalade.

Part IV: Into the Mixing Bowl

Simple rich cakes and pies are the stars of Chapter 10. A dense, nutty Pecan-Cream Cheese Pound Cake resides there. An old friend, Bountiful Fruitcake, gets a makeover with an Edible Almond Paste "Wrapping Paper." I also provide tips for testing a cake for doneness and techniques for making a flaky pie crust. All the satisfaction that comes from baking breads is captured in Chapter 11, including quick breads like Banana-Blueberry or savory Prosciutto-Fig. Follow the steps to prepare a proper cup of tea to go with the Pineapple-Ginger Scones. If you've never attempted a yeast bread before, Chapter 11 can guide you through the steps to producing an Oat and Ale Bread or Jumbo Pretzels.

The party begins in Chapter 12. Spread the fun around with Red Pepper Hummus or Pâté 101. And don't forget the Curried Cashews and Marinated Olives. Chapter 13 contains timesaving mixes for interesting things like Thai Bean Soup, Rise-and-Shine Waffles, and Mulled Cider.

Part V: Tying Up Loose Ends: Wrapping, Packaging, and Mailing

Chapter 14 helps you to package your food gift — in a nature-made container, in a homemade wrapping like a Chocolate Nest, or in a unique find from a flea market. Leave the kitchen behind in Chapter 15 as you organize delivering your food gift, whether that means over the river and through the woods or across the ocean.

Part VI: The Part of Tens

All families have traditions, and the Part of Tens is a tradition in the Dummies family. *Gifts from the Kitchen For Dummies* is no exception. This section contains ideas for gift baskets to carry through a theme with your food present, as well as numerous references to help you find recipe ingredients, cooking equipment, and wrapping/packaging resources. It's all there in quick reference form.

Icons and Symbols Used in This Book

Icons are the attention getters in the left-hand margin of many pages. They are there to alert you to special information, as I explain below.

This icon lets you know that I'm offering additional useful information to help you with recipe preparation (or with anything else, for that matter), based on my experience.

Take notice. Something is happening, or could happen, that could affect your health or safety.

This icon points out an important bit of information that you can carry over to other cooking endeavors.

If you're looking for an idea or suggestion that will help to make a good food gift even better, watch for this icon.

This icon points out purely whimsical facts about food intended to stupefy, edify, or delight.

A Few Guidelines Before You Begin

I'm not standing on a soapbox and not trying to preach absolutes; I just want you to enjoy being in the kitchen. And in order to do that, you need to pay attention to a few universal truths that I wish someone had told me along the way:

- ✔ Read the recipe all the way through — really, all the way through.
- ✔ Have all the ingredients measured out in front of you.
- ✔ Keep your knives sharp.
- ✔ Check your oven with an oven thermometer.
- ✔ Do any task in the kitchen with a huge pinch of humor and common sense.

In addition, here are a few bits of information that apply specifically to the recipes in this book:

- ✔ All eggs are large.
- ✔ All black pepper is freshly ground unless otherwise noted.
- ✔ All recipes were tested with unsalted (also called sweet) butter.
- ✔ All oven temperatures are Fahrenheit.
- ✔ All flour is all-purpose unless otherwise noted.

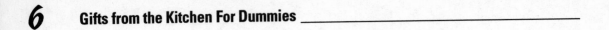

Part I
Getting Started: The Why, What, When, and How

"Okay, Cookie — your venison in lingonberry sauce is good, as are your eggplant souffle and the risotto with foie gras. But whoever taught you how to make these balsamic vinegar candies should be shot."

In this part . . .

Giving food gifts can be an anytime, joyous event rather than a major hassle at the holidays. In this part, you discover all the seasons and all the reasons to make a gift from the kitchen, plus the ingredients and tools you need to make it happen. Also, you and I have a basic kitchen conversation about some indispensable techniques like chopping and measuring, with a few helpful safety tips thrown in.

Chapter 1

It's More Than the Thought That Counts

. . . .

In This Chapter

▶ Sending a message with food

▶ Getting revved up to go into the kitchen

▶ Coming up with insightful reasons and creative seasons to give a food gift

▶ Making your gift presentable

. . . .

Admit it. Food pervades your life. You see it, shop for it, hear about it, read about it, stuff yourself with it, deprive yourself of it, and dream about it. But most important, food makes you happy. Food makes other people happy, too — no doubt about it, food makes a great gift. I'll go out on a limb here and say that no one has ever been unhappy about receiving a gift of food. (Well, there was that unfortunate incident in the Garden of Eden.) Getting a gift of food isn't like receiving monogrammed, battery-operated his and hers toenail clippers that you couldn't possibly ever return. Food gifts are unique — they're rarely inappropriate, and one size does fit all because the most important ingredient in all these recipes, the only one you have to supply, is heart. And a gift from your heart is tailor made — no department store will ever stock it. So read on, and discover all the ways this book provides to spread the happiness.

Discovering the Joys of Making Your Own Gifts

People have been giving the gift of food for thousands of years. In this faster-than-lightning, high-tech cyberworld, the tradition of giving homemade gifts may seem like an old-fashioned dinosaur. After all, companies spend big bucks on researching their target markets, figuring out exactly who wants what they have to sell, and trying to convince you to buy their products. With all the advertisements for the latest gadgets you see every day, you may have even forgotten that making something from scratch is an option!

Food communicates a message. In gentler times, Romans used herbs to relay sentiment. Rosemary signified remembrance; parsley symbolized bad luck. Early American sea captains impaled pineapples on their gateposts as a sign that they had returned from the sea and that all were welcome to visit. Today, Jews still celebrate the tradition of Passover with symbolic foods: Saltwater symbolizes tears, and *harosset*, a thick mixture of fruit, nuts, and wine, is the "mortar" between *matzoh* (unleavened bread) "bricks."

Your homemade food gifts don't have to be symbolic, but you can rest assured that they say something far beyond "I have to give you a gift." Homemade No-Bake Black Forest Bites (see Chapter 5) or Banana-Mango Chutney (see Chapter 9) say that you cared enough to take the time to make something with your own two hands. Maybe Donna Reed said it best in the movie *It's a Wonderful Life:* "Bread, that your house may never know hunger; salt, that life may have flavor; wine, that joy and prosperity may reign forever."

Gaining the Confidence to Get Started

Nobody strides into the kitchen for the first time and declares, "I think I'll whip up a little beef Wellington with Madeira sauce tonight." Like any other undertaking, whether it's belly dancing or snowboarding, cooking starts with a few basic building blocks. Some people are afraid of working with all those gadgets and gizmos found in the kitchen. Other people hesitate to set foot in the kitchen because they're afraid that what they make won't be good enough to give as a gift. But no matter what's giving you pause, you can find a way of dealing with it.

I have a friend Helen, whose elder sister lived with her and did all the cooking for the two of them. When retirement time came, Helen wanted to stay up north; her sister wanted the sunshine of Florida. Helen was left to cook for herself, never having done so before. When I asked her how she would begin learning to cook, she said, "I can read, can't I?" Helen had the one key ingredient that every cook needs: attitude. Cooking isn't rocket science — the recipes in this book prove that fact to you if you aren't convinced. All it takes is practice, and even if you've never set foot in the kitchen except to ask, "What's for dinner?" you can make gifts that will delight your friends and family.

Whatever your skill level in the kitchen, you'll find tasty recipes in this book that you can make. Each chapter contains tips and guidelines that offer sage advice to cooks of all skill levels. You can pick and choose the recipes that appeal to you.

Finding Reasons to Give the Gift of Food

I can't think of anyone who wouldn't enjoy homemade gifts from the kitchen any time of year — whether you have a reason for giving or not. But if you're not sure when homemade goodies are appropriate, pull your calendar off the wall or open your datebook and read on.

To celebrate holidays

You're rushing through the supermarket (you're always rushing through the supermarket), trying to get home to put supper on the table. Halfway down the baking goods aisle, a package of brownie mix catches your eye. Warm and fuzzy thoughts about making something homemade for your sweetie creep into your mind. Great! You've thought of your own reason to give a food gift. But your honey's birthday was three months ago, and you feel guilty that you didn't do it then. Be inventive. Make up a reason.

Holidays are like constellations: Some are major, and some are minor. Anyone can spot the Big Dipper, but what about Pleiades? In the same spirit, anyone can think of gingerbread men for Christmas and potato pancakes for Chanukah. But you want more holidays to celebrate with food! Here are a few holidays you can mark, along with some suggestions for recipes from this book to mark them with:

- ✔ **Chinese New Year (sometime between January 21 and February 21):** Fortune Cookies (Chapter 7)

- ✔ **Groundhog Day (February 2):** Provençal Cheese and Olive Bites (Chapter 12)

- ✔ **Valentine's Day (February 14):** White Chocolate Coeur à la Crème with Fresh Strawberry Balsamic Sauce (Chapter 5)

- ✔ **Teflon Invented (April 6):** Banana-Blueberry Bread (Chapter 11)

- ✔ **Hug an Australian Day (April 26):** Anzac Granola Bars (Chapter 7)

- ✔ **Mother's Day (the second Sunday in May):** Pineapple-Ginger Scones (Chapter 11) and Rhubarb-Fig Conserve (Chapter 9)

- ✔ **National Hot Dog Month (July):** Hot Diggity Dog Relish (Chapter 9)

- ✔ **National Fresh Breath Day (August 6):** Easy Alabaster Mints (Chapter 6)

- ✔ **National Dog Week (last full week of September):** Fido's Fetching Bones (Chapter 7)

- ✔ **Johnny Appleseed's Birthday (September 26):** Toast-of-the-Town Big Apple on a Stick (Chapter 6)

- **Leif Erickson Day (October 9):** Downtown Lox Spread and Uptown Smoked Salmon Spread (Chapter 12)
- **Columbus Day (October 12):** Orange Cannoli Pie (Chapter 10)
- **World Kindness Day (November 13):** Anything!
- **Kwanzaa (December 26 through January 1):** Benne Seed Candy (Chapter 6)

Maybe you don't have the luxury of *searching* for a holiday on which to give your homemade treats. Maybe the end-of-year holidays have snuck up on you, and you have no idea what to give all the people on your list. A gift from your kitchen renews true holiday spirits — for both you and the lucky recipient. Here's just a sampling of the people you can delight with scrumptious gifts:

- Unexpected guests
- The hairdresser who got bubble gum out of your hair
- The postman (after all, the bills aren't *his* fault!)
- The people in your church choir (or on your ice hockey team)
- Uncle Albert's heir apparent, the dog
- Your son's college roommate (truffles won't get caught in his lip ring)
- The babysitter (she already ate part of the gift anyway)
- Santa and his eight tiny reindeer

You can also use homemade gifts as stocking stuffers or party favors. Or you can bring them as a thank-you gift to all the holiday parties you attend.

And if all this talk of holidays is making you break out in hives, you can always make something for a non-holiday special occasion. For example, if you've been invited to a tailgate party before the big game, you can bake some Jumbo Pretzels (Chapter 11). Or you can surprise your poker buddies by bringing along some Barbecue Almonds (Chapter 12) to liven things up.

For no reason at all

When you start cooking and baking, you may find it addictive. So don't let the fact that a major (or minor) holiday isn't on the horizon stop you from sharing the fruits of your labor. You can give gifts for no reason at all. Here's a list of some excuses you may find yourself using:

- Knitting a sweater takes too long.
- The department store closed earlier than I thought.
- I just wanted to — that's all.

✔ It'll cheer someone up.

✔ I can't afford a store-bought present.

✔ It makes someone feel special.

✔ Homemade tastes better than store bought.

✔ I like to be unique.

✔ I'm old-fashioned.

✔ My dog chewed up the store-bought present.

✔ I'm trying to cater to someone's dietary needs.

✔ I like someone.

✔ I like someone a lot.

✔ I love someone.

Packaging It Up and Sending It Off

Part of the fun of making your own presents is packaging them and sending them off. You'll want to put just as much care into the way you package your gift as you do into making it in the first place. Whether you're mailing your gift or presenting it in person, you may want to follow some of these suggestions:

✔ Add little details, like dried flowers, to make gift wrapping special.

✔ Search flea markets and antique stores for added details, such as doilies.

✔ Be creative. Look in unusual places — like hardware stores — for packaging.

✔ Give a gift in a reusable container.

✔ Look to nature for interesting containers, and make your own edible containers. (See Chapter 14 for examples).

✔ Make the wrapping as big a deal as the gift.

And if you're shipping your presents, make sure to do the following:

✔ Use plenty of protective materials.

✔ Insulate a gift box inside a strong shipping box.

✔ Weatherproof your labels.

✔ Ship in plenty of time.

Gift-giving etiquette

I'm sure that your parents tried their darnedest to teach you a few manners, and I'm sure that you meant to pay attention. But just in case advancing years, the faulty ozone layer, or low blood sugar has caused you to forget, here are a few things you may want to keep in mind before you gleefully show up at someone's door with gift in hand:

✔ **If you bring your food gift to the hosts of a party, they aren't required to serve it immediately.** They've put great thought and consideration into their celebration, and your South-of-Somewhere Salsa (Chapter 12), though delicious, probably doesn't go with their cherry-glazed Cornish hens. However, if the menu includes cocktail hot dogs, maybe they think putting out the salsa is a great idea. Either way, it's their call — don't make them feel guilty if they don't serve your dish.

✔ **If the event you're taking a food gift to is a large gathering, make sure that your package has a gift tag.** With the distractions of refilling nut dishes, saving the dog from Cousin Edna's twin boys, or extinguishing the napkin that caught on fire, a host can easily overlook who brought the delicious Prosciutto-Fig Quick Bread (see Chapter 11) and never know whom to call and thank the next day.

✔ **If you don't know the recipients of the gift very well, you may want to include the ingredients on the label.** You never know whether they have a vegan in their midst, or whether someone is allergic to nuts. Also note if it needs refrigeration.

✔ **If you accompany a food gift with a bread knife (or other sharp object), and you're at all superstitious, have the recipient give you a coin so that your friendship isn't severed.** According to folklore, giving a sharp object will end a friendship. But paying for it (no matter how little) makes the gift an acceptable exchange. Better safe than sorry!

When your presents arrive — whether by mail or in person — your friends and family are sure to be impressed! And, more important, they'll know that you've put great care into what you're giving.

Freshness is a big part of a food gift. Give gifts shortly after preparing. If you're mailing, ship overnight to assure best quality.

Chapter 2

To Market, To Market: Stocking Your Pantry

- -

In This Chapter

▶ Going "gourmet" — buying the best ingredients

▶ Selecting perishables and nonperishables

▶ Stocking up on ingredients for last-minute gifts

- -

This chapter is about buying the basic ingredients for the recipes in *Gifts from the Kitchen For Dummies*, and in this department, I follow the advice of people like poet and playwright Oscar Wilde, who said, "I have the simplest of tastes — I am always satisfied with the best." If that sounds rather hoity-toity and, oh my gosh, "gourmet," then I call upon chef Julia Child who basically says that gourmet is just good food prepared properly. Wow — what a simple concept!

Of course, whenever you talk about ingredients, the subject of substitutions comes up. Can you or can't you use this instead of that? It depends. Consider this cautionary tale: A friend once asked for my sour cream apple pie recipe, which she loved. I happily gave it to her, but she later told me hers tasted very different. She wondered whether I possibly had left out an ingredient on the copy of the recipe. I hadn't, so I asked her what apples she used. She had switched from the Golden Delicious that I use to Granny Smith — apples so different in taste that it's no wonder the pie wasn't the same.

Now don't get me wrong: I'm all for experimenting, and you'll enjoy doing it, too. But sometimes you can substitute ingredients, and sometimes you can't.

Using the Best Ingredients

When shopping for ingredients for your gifts from the kitchen, choose good-quality products. Of course, having a champagne taste and a beer budget can be exasperating, but always buying the best you can afford is not necessarily an indulgence. Especially when you're making a simple dish, you have fewer places to hide poor quality, so better ingredients can greatly affect the final result. Now that you have a whole cookbook dedicated to giving good things to friends, make all your time and efforts shine by using only quality ingredients.

Pantry pride, fortunately, is not one of the seven deadly sins. I do love going to my pantry and finding an ingredient I was pretty sure was there. Having basic ingredients — and often some not-so-basic ingredients — on hand makes the cooking process a little easier. Nothing is more frustrating than starting a recipe and finding that the last egg became rocket fuel for Junior's science project.

I divide the discussion of ingredients into perishable and nonperishable. Most of the ingredients are used somewhere in the recipes in this book, but you also may find a few extra morsels of information that you can carry with you in your future cooking escapades. Understanding ingredients can keep you out of hot water in the kitchen.

Perishable stuff

Most perishables require you to rush home from the market on a hot summer day. They are the basic dairy ingredients needed for many of the recipes in this book. The vegetable produce doesn't require refrigeration if you have a cool, dry place to store it.

Butter

Butter is available in unsalted (also called sweet) and salted. All recipes in this book were tested with unsalted butter. It has a fresher flavor and allows control of the salt level in a recipe.

Butter freezes very well (tightly wrapped for up to 4 months). You can store extra for making those holiday gifts.

Buttermilk

Some people gag on buttermilk. Others think it is velvety nectar of the gods. One thing is certain: Buttermilk, a slightly thick, tangy, lowfat milk, helps make baked goods moist.

Cream cheese

Cream cheese is a soft, unripe spreadable cheese. Neufchâtel (one-third reduced-fat) cream cheese was used in some recipes because it is softer still than cream cheese and easier to blend into a recipe. Cream cheese is also available in lowfat and no-fat versions.

Eggs

Eggs are graded small, medium, large, extra large, and jumbo. All recipes in this book were tested with large eggs. Don't substitute one for the other, because doing so can make a disastrous difference.

Most recipes use large eggs unless otherwise specified. However, do check the author's note in any cookbook you use to double-check which size egg to use.

Heavy cream

Heavy cream has the highest fat content, between 36 and 40 percent, of all the creams. See Chapter 10 for more details.

Lemons, limes, and oranges

Citrus fruits are always good to have on hand. Their zest and juice find a home in many recipes. See Chapter 8 for information about grating citrus fruit.

Onions and garlic

These related bulbs are cornerstones of some of the savory dishes in the book. See Chapter 9 for more details about onions.

Choose only garlic heads that are firm and without bruises. Garlic should not be sprouting.

Sour cream

A thick, smooth dairy product with a tart taste, sour cream helps make baked goods moister. You can use it in virtually any aspect of cooking. It is available in light and nonfat versions. I used regular sour cream in the recipes in this book.

The worst place to store milk, eggs, and butter is on the refrigerator door. The opening and closing of the door expose the dairy products to unnecessary heat. If possible, place them toward the back of a shelf.

Not-so-perishable stuff

These are the bankable ingredients. Like money in the vault, they're available when you need them. You may use them initially for recipes in this book, but you'll surprise yourself one day when you open the pantry door and start browsing for something to add to stew.

Baking soda and baking powder

Both baking soda and baking powder are *chemical leavening agents.* This term may sound like something to do with global warming but actually is the technical explanation of how these ingredients work to raise quick breads, cookies, and cakes. Baking soda, however, works primarily in the presence of acids like buttermilk and sour cream. See Chapter 11 for more details.

Chocolate

Chocolate comes in many forms for many uses and taste preferences. In descending order of sweetness, the types of chocolate are white chocolate, milk chocolate, semisweet chocolate, bittersweet chocolate, and unsweetened chocolate. All you chocoholics can go directly to Chapter 5 for more information (and recipes!).

Cocoa

Cocoa is unsweetened and is available in Dutch processed and regular varieties. See Chapter 5 for more information on using cocoa in recipes. The two types of cocoa aren't interchangeable, and recipes specify which kind you should use.

Don't confuse cocoa with cocoa mix. Cocoa mix is a beverage with sugar and milk solids in it.

Evaporated milk and sweetened condensed milk

Evaporated milk is unsweetened milk from which 60 percent of the water has been removed. Sweetened condensed milk has been heated with a huge amount of sugar in it, so, as a result, it's very thick and very sweet. It's used mostly in desserts. Recipes that call for one of these ingredients usually caution you not to use the other one, so obviously they are not interchangeable.

Extracts

Vanilla and almond extracts are the two most commonly used extracts in this book. Many other extracts are also available, including double vanilla, lemon, orange, maple, chocolate, walnut, and peppermint. You may want to experiment with some of them.

Always buy real extracts. The imitations are exactly that and usually poor tasting. It's not worth investing in other good ingredients only to spoil the final taste of a recipe with an imitation flavor.

Flour

There are many types of flour, and each one has a characteristic that suits it better to one job rather than another. I use only two types of flour in this book: all purpose and whole wheat. All-purpose flour is a blend of high-gluten wheat (good for yeast breads) and low-gluten wheat (good for cakes). It is available in bleached or unbleached forms, which are interchangeable. Whole-wheat flour contains bran and germ from the kernel.

Whole-wheat flour should be stored in the refrigerator because it goes rancid quickly.

Herbs

The herb racks in the market keep edging outwards as manufacturers realize more and more customers are dabbling in different ethnic cuisines. Here is a list of the most popular to get you started.

- ✔ **Basil** is one of the most popular herbs and has 50 to 60 species. It's a major ingredient in pesto sauce, loves tomatoes, and plays well with other herbs.

- ✔ **Bay leaf** is an intensely flavored leaf of the Laurel family. Labeled Turkish or California (slightly stronger), it likes to swim in stews and soups. Poets and victorious warriors wore a crown of this leaf in ancient times — it is where we get the term *poet laureate.*

- ✔ **Chives** are members of the onion family. These svelte hollow stalks have a mild, delicate taste.

- ✔ **Cilantro** is also known as coriander (the fresh kind, not the seeds) and Chinese parsley. It speaks with a Latin American and Southeast Asian accent (not to mention a Tex-Mex drawl), whose foods it extols.

- ✔ **Dill** is one of the oldest herbs. Scandinavians love this feathery frond for the invigorating zing it brings to their long, dreary winters. It is also a major player in pickle preparation.

- ✔ **Marjoram** or sweet marjoram has a delicate flavor. It's a good alternative for stuffings if you find that sage tastes too strong. Marjoram is a symbol of honor in Crete.

- ✔ **Mint** is a fragrant herb with about 25 varieties. It has an agreeable personality that teams up with everything from meat to melon — as well as those juleps that Southerners are so fond of.

- ✔ **Oregano** is from Mexico or the Mediterranean (including Greece and Turkey). The Mexican variety is stronger. Like all teenagers, oregano loves pizza.

- ✔ **Parsley** is available in both flat-leaf, or Italian, and curly-leaf varieties. Although the curly-leaf type appears to be everywhere, the flat-leaf variety has both more flavor and vitamins. Parsley has been cultivated for at least 2,000 years, and in that time has seen and done it all. It's a busybody found in seemingly every dish or gallantly standing alone as a garnish.

- ✔ **Rosemary,** the original "punker," is a spiky herb with lots of flavor. A little goes a long way. It has long been the symbol of remembrance.

✔ **Sage** is best known for its use in stuffing and sausage meats. It also goes well with veal and pork. The English have even put it in a cheese (Sage Derby).

✔ **Tarragon** is an anise-flavored herb that is a supporting player in béarnaise sauce as well as in flavored vinegar. It is loved in the French kitchen and is one of the characters in *fines herbes,* a French seasoning mixture.

✔ **Thyme** is a trusty little leaf that's the all-round switch hitter. You can put it in just about anything and come up a winner.

Nonstick cooking spray

Cooking sprays, such as PAM, are a boon to baking. They make releasing cakes from pans a whole lot easier, and they're also good for lightly coating sauté pans.

Oils

Oils come from a variety of plants, nuts, and seeds. Always keep vegetable oil and extra-virgin olive oil in your pantry. Use the olive oil for making flavored oils and in places that best highlight its flavor, including salads, dipping bread, and drizzling over vegetables. See Chapter 9 for more information on olive oils. At other times when flavor is not as important, vegetable oils are good for general cooking purposes, such as sautéing and frying.

Pepper

All pepper in the book is freshly ground black pepper, unless otherwise noted. There really is no comparison to the pre-ground pepper. Invest in a good pepper mill that grinds the peppercorns evenly.

Salt

Anytime salt is called for in this book it is always table salt unless otherwise noted. A few exceptions call for sea salt or kosher salt. These are coarse-grained salts that are added at the end of a recipe. These types of salt measure differently than table salt and should not be interchanged.

Spices

Spices give a recipe character. Some of the basic spices you'll want to have on hand include the following:

✔ Allspice

✔ Cardamom

✔ Cayenne

✔ Chili powder

✔ Cinnamon

- ✔ Cloves
- ✔ Cumin
- ✔ Ginger
- ✔ Nutmeg

Dried herbs and spices are most flavorful when fresh. Buy them in the smallest quantity possible and replace them every 6 months. Heat is the worst enemy of herbs and spices; keep them away from the cooktop and in a cool, dark place.

Sugar

In this book, *sugar* without qualifying words always means white granulated sugar. It is a principal sweetener that contributes to browning and crisping as well. Other sugars to note include the following:

- ✔ **Brown sugar** is white sugar mixed with molasses. Dark brown sugar has more molasses than light brown sugar. These sugars are usually interchangeable, but sometimes you may prefer one over the other to give a recipe the right appearance or taste.
- ✔ **Confectioners' (or powdered) sugar** is granulated sugar that has been finely ground and to which a small amount of cornstarch has been added to prevent lumping. Also known as 10X sugar, it is usually used in desserts and icings.
- ✔ **Superfine sugar** is very finely ground granulated sugar. It dissolves very quickly.

Vegetable shortening

Vegetable shortening is solid vegetable fat. It is used in place of lard in pie crusts to make them flaky and is used in quantity for deep-frying.

Vinegar

Have red and white wine vinegars on hand for making salad dressings and marinades. Also keep some cider vinegar, which has an apple flavor, and harsher, distilled white vinegar in the pantry. See Chapter 9 for more information.

Dried versus fresh herbs

Listen up. This is the most important fact you need to know about the use of herbs: Dried herbs are almost three times stronger than fresh herbs. To this day I hate tarragon because I didn't know the difference between fresh and dried herbs. If a recipe says, "¼ cup chopped parsley," it usually means fresh. It should say dried if it means dried. But it is *always* a good idea to read the author's notes to be sure.

Yeast

Yeast is one of the leaving agents used for breads. It is available in granular and cake form. See Chapter 11 for more details.

Storing Extra Ingredients for Making Last-Minute Gifts

This list of ingredients isn't exactly basic, but they do enable you to make the last-minute gifts I describe in Chapter 1. Most of the ingredients will keep for a good long time, like "bench players" in reserve in case the game plan changes — or the boss's open house sneaks up while you aren't paying attention.

- Balsamic vinegar (see Chapter 9)
- Buttermilk powder
- Candied ginger
- Cheeses, especially Parmesan and cheddar
- Cornmeal
- Cornstarch
- Cream of tartar
- Gelatin
- Instant espresso coffee granules
- Light corn syrup
- Nuts, especially walnuts, pecans, and almonds
- Raisins and other dried fruits, including dried pineapple
- Sugar cubes

Putting your stamp on everything

Though it's not an "ingredient," an indelible marking pen is an essential part of every kitchen — yes, a marking pen. Use it to label everything that goes in your pantry with a date (the month and the year are all you need). Cans have a way of sashaying to the back of a shelf. And spices have a way of growing old before your eyes. And lest you think me totally insane, consider the fashion industry. Ralph Lauren puts a label on everything, and so should you.

Chapter 3

Selecting Tools for Your Kitchen

· ·

· ·

Kitchen stores have turned into super toy stores for adults. You can choose from so many utensils, pans, and gadgets, and of course, you want them all. And you think you need them all, but you don't. Assess what and how much you want to cook before you go into debt buying cooking tools. Kitchen tools are addictive. But do try to go for quality rather than quantity, especially if you're just starting out. An experienced cook can improvise with whatever is at hand. As a neophyte, however, you don't want to work in a kitchen where flimsy pans burn food, dull knives make chopping tedious, or thin baking sheets warp and send cookies flying in the oven.

Do a little homework before shopping for kitchen tools. Read this chapter, surf the Internet, go to gourmet shops or department stores, and talk to salespeople. Find out what suits your needs.

Your handiest kitchen tool is the best kitchen tool

Believe it or not, you already possess the best piece of equipment you'll need in your kitchen. It shreds, pokes, peels, prods, grabs, shapes, kneads, pinches, gauges, separates, and crumbles. And you always know where to find it. Yup, your hands. No utensil is quite as dexterous or durable as those ten digits on the end of your wrists. Use them.

My grandmother always taught me to plunge in with both hands (although I learned to try and keep one hand reasonably clean in case the telephone rings). If you do, you'll find that you don't need a lot of gadgets. Between your hands and a good knife, there isn't much you can't get accomplished in the kitchen.

Getting to the Point about Knives

To start out, you only really need three knives: a chef's knife, a paring knife, and a bread knife. They can accomplish all the tasks you have to do in a kitchen. You can buy specialty knives later if you're so inclined, but for now, these three will do. Don't skimp on quality, however. Buy the best. High-end knives last many, many years. They are the workhorses of the kitchen and make the jobs go that much smoother.

The best knife is a sharp knife. Regardless of what brand of knife you choose, that is the most important thing you need to know about cutlery. If you're thinking about purchasing knives, here are some other things to consider:

- ✔ **A high-carbon stainless steel blade is the best choice.** It takes and keeps an edge well and doesn't rust like carbon steel.
- ✔ **The blade of the knife should continue between the two handle pieces.**
- ✔ **The handle should have rivets going through it, securing the blade in place.**
- ✔ **The knife should feel comfortable in your hand.** Chef's knives come in several sizes, and none of them are right or wrong. Pick the one that feels best.

Caring for knives

You're going to drop a pretty penny on really good-quality knives, so try to give them a little TLC by following this advice:

- ✔ **Don't put knives with wooden handles in the dishwasher.**
- ✔ **Don't leave knives with wooden handles soaking in the sink.**
- ✔ **Always use a cutting board, never a counter surface.**
- ✔ **Store knives in a knife block, rack, or drawer fitted with slots.** Never leave them loose in a drawer. It's not good for them, and it's certainly no good for your fingers.
- ✔ **Don't use your knives as letter openers, dry paint scraper-uppers, package slitters, and jar pryer-openers.**

Keeping 'em sharp

Keep your knives sharp. You can sharpen them with any of the following tools:

✔ **A sharpening steel.** It is a long, slightly rough, metal rod with a handle used for touch-up sharpenings.

✔ **A whetstone.** This is a fine-grained, rectangular stone wet with oil, used to reestablish and maintain a blade's sharpness.

✔ **A three-stage electric knife sharpener.**

Occasionally, you may want to have your knives sharpened professionally — but not often because this rapidly wears down the blade.

You're less likely to cut yourself with a sharp knife than a dull knife. The explanation is simple: The harder you push on a dull blade, the greater the chance the knife will keep on going (into a finger) once all that energy finally cuts through, say, tomato skin. On the other hand, you use very little energy with a sharp knife, and the weight of the blade does some of the work.

Cuts suffered from a sharp knife are cleaner and heal better than cuts from a dull knife. Isn't that a great reason to keep your knives sharp?

Shopping for Pots and Pans, or As They Say in Paree, "Batterie de Cuisine"

Batterie de cuisine is a two-dollar French phrase that just means kitchen stuff, including pots and pans. In this section, I give you information about what to look for in cookware and what pots and pans you should have.

Start with what you need. Don't worry about not owning every pot and pan known to mankind right away; in no time, you'll have so much stuff you won't know where to put it.

Here are some tips when shopping for cookware:

✔ You may not have been a fan of heavy metal before, but you will be now. Heavy is good. Pots and pans should have a substantial heft when you pick them up. The bottoms should be thick. Cookware with a copper core is even better because it helps distribute the heat more evenly and prevents hot spots that encourage foods to burn when you're not looking.

✔ Pick up pans before you buy them. The balance and length of the handle should feel comfortable to you.

✔ Handles should be riveted, not screwed, to the pot or pan.

✔ Lids should fit well, and knobs or handles should be securely fastened.

Basically, you need three saucepans, ranging in size from 1 quart to 4 quart, plus the lids. A 1½-pint saucepan is sometimes handy for melting butter or dissolving gelatin, but it's not a necessity. A 6- to 8-quart pot is good for boiling pastas and braising. Eventually, you may want to get a 10-quart stockpot. You also may want to buy sauté pans in 9- or 10-inch and 12-inch sizes to round out your arsenal.

Okay, what's the difference between a pot and a pan? A pan has one long handle, but a pot has a short handle on both sides. Well, of course, you knew that!

You should consider having at least one nonstick pan, which is handy for foods that like to be annoying and stick and also if you do lowfat cooking. Steamer inserts are nice, but you can buy an expandable fanlike steamer in a cook shop that adjusts to pans of different sizes. A double boiler is occasionally useful, but you can use a bowl on top of a pan if you don't want to invest in the real thing.

You pay a price for quality cookware, but the pans will last. If you buy cheaper cookware, you'll probably be paying a greater price in ruined foods and having to replace your set a few times. Spend some time looking and hefting. Definitely do comparison shopping. Many companies offer sets of cookware, but this is a good deal only if the set includes all or most of the pans you want.

Measuring, Mixing, and Other Helpful Tools

In addition to pots and pans, you need an assortment of other kitchen tools. Here's the rest of the crew that should show up in your kitchen:

- ✔ **Graduated dry measuring cups:** Choose from metal or plastic nesting cups that come in four standard sizes: 1 cup, ½ cup, ⅓ cup, and ¼ cup. You can purchase 2-cup and ⅛-cup sizes separately. As their name implies, use these cups only for measuring dry or solid ingredients. (See Chapter 4 for a fuller explanation of these tools and tips on using them.)

- ✔ **Liquid measuring cups:** These cups are available in glass or plastic and come in a variety of sizes, ranging from 1 cup to 8 cups. Having these cups in a few different sizes is a good idea.

Liquid and dry measuring cups are not interchangeable. Dry is dry and wet is wet, and never the twain shall meet. (See Chapter 4 for a full explanation.)

✔ **Graduated measuring spoons:** These spoons come on a ring in a set of four sizes: 1 tablespoon, 1 teaspoon, ½ teaspoon, and ¼ teaspoon. Some sets come with other sizes, like ⅔ teaspoon, but I find them confusing. Standard measurements are important in baking — a fairly precise science — so using measuring spoons (and cups) yields better results.

✔ **Bowls:** Ideally, you should have a range of sizes of bowls, both stainless steel and glass. In addition to all their other duties, a bowl can substitute as a double boiler. (You can even invert one and bake a gingerbread bowl on it, as I explain in Chapter 14.) Glass bowls are handy for the microwave.

Plastic bowls love to hang on to grease. I don't recommend using them when beating egg whites. Even the smallest amount of grease prevents egg whites from reaching their full volume when whipped.

✔ **Cutting board:** Available in either wood or plastic, cutting boards make chopping easier and protect your knives. Wood traditionally is harder to keep clean (wash with hot, soapy water and an occasional bleaching), but you can pop the plastic ones in the dishwasher. Use only plastic boards for cutting raw fish, poultry, or meat. In either case, keeping the boards free from bacteria is essential.

Mark one side of the cutting board with indelible marker. Use this side to chop only garlic and onions, and save the other side for chopping ingredients such as nuts for a dessert. That way, those savory flavors won't affect your sweet dishes.

✔ **Rubber spatulas:** These items come in a variety of sizes (and now colors!). I'm particularly fond of the high-heat-resistant ones.

Rubber spatulas are grease magnets as well. Wash them well before using them with egg whites.

✔ **Whisks:** Wire whisks come in a variety of shapes and sizes. They're handy for blending, occasionally getting out lumps, and even for whisking dry ingredients together.

✔ **Wooden spoons:** Kitchen tools don't get any more utilitarian than this. I really like the flat-ended ones that scrape a wide path on the bottom of a pan.

Don't stir something and then leave a wooden spoon in the pot. The spoon will pick up all sorts of flavors, and the wood probably doesn't do much for the taste of what's cooking, either. When you want to taste to adjust the seasonings, use a metal spoon, which gives you a more accurate taste.

- **Grater:** A box grater with a different size opening on each of its four sides is a good basic choice. You may want to later add a mouli drum grater for easy shredding of cheese and grating of chocolate. The Microplane zester (available through catalogs and in cookware stores) makes zesting citrus peel a snap. (See Chapter 8 for more information.)

- **Strainer:** This tool does many kitchen chores, from draining wet fruit to rescuing lumpy gravy to sifting dry ingredients to sprinkling confectioners' (powdered) sugar on a tart.

- **No. 100 scoop:** This is a very small — 1⅛-inch — metal "ice cream" scoop that can help you measure candies and dough evenly and quickly.

Baker's Delights

The concept of heavy that works so well in pots and pans works equally well in baking equipment. If you love baking as much as I do, you'll want equipment that stands up to batches and batches of Christmas cookies. Here are some basic baking tools that you should have:

- **Baking sheets:** These are also known as cookie sheets and come in a variety of sizes. I used the standard size sheet, 14 x 17 inches, for the recipes in this book. As a rule, the baking sheet should fit in your oven and still allow 2 inches all around for air circulation. I like the ones that have a lip on only one end, giving you something to grasp when removing the sheet from the oven. These baking sheets also make it easy to slide things off in any direction.

- **Cake pans:** I used 8-x-8-inch, 9-x-9-inch, 13-x-9-inch, and 8-inch round pans for the recipes in this book. The heavier the pan, the better.

- **Cooling racks:** These items are a must in baking, so you should have a few on hand. Cookies and breads cool crisper on them, and they make handy trivets to rest the baking sheet on when you take it out of the oven.

- **Digital thermometer:** An instant-read digital thermometer comes in handy when you're trying to get the water temperature right to proof yeast and when you're making candy. The nondigital instant-read thermometers are also fine to use but aren't as precise as the digital kind.

- **Jelly roll pans:** These pans are like baking sheets but have sides all around. Their real job is to hold the ingredients for a sponge cake for jelly rolls, but you also can toast nuts on them without scattering them all over the oven.

- **Loaf pans:** You should have at least two 9-x-5-x-3-inch loaf pans. If your collection includes two 8½-x-4½-x-2½-inch pans, that's even better.

- **Pastry bags and tips:** Only a few recipes in this book call for pastry bags and tips, and it's purely your choice whether to use them. (See Chapter 6 for more information.) Pasty bags and tips are available at cookware shops, large discount stores, and craft stores and through catalogs.

- **Pastry blender:** This torturous-looking implement is used to cut shortening into flour for pie crusts. It usually is made of five or six stiff looping wires attached to a handle. (See Chapter 10 for more details.)

- **Pie plate:** I used a standard 9-inch glass pie plate for the recipes in this book.

- **Rolling pin:** You can find several different models of rolling pins. Test-drive a few and see which is comfortable. I use my grandmother's simple solid wooden rolling pin and just wouldn't dream of using another, but you may want to try the one with little ball bearings. The handles stay still when you roll, and the center pin glides smoothly.

- **Tart pan:** I used a tart pan with a removable bottom for the recipes in this book. Tarts always seem more elegant than pies, and they're so much easier to make than pies because you don't have to flute the crust.

- **Tube pan:** This round cake pan has high sides and a hollow tube attached to a removable bottom. (I've also seen square versions of the tube pan.) It is usually used for angel food or chiffon cakes, but it also promotes even baking in very high, dense cakes such as pound cake. A Bundt pan is a fancier variation of the tube pan but with a non-removable bottom.

Three small but mighty tools

You probably don't think that the three kitchen tools I mention in the following list are important. They may seem incidental, but they all can avert one disaster or another. I'm betting that it never occurred to you to buy at least two of them.

- **Oven thermometer:** Don't leave the store without one. Your oven is most likely at least 25 degrees too hot right now. If you know about it, you can compensate for it, as I explain in Chapter 4. Cooking has too many variables, so at least know that your oven is on your side.

- **Timer:** You may think you'll remember what time the bread comes out of the oven, but the phone, the doorbell, that new catalog that came in the mail, or the message that soccer practice was canceled can divert your attention. Often you're doing more than just one thing in the kitchen. Set a timer. That way, there's one less thing that can go wrong.

- **Potholders or oven mitts:** Get real ones. Kitchen towels just don't do the job. Yeah, professional chefs use towels and aprons, but I swear their hands are made from asbestos. Remember never to use a potholder that's wet. It does nothing but conduct pain.

Plugged In: Choosing Electric Appliances

Oh, thank you, Mr. Edison — and all the other inventors who make life in the kitchen so much more pleasurable today. The following appliances will speed you through a number of steps in the recipes in this book.

✔ **Blender:** Nothing beats a blender for pureeing and liquefying foods. You don't, however, need one with a million buttons. A basic model with a few functions and a good motor gets the job done.

✔ **Food processor:** This small appliance is one of the greatest boons to the home kitchen. Tasks of chopping, shredding, julienning, and slicing are simplified with this machine and its multiple blades. It also purees but not as smoothly as a blender.

✔ **Mixer:** You can choose from hand, stand, and heavy-duty professional varieties. A hand mixer with a good motor can get a lot done in the kitchen, including whipping cream and beating most cookie doughs and cake batters. Sometimes I like the control of being able to tilt it where I want. The stand mixer makes the going easier because the motor is more powerful and you don't have to stand there holding it. The souped-up version of the stand mixer is a heavy-duty mixer, such as one made by KitchenAid, which comes with a 4½-quart, 5-quart, or 6-quart bowl — the choice is yours, depending on how extensive your cooking is. Its heavy motor copes with the thickest cookie doughs or stiffest bread doughs. It comes with a flat beater or paddle for batters, a wire whisk for meringues, and a dough hook for yeast breads.

Always insert the beaters into the mixer before plugging it in.

✔ **Spice grinder:** This gadget isn't one of the heavy hitters in the electric lineup, but it is a great little addition to the "batterie." It grinds whole spices and chops small amounts of herbs or nuts.

Chapter 4

Technique 101

● ●

In This Chapter

▶ Measuring dry and liquid ingredients

▶ Sifting dry ingredients

▶ Using a knife safely and effectively

▶ Separating an egg, creaming butter, and folding in egg whites

▶ Getting your pans ready for the oven

▶ Knowing how to make your stove and oven work for you

▶ Taking your oven's temperature

● ●

*Y*ou'll be happy to know that this book isn't about "pressure" cooking. You don't have to get dinner on the table by six. This book is about doing something nice for friends and family. The recipes don't require highly intricate techniques or years of cooking experience. But they do assume that you've dabbled in a few basic cooking and baking tasks.

In this chapter, I give you a primer on the cooking techniques, like chopping and slicing, separating an egg, or sifting flour, that you'll use over and over again throughout your cooking life. You'll probably want to look through the chapter now, but always feel free to turn back whenever you need a refresher course.

The first thing you should do when you walk into the kitchen is wash your hands. Doing so protects everyone from creatures of the invisible underworld. Also, the experts say that frequent hand washing cuts down on colds. So everyone wins!

Use common sense. The kitchen is a land mine of things that can cut, burn, puncture, poison, slice, scald, and generally discombobulate your life. Not surprisingly, most household accidents happen in the kitchen.

Measuring

Measuring ingredients is the most fundamental part of any recipe. You will do it a gazillion times. Whether you're baking cookies or making jam, the recipe requires you to accurately measure ingredients, liquid and dry.

Dry ingredients

To measure dry ingredients, use — drum roll, please — *dry measuring cups*. By dry measuring cups, I mean the metal or plastic cups made specifically for measuring dry ingredients.

Two main methods are used to measure dry ingredients, "dip and sweep" and "spoon and sweep." Dip and sweep is the method I use in this book, but here's how both of them work:

- ✔ **Dip and sweep:** In this method (which I used in creating the recipes in this book), I recommend that you do at least one "dive" into the ingredient before you start to measure. Loosen it up by lifting up a cupful and sprinkling it back into the container (this is not necessary with granulated sugar). Then dip the measuring cup into the container holding the ingredient and remove a slightly mounded cupful. Run a straight metal spatula or knife across the top edge of the cup, leveling the ingredient. Don't shake or tap the cup.

- ✔ **Spoon and sweep:** Another method for measuring dry ingredients requires you to use a spoon to scoop the ingredient into the measuring cup, mounding slightly. Then run a straight-edged metal spatula or knife across the top edge of the cup to level the ingredient. Don't shake or tap the cup.

When using other cookbooks, check the author's instructions to see which measuring method she specifies, if any.

For most dry ingredients (such as flour and confectioners' sugar), you should lightly scoop the ingredient and never pack it down into the cup. One exception to this rule is brown sugar. Recipes usually indicate a certain amount of *firmly packed brown sugar* — this means that, as you scoop the brown sugar into the cup, you press it down into the cup with your fingers or a spatula. It doesn't mean bench-pressing the sugar into the cup; it's more like building a sand castle. Then level it off.

Level the ingredients in measuring cups or spoons over a piece of wax paper or parchment. Use the paper to funnel any excess back into the container — this way, nothing goes to waste. It's also a good idea to measure all the ingredients first, leaving them in little piles. Then add them all at once. That way, if life interrupts your cooking, you have a visual reminder of what already has been measured.

Remember that old cliché, "Haste makes waste"? The trouble with clichés is they're usually right. Don't try to save time by measuring or leveling ingredients over the mixing bowl. If you do, I guarantee that will be the time the top falls off the salt shaker and you wind up with a saltier taste than planned.

Pay attention to what the recipe calls for. There is a difference between *1 cup sifted flour* and *1 cup flour, sifted*. In the first measurement, the flour is sifted and *then* measured. In the second, the flour is measured and *then* sifted. Although they sound very similar, the end result isn't. A cup of flour that has been measured first and then sifted is greater than a cup of flour that was sifted first. (By the way, this rule applies to chopped and sliced ingredients as well. If a recipe calls for "1 cup chopped broccoli," you chop the broccoli first. If it calls for "1 cup broccoli, chopped," you measure the broccoli first and then chop it.) For more on sifting, see the section on sifting later in this chapter.

Liquid ingredients

Just as you use dry measuring cups to measure dry ingredients, you use liquid measuring cups to measure pourable ingredients. Simple you say. And so it is. All you have to remember is, they are not interchangeable — never, ever, no way. Thank you! To use a liquid measuring cup accurately, place the measuring cup on a level surface, such as a countertop. Pour the liquid into the cup. Bend over — yes all the way over — and look at the amount at eye level, making sure that the liquid is level with the line indicating the amount you need.

Use a measuring cup that's close in size to the amount you want to measure. For example, if you're measuring 1½ cups of an ingredient, use a 2-cup measuring cup, not a 4-cup one. This advice is particularly important with smaller amounts of liquid — ¼ cup will not measure accurately in a 4-cup measure.

Graduated measuring spoons

Measuring in spoons differs from measuring in cups in that you use the same kinds of measuring spoons whether you're measuring dry or wet ingredients. Otherwise, the method you use to do the measuring is the same as you use with measuring cups.

Remember: Always use measuring spoons to measure teaspoon and tablespoon measurements called for in a recipe. Don't use the teaspoons that come with your silverware (unless the recipe specifically tells you to do so).

Pour hot liquids away from you so that you don't need to go running for the burn ointment every time you cook. Pouring away from you is actually a good habit to get into anytime you transfer something from one container to another, even if it's just cake batter. This way, you have a good chance of being able to continue wearing the outfit you started the day with, instead of having to change clothes because you splattered food all over yourself.

Sifting

Most flour is already presifted. If a recipe calls for sifting, however, you need to sift the flour (whether it's been presifted or not).

To sift flour, use a sieve (strainer) or a *flour sifter* (that funny-looking, coffee-can-shaped utensil with a crank on the outside and screening on the inside). After sifting the flour, spoon it into a measuring cup until slightly mounded. Level off the flour by running a straight-edged metal spatula or knife across the top edge.

Besides sifting flour, recipes sometimes call for sifting as a way to combine dry ingredients thoroughly. (If this is the case, the recipe says something like, "Sift together the flour and spices.") Sifting is also used to declump stickier dry ingredients, such as brown sugar.

As long as you aren't working with any lumpy ingredients, you can use one of two shortcuts for combining dry ingredients:

- ✔ Combine all the dry ingredients in a bowl and whisk thoroughly with a wire whisk.

- ✔ Combine all the dry ingredients in a resealable plastic bag. Close the bag, making sure that it's sealed, and shake thoroughly. (This approach is particularly handy if you do measuring ahead of time, because you can leave the ingredients in the plastic bag until you're ready to use them.)

Slicing and Dicing

Whether armed with newly purchased knives or trusty hand-me-downs, you can begin dicing, chopping, mincing, and julienning (see Table 4-1) after only a little bit of practice. Just as with all kitchen techniques, slicing and dicing require a little know-how and a lot of common sense.

Table 4-1	Slicing Terminology
Technique	*End Result*
Chopping	Irregular pieces about ¼ inch in size (about the size of a pea)
Mincing or finely chopping	Irregular pieces about ⅛ inch in size
Dicing	Tidy ¼-inch squares
Julienning	Thin strips about the size of matchsticks

When you're slicing, be sure to protect the hand that *isn't* holding the knife. Tuck the thumb of that hand behind the other fingers and keep it there. (The worst cut I ever gave myself was when I didn't follow that bit of advice.) Curl your fingernails slightly under your thumb. This basically forms a straight "wall" between the first and second joints of your fingers, which becomes the guide that your knife follows. Your curled-under fingers steady whatever ingredient you're slicing. Slice through the ingredient with the knife blade, pushing away from you slightly. With some practice, you'll be able to cut beautifully even slices.

The technique for chopping is slightly different from slicing. Here's how to do it:

1. **Grip the knife handle in one hand.**

2. **Rest the fingers of your other hand flatly on the *spine* of the knife (the side of the blade opposite the sharpened edge), near the point.**

   If you prefer, instead of resting your hand on the spine, you can lightly pinch the spine with your thumb and one or two fingers.

3. **Chop the ingredient while holding the point in the same place. Simultaneously work the handle back and forth in a 30- to 45-degree arc (still holding the point in the same place).**

Always assume that a knife is very sharp. It is, after all, a weapon. In fact, respect all sharp objects, including food processor blades. Wash and properly store them right away. And don't put a blade of any kind in soapy water just to soak. It's a hidden danger to the unsuspecting soul who may be kind enough to wash your dishes.

Avoid cross-contamination. Use a plastic cutting board for raw meat, poultry, or fish. Wash the cutting board (preferably in the dishwasher) and knife before you use it to chop vegetables.

Store food properly. My husband thinks anything that has salt or curry in it is automatically preserved for life. No such luck. If this is a light bulb moment for you, know that perishable foods should not remain outside the refrigerator any longer than 2 hours. This advice also applies to cooked foods (other than baked goods) that aren't eaten immediately. When in doubt, throw it out. If you question the safety of a food, don't eat it. It's not worth the risk of food poisoning.

Separating Eggs

Did Humpty Dumpty leave you intimidated by the thought of separating eggs? If you still have visions of a goopy, shell-riddled mess, follow this simple technique — it's really not that difficult:

1. **Using a small bowl, gently crack the shell of an egg straight from the fridge (as opposed to an egg that's been sitting out for a while).**

2. **Carefully pass the egg back and forth between the two halves of the shell, keeping the yolk in the shell and allowing the white to fall into the bowl.**

3. **After each separation, add the single egg white in the bowl to the larger bowl of accumulated whites to be whipped.**

Avoid passing the egg over any sharp edges on the cracked shell — you're less likely to cause the yolk to break. If the yolk does break, you'll have to start over with a new egg. But that's why it's a really good idea to break one egg at a time over a small bowl instead of risking messing up a large bowl of egg whites with a little bit of wild yolk.

Unbroken egg yolks not needed in a recipe can be placed in a small custard cup filled with water. Cover the cup with plastic wrap and store in the refrigerator for up to two days. Extra yolks can be used to make custards or chiffon cakes.

Professional chefs don't use the shells to help separate the whites. After cracking the shell, they pour the egg into a cupped hand and allow the white to ooze between their fingers while the yolk stays in their hand. Unappealing as it sounds, this technique works extremely well.

Mixing Ingredients

So you just throw all the ingredients into a bowl and stir 'em round and round, right? Not exactly. Different situations call for different approaches to mixing. Two techniques you need to know are creaming and folding.

Creaming

Creaming is beating butter or some other shortening to incorporate sugar. This technique calls for you to beat the butter with an electric mixer until it's light and fluffy.

Don't skimp on this step. It creates an army of air bubbles that help the cake to rise to great heights. Pound cakes in particular depend on proper creaming.

When you're creaming, make sure that the butter or shortening is at room temperature. It will beat up lighter and faster, and you won't have to fight through a hard chunk of butter.

Folding

Folding is a technique used to combine two mixtures (usually one lighter than the other) while trying to maintain all the little air bubbles you worked so hard to create in the lighter one. After you spoon or pour the lighter mixture into the heavier mixture, follow this drill, thinking of the bowl as the face of a clock:

1. **Draw a rubber spatula, with the narrow edge coming toward you, from the 12 o'clock position to the 6 o'clock position, slicing down through both mixtures.**

2. **As you approach the 6 o'clock position, hang a left toward 9 o'clock.**

3. **Somewhere around 7 o'clock, twist the spatula broad side up and start to lift some of the underneath mixture up and on top of the lighter mixture.**

4. **Give the bowl a quarter turn and keep repeating until the mixtures are combined, with the batter still light and full of air.**

When you fold beaten egg whites into a heavier mixture, it is accepted practice to *forfeit* one-fourth of the whites. In other words, fold one-fourth of the whites into the heavier mixture as best you can. Assume that most of it will deflate, but forfeiting serves the purpose of lightening up the heavier mixture. Then add the remaining egg whites and continue folding in the steps described in this section.

Preparing Pans

If you see a direction in a recipe telling you to *prepare the pans*, it means that you should grease the baking pan and dust it with flour. Take a look at Figure 4-1 and follow these directions:

1. **Start by lightly greasing the pan with shortening. Spread a thin layer of grease over the bottom and sides of the pan.** Any way is a good way to spread the grease. Use a crumpled paper towel or wax paper or a brush. Or just use your fingers — whatever suits your style.

2. **Sprinkle a small amount of flour into the pan.**

3. **Tilt and rotate the pan to get the flour everywhere.**

4. **Invert the pan and tap out any excess flour.**

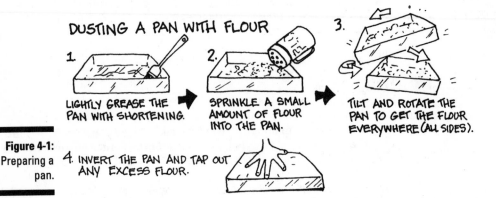

DUSTING A PAN WITH FLOUR

1. LIGHTLY GREASE THE PAN WITH SHORTENING.

2. SPRINKLE A SMALL AMOUNT OF FLOUR INTO THE PAN.

3. TILT AND ROTATE THE PAN TO GET THE FLOUR EVERYWHERE (ALL SIDES).

4. INVERT THE PAN AND TAP OUT ANY EXCESS FLOUR.

Figure 4-1: Preparing a pan.

Pans can also be dusted with ingredients such as cocoa or cornmeal, instead of flour — depending on what's in the recipe. The dusting ingredient often depends on what the final state of the recipe is. Chocolate cakes that don't get iced look better with cocoa rather than a white ring of flour.

You just never know when a cake is going to be in a cranky mood. Sometimes it doesn't want to leave the pan. Lining a pan beforehand with parchment or wax paper becomes a gentle persuader. Large flat cakes baked in a 9-inch-x-13-inch pan (like the Buttermilk-Streusel Coffee Cake in Chapter 10) are usually good candidates for lining (as shown in Figure 4-2). Follow these steps:

1. **To cut the liner, lay the pan on top of the paper and trace the outline with the tip of a pair of scissors. (Don't use a knife for this task, especially if you've just invested a lot of money in a new set.)**

2. **Cut out the shape.**

3. **Grease the pan lightly.**

4. **Place the paper in the pan.**

5. **Continue according to the recipe instructions, greasing or greasing and flouring.**

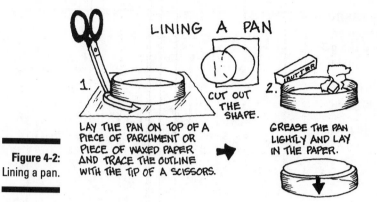

LINING A PAN

1. LAY THE PAN ON TOP OF A PIECE OF PARCHMENT OR PIECE OF WAXED PAPER AND TRACE THE OUTLINE WITH THE TIP OF A SCISSORS.

CUT OUT THE SHAPE.

2. GREASE THE PAN LIGHTLY AND LAY IN THE PAPER.

Figure 4-2: Lining a pan.

With few exceptions (like Bundt pans), I routinely line any pan I'm using. The extra minute or two it takes usually makes life easier in the end, especially if I'm trying an unfamiliar recipe.

Using the Stovetop and Oven

The cooktop (or stovetop) and the oven are the places where molecules start to spin and chemistry happens. This is where the preparations start to turn into something edible. Serious cooks and professionals prefer a gas cooktop. Just like a little red sports car, a gas cooktop is very responsive to adjustments. It can go from low to high in a matter of seconds. Bakers like electric ovens. Just like a '59 Caddie, electric ovens are solid and even. (If you're in the market for a new cooktop/oven, you can have both in one appliance: It's called dual fuel. Of course, you can also buy separate units.)

To get you rolling, here are some stovetop-related terms you're sure to come across as you read the recipes in this and other cookbooks:

- **Simmer:** Heat liquid to just below boiling; small bubbles start rising to the surface.

- **Boil:** Heat liquid until it is more agitated, with moderate bubbles breaking the surface one after another.

- **Rolling boil:** Heat liquid until it appears angry; bubbles rapidly rise over each other.

- **Blanch:** Dunk an ingredient in boiling water for a short period of time and then plunge it in ice water to stop the cooking (a useful technique for skinning nuts or tomatoes and bringing out color in vegetables).

- **Sauté:** Cook food in a pan over moderate-high to high heat in a small amount of oil or butter with frequent stirring or tossing; this is usually done just for a short period of time.

Location, location, location

You're always told to rotate your car tires, but rotate your baking pans? Yep, for much the same reason: even distribution. Your oven has hot spots (mine is right-rear), and you need to shift things around in the oven so that everything bakes evenly. (Rotation is especially important for cookies, but it's also a good idea to give big items such as turkeys a 180-degree turn.)

Loaf pans, cake pans, and the like should not touch each other. Rotate them once during baking. But do wait until they're at least halfway through the cooking time before you rotate.

When using two baking sheets, put them on separate racks in the oven. They should be staggered, not lined up one over the other. You should also leave a generous space between the two racks. Rotate them top to bottom as well as front to back once during baking.

Don't leave the stove unattended. At best, things boil over and look like the Vesuvius lava flow. At worst, they burn and catch fire.

Keep a fire extinguisher in the kitchen. Check the gauge regularly and know how to use it. Keep a container of salt or baking soda within reach, too. Pour either on spills in the oven. They stop oven spills from smoking and possibly catching on fire. And it also makes cleanup easier when the oven is cool.

Keep potholders handy. One is good; two are better. Don't try juggling a hot, heavy object with one potholder — that's courting disaster. And don't ever use a wet potholder; it won't protect you from the heat.

All ovens need to have their temperature taken, whether they're under the weather or not. Save yourself a lot of grief — invest in an oven thermometer. The oven thermometer tells you how hot your oven actually is (as opposed to what the dial says), and you can compensate accordingly. You can test your oven by setting the dial to a certain temperature — 300 degrees, for example. Wait at least 15 minutes and check your oven thermometer. If it reads 300 degrees, you don't have to worry about making any adjustments. But if the thermometer reads 325, then you know that your oven is running 25 degrees warmer than the dial says. So if you have a recipe that calls for the oven to be set at 350, you should set your oven to 325. (This advice works in reverse, of course, if your oven is running cooler than it should be.)

When you're using the oven, temperature is your major concern. Most recipes call for the oven to be preheated. (You'll want to check to be sure.) Whether your oven is gas or electric, set it to the recipe's temperature about 15 minutes before you put the dish in the oven. Preheating ensures that you're working with a fully heated oven.

If your oven temperature is off greatly, have an authorized repair technician adjust it.

In general, lighter and smaller foods should be placed higher in the oven; heavier and bigger foods should be placed lower in the oven. Exceptions are foods that need to be browned on top, such as casseroles — they should be placed higher up. Foods such as quiches that need more heat on their bottoms should be placed on a lower rack. However, if a recipe calls for a specific rack position, that is the one you should use.

Part II
Magnificent Mouthfuls

The 5th Wave
By Rich Tennant

@RICHTENNANT

"Oh, let me help, dear. If you're going to wrap and send a nice fish to someone, use some pretty wrapping paper, not some old newspaper. And here, let me get you a nice bow..."

In this part . . .

On to the good stuff! Chocolate leads the way with recipes for everyone. If the chocolate chapter doesn't suffice in the way of sweets, take a stroll through the candy chapter — or fill your cookie jar with goodies from the cookie chapter. You can find a delectable treat here for every member of the family, including Fido.

Chapter 5

Chocolate: Life Vest for the Soul

*U*nfortunately, Shakespeare wrote no sonnets about chocolate. But this was not a grave oversight on his part. Cacao, the chocolate beverage, did not arrive on Britain's shores until just after his death in 1616 (although Spain had been keeping it a secret for years). History proves that Will's writing is pretty good but, alas, wouldn't you have loved it even more if Juliet had drunk chocolate instead of poison, and lived happily ever after?

You, on the other hand, have the benefit of the past few centuries of chocolate refinement. It comes in many shapes, sizes, and assortments. You can find milk chocolate, dark chocolate, white chocolate, and bittersweet chocolate. Don't forget plain, nutty, fruity, melted, frozen, chopped, curled, shaved, moussed, and baked. Chocolate is paired with everything from the sublime to the ridiculous. Pumpkin, green tea, and pomegranate have all kept the company of chocolate.

A "gift of the gods," chocolate deserves a chapter all its own. Whether you choose the utterly decadent truffles or the handy tote-along biscotti, your chocolate cravings will find a soul mate in this chapter to help smooth out life's little bumps.

Introducing the Varieties of Chocolate

Lucky for us, chocolate comes in many forms — all the better to buoy up your soul and give flight to your spirits. Here are the main types of chocolate:

- **Unsweetened chocolate:** Basic chocolate that gets the job done. Also known as *chocolate liquor* by professionals (it sounds better than it tastes), it contains cocoa butter but no sugar, which gives it flexibility in recipes. But you'd never want to bite into unsweetened chocolate by mistake — it's not a taste sensation you'd want to experience.

- **Semisweet or bittersweet chocolate:** Basic unsweetened chocolate with varying amounts of sugar added. Each manufacturer has its own blend. So don't expect that all bittersweet or even all semisweet chocolates will taste the same. If you sample this category, you'll find a great range in flavors, from nutty to almost fruity.

- **Milk chocolate:** Unsweetened chocolate that has had milk powder and sugar added. It's lighter in color and milder in taste than dark chocolate.

- **Sweet chocolate:** A stronger chocolate than milk chocolate, with lots of sugar added.

- **White chocolate:** The great pretender, this is technically not a chocolate but a mixture of cocoa butter, milk solids, and sugar.

- **Compound coating chocolate:** Also known as summer coating or molding chocolate, it is made from vegetable oil rather than cocoa butter. It is easier to work with, although it definitely doesn't have the taste of its cocoa butter-filled cousins.

- **Unsweetened cocoa:** The powdery residue left after the cocoa butter has been pressed out of chocolate liquor. Cocoa can be *natural,* which is stronger in taste but lighter in color, or *Dutch-processed,* which is milder in flavor but darker in color.

If a recipe calls for Dutch-processed cocoa powder, don't use natural cocoa. Dutch cocoa needs to be paired up with baking powder in order to achieve its true potential.

The sole purpose of hot chocolate or drinking cocoa is to make tummies happy. Don't substitute it for cocoa powder in a recipe because it contains sugar and powdered milk. It is often seen in the company of marshmallows.

Baker's German Chocolate is not at all German but a sweet chocolate named after an employee named Sam German who developed the chocolate.

Preparing to Melt Chocolate

When you're preparing chocolate for melting, it needs to be finely chopped so it spends as little time as possible over the heat (a place that chocolate doesn't want to be anyway). Here are a few ways to approach this task:

✔ **Chopping:** Use a chef's knife to cut up the chocolate with the method described in Chapter 4, but with one modification: Because chocolate is harder than most ingredients you'll chop, place the heel of your palm on the spine of the knife, near the tip, to steady it and help apply more pressure.

✔ **Using a food processor:** Coarsely chop the chocolate with a knife. Place the chocolate in the bowl of a food processor fitted with a metal blade. Pulse it on and off until the chocolate is finely chopped.

✔ **Grating:** Chocolate can be grated easily with a nifty tool called a mouli. A *mouli* is a hand rotary grater outfitted with interchangeable drums, often used for grating Parmesan cheese. You can also rely on your old faithful box grater if you don't have a mouli lying around.

✔ **Using a chipper:** Use this six-pronged device (that looks like it came straight out of a medieval torture chamber) to break up the chocolate. (See Chapter 18 for a list of places to buy cooking tools like this one.)

Melting chocolate

Chocolate melts basically at body temperature. You won't need much more heat than the temperature of your hot little hands to melt chocolate. (That's why children so often have chocolate smeared across their faces.) This is an image to keep in mind when you start to melt chocolate in the kitchen.

Because chocolate has an aversion to heat, the less time it spends near heat, the better. After the chocolate is finely chopped, place it in a double boiler over, but never touching, the water. The water itself should be barely simmering. Because chocolate detests water as much as it detests heat, make sure that all your utensils are dry. If the smallest amount of water gets into the chocolate, it will cause it to *seize*. In a heartbeat, the chocolate will go from a smooth consistency to something grainy and alien, stuck on the end of your spatula. If this happens, your best option is to start over again.

Steam is water. If the water in the double boiler is too hot, steam will leak around the rim and can affect the chocolate. Also, remove the chocolate pot from the water pot quickly, because steam will escape when you separate the two pots.

Milk chocolate and, especially, white chocolate are even more sensitive to heat. When melting these chocolates, bring the water in the saucepan to a simmer and then turn off the heat. Then place the finely chopped chocolate in the top of the double boiler, just allowing the heat of the water to melt it.

Recipes that incorporate melted chocolate into a mixture require a little less coddling. Chocolate loves fat. (Don't we all?) If the recipe calls for melting chocolate with a high-fat ingredient like butter or heavy cream, it can be done directly in a heavy-bottomed saucepan over very low heat, with constant stirring.

Microwaving chocolate

When you melt chocolate in the microwave, you encounter a number of variables — the kind of chocolate, the amount of chocolate, the power of the microwave — so the best advice is to go slowly. Put finely chopped chocolate in a microwave-safe measuring cup or bowl. Do not cover. Adjust the power to medium (or 50 percent) and start with 30 to 45 seconds for a small quantity. Stir and then go with shorter bursts of about 10 to 15 seconds, stirring after each burst. When only a few little chunks of chocolate are left, remove the bowl from the microwave and stir until the chunks melt. (Keep in mind that milk chocolate and white chocolate may require even shorter times to melt in the microwave.) Check package labels for manufacturer's directions.

Many chocolates (except unsweetened) retain their shape while softening in the microwave. Don't be fooled into thinking that it's not melting.

Tempering chocolate

The process of fully tempering chocolate (*tempering* is a melting and cooling process that stabilizes chocolate and gives it a sheen) is rather involved and actually not required for any of the recipes in this book. What you need to know is a quick-temper method, which helps chocolate that has been melted keep its luster.

Figure 5-1 gives you the tempering picture at a glance. Start by finely chopping good-quality dark (bittersweet, semisweet, or unsweetened) chocolate. Place about three-fourths of it in the top of a dry double boiler or bowl over, but not touching, water that's just simmering. Make sure that there isn't any moisture on the spatula and that no steam escapes around the pot.

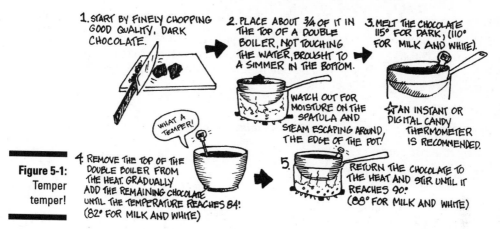

QUICK TEMPERING CHOCOLATE

1. START BY FINELY CHOPPING GOOD QUALITY, DARK CHOCOLATE.

2. PLACE ABOUT ¾ OF IT IN THE TOP OF A DOUBLE BOILER, NOT TOUCHING THE WATER, BROUGHT TO A SIMMER IN THE BOTTOM.

3. MELT THE CHOCOLATE 115° FOR DARK, (110° FOR MILK AND WHITE).

WATCH OUT FOR MOISTURE ON THE SPATULA AND STEAM ESCAPING AROUND THE EDGE OF THE POT!

AN INSTANT OR DIGITAL CANDY THERMOMETER IS RECOMMENDED.

WHAT A TEMPER!

4. REMOVE THE TOP OF THE DOUBLE BOILER FROM THE HEAT. GRADUALLY ADD THE REMAINING CHOCOLATE UNTIL THE TEMPERATURE REACHES 84°! (82° FOR MILK AND WHITE)

5. RETURN THE CHOCOLATE TO THE HEAT AND STIR UNTIL IT REACHES 90°. (88° FOR MILK AND WHITE)

Figure 5-1: Temper temper!

Melt the chocolate to a temperature of 115 degrees for dark chocolate or 110 degrees for milk chocolate or white chocolate. (Use an instant-read or digital candy thermometer to measure the temperature.) Remove the top of the double boiler or bowl from the heat. Gradually add the remaining chocolate until the temperature reaches 84 degrees for dark chocolate or 82 degrees for milk chocolate or white chocolate.

Return the chocolate to the heat and stir until it just reaches 90 degrees for dark chocolate or 88 degrees for milk chocolate or white chocolate.

Oh, Fudge — It's Grainy!

Even veteran candy makers can have one of those days. Your trusted fudge recipe has betrayed you. Not to worry. You can take a lesson from chef Julia Child. Her sage advice was that if you're making a corn soufflé, a culinary land mine if ever there was one, don't mention it beforehand. That way, if it should collapse before it reaches the dinner table, you can proudly present it as your wonderful "corn pudding"! You can adapt that advice for your fudge recipe. If your fudge turns out grainy, simply tell your friends that you made "textured fudge," "assertive fudge," "designer fudge," or even "Gram's secret fudge" — whatever name strikes your fancy. Don't ever let on that the "grain" isn't supposed to be part of the recipe.

O.M.G. Fudge

O.M.G. can stand for "oh, my gosh" or "original meal of the gods" or "one more gobble" — all are fitting. This fudge has an extra helping of chocolate in it to make it exceptionally rich. It's an old-fashioned fudge reminiscent of general stores and quaint vacation towns — the way fudge was meant to taste.

Special equipment: *Candy thermometer*

Preparation time: *15 minutes, plus 30 to 45 minutes cooling*

Cooking time: *30 minutes*

Yield: *Sixty-four 1-inch pieces*

6 tablespoons butter	*¼ cup light corn syrup*
4 ounces unsweetened chocolate, coarsely chopped	*Pinch of salt*
1 cup evaporated milk (not sweetened condensed milk), well shaken	*1½ teaspoons vanilla extract*
3 cups superfine sugar	*1 cup chopped walnuts*

1 Cut the butter into ½-inch cubes. Keep refrigerated.

2 Melt the chocolate and evaporated milk in a heavy-bottomed medium pan over low heat, stirring constantly.

3 Add the sugar, corn syrup, and salt. Increase the heat to medium-low and stir the mixture until the sugar dissolves. Wash down any sugar crystals on the side of the pan. (See Chapter 6 for more information on this technique.) Clip the candy thermometer on the pan and increase the heat to medium-high.

4 Cook until the candy thermometer reads 238 degrees. Occasionally stir gently just to scrape the bottom. Remove the pan from the heat. Add the vanilla. Do not stir. Dot the surface of the chocolate with the butter. Do not stir. Allow to cool, undisturbed, to 110 degrees, about 30 to 45 minutes.

5 Meanwhile, line an 8-x-8-inch pan with aluminum foil, leaving a 2-inch overhang. Lightly grease.

6 Stir the chocolate with a wooden spoon until it starts to thicken. Quickly add the walnuts and pour into the pan. Cool completely. Store in an airtight container for up to 2 weeks.

Vary It! *You can leave out the walnuts and replace them with 1 cup of pecans, pistachios, dried sweetened coconut, or dried fruit.*

Per serving: *Calories 74 (From Fat 32); Fat 4g (Saturated 2g); Cholesterol 4mg; Sodium 8mg; Carbohydrate 11g (Dietary Fiber 0g); Protein 1g.*

Easy Chocolate Treat

Chocolate is special no matter what the occasion. If you're looking for a way to share chocolate as a gift, try the one-bite wonder in this section.

1-2-3 Milk Chocolate Chunky Clusters

This recipe is as easy as one, two, three. Just melt the chocolate, add the raisins and nuts, and drop in a cluster. Oh, there is a Step 4: Eat! To tempt your appetite, see the picture in the color section of this book.

Preparation time: *25 minutes, plus cooling time*

Cooking time: *5 minutes*

Yield: *About 44 clusters*

1 pound good-quality milk chocolate, finely chopped

1¼ cups golden raisins

1 cup unsalted roasted peanuts

1 Line 2 baking sheets with wax paper or parchment paper. Set aside.

2 Place the chocolate in a double boiler over (but not touching) hot water. Bring to a simmer over low heat. Remove from the heat. Continue to stir the chocolate until melted. Remove the top half of the double boiler.

3 Stir the raisins and peanuts into the melted chocolate. Allow to cool for 5 to 10 minutes, until it starts to thicken. Drop by heaping teaspoonfuls onto the baking sheets. You can place them in the refrigerator for 20 minutes to set. Store in an airtight container in a cool place, for up to 2 weeks.

Per serving: *Calories 89 (From Fat 45); Fat 5g (Saturated 2g); Cholesterol 3mg; Sodium 8mg; Carbohydrate 10g (Dietary Fiber 1g); Protein 2g.*

Brownies, Cupcakes, Black Forest Bites

The first recipe in this section is the classic summer-camp care package. Send a batch of brownies to a camper. Put them in an airtight tin for protection against midnight raiders of the four-legged kind. You can also enclose a stamped, self-addressed postcard to make it easier to find out what's happenin'!

Not-So-Basic Brownies

From pot to pan to mouth — a good plan if ever there was one. The two kinds of chocolate in this recipe make for an intensely fudgy brownie. But because you really shouldn't live by chocolate alone, you can add all sorts of ingredients to vary the experience, and make this brownie anything but basic. The all-in-one-pot cooking method makes cleanup easy enough that you'll want to try every one of the ways to vary the flavor.

Special equipment: *Parchment paper*

Preparation time: *20 minutes*

Cooking time: *26 to 28 minutes*

Yield: *Sixteen 2-inch squares*

½ cup (1 stick) butter

2 ounces good-quality semisweet chocolate, coarsely chopped

¾ cup sugar

2 eggs, at room temperature

1 teaspoon vanilla extract

⅔ cup flour

2 tablespoons unsweetened cocoa, sifted

Pinch of salt

¾ cup chopped walnuts

1 Preheat the oven to 350 degrees. Line an 8-x-8-inch pan with parchment or wax paper. Grease lightly. Set aside.

2 Melt the butter and the chocolate over low heat in a medium heavy-bottomed saucepan, stirring constantly. Remove from the heat. Stir in the sugar.

3 Add the eggs, one at a time, stirring until incorporated. Add the vanilla; stir. Add the flour, cocoa, and salt. Stir until smooth. Add the nuts.

4 Pour into the prepared pan. Bake for 26 to 28 minutes. Test with a wooden toothpick. A moist, not wet, crumb should cling to the toothpick when removed (see Figure 5-2).

5 Remove from the oven. Cool on a wire rack. Cut into 16 squares. Store in an airtight container for up to 4 days.

Vary It! *Leave out the walnuts and put in any one of the following ingredients or a combination of the following ingredients to equal ¾ cup: semisweet chocolate chips, chopped pecans, peanuts, pistachios, almonds, coconut, raisins, dried cherries, dried cranberries, dried apricots (chopped), dried pears (chopped), mini chocolate-covered candy pieces, or chocolate-covered raisins. If you want to experiment even further, put ½ cup of the ingredients in the batter and sprinkle the remaining ¼ cup on top of the batter for an attractive presentation.*

Vary It! *Exchange any other extract — peppermint, almond, rum, orange, or coconut, for example, — for the vanilla.*

Per serving: *Calories 171 (From Fat 104); Fat 12g (Saturated 5g); Cholesterol 42mg; Sodium 18mg; Carbohydrate 16g (Dietary Fiber 1g); Protein 3g.*

BROWNIES:
TESTING FOR
DONENESS

Figure 5-2: WITH A WOODEN TOOTHPICK,
Brownie TEST FOR DONENESS
testing. MOIST, NOT WET, CRUMBS
WILL CLING WHEN THE
TOOTHPICK IS REMOVED.

Brownies were first mentioned in print in the 1897 Sears, Roebuck catalog.

No-Bake Black Forest Bites

Somewhere between a cookie and a truffle, these bites are a delight of Old World charm, with all the tastes of Black Forest cake — moist chocolate and tangy sweet cherries rolled into one. Take a look at the photo in the color section of this book.

Special equipment: #100 scoop, mouli grater

Preparation time: 45 minutes, plus 5 minutes cooling

Cooking time: 5 minutes

Yield: 64

6 ounces good-quality semisweet chocolate, chopped	¾ cup spreadable cherry or black cherry fruit jam (Smucker's Simply 100% Fruit)
4 tablespoons butter	¼ teaspoon almond extract
9-ounce box chocolate wafers, finely crushed	7 ounces good-quality white chocolate, finely grated
1½ cups dried cherries, chopped	

1 Line a tray or jelly roll pan with wax paper.

2 Melt the semisweet chocolate and butter in a medium-sized saucepan, stirring constantly over low heat. Remove from the heat.

3 Stir in the chocolate wafers, cherries, cherry fruit spread, and almond extract.

4 Scoop the mixture and roll into 1-inch balls. (They will look a little greasy.) Roll the balls in the white chocolate. Refrigerate in an airtight container for up to 1 week. Bring to room temperature before serving.

Per serving: Calories 76 (From Fat 30); Fat 3g (Saturated 2g); Cholesterol 3mg; Sodium 28mg; Carbohydrate 11g (Dietary Fiber 1g); Protein 1g.

Peanut Butter and Chocolate Dimple Cupcakes

One of the most important pieces of information I discovered early on at school was what day of the week the bookstore received its shipment of peanut butter cups. You had to be fast to get an adequate supply for the week. Although I no longer allow them in the house, the combination of chocolate and peanut butter has not lost its allure. These cupcakes have a slightly sunken center of dense peanut butter, surrounded by intense chocolate cake. Shirley Temple's dimples weren't this appealing.

Preparation time: *30 minutes*

Baking time: *25 to 27 minutes*

Yield: *18 cupcakes*

Filling:

½ cup smooth peanut butter

2 tablespoons light brown sugar

1 tablespoon flour

½ cup milk, at room temperature

Cake:

1⅔ cups flour

3 tablespoons unsweetened cocoa (not Dutch-processed cocoa)

1 teaspoon baking soda

¼ teaspoon salt

1¼ cups light brown sugar

1 cup water

¼ cup vegetable oil

1 tablespoon distilled white vinegar

1½ teaspoons vanilla extract

¼ cup roasted unsalted peanuts, chopped

1 Preheat the oven to 350 degrees. Line 2 muffin tins with muffin papers. Set aside.

2 To make the filling, mix the peanut butter, brown sugar, and flour in a small bowl until smooth. Add the milk, mixing until combined. Set aside.

3 To make the cake, combine the flour, cocoa, baking soda, and salt. Set aside.

4 In a medium bowl, combine the brown sugar, water, oil, vinegar, and vanilla. Whisk until smooth. Add the flour mixture. Whisk until smooth. The batter will be thin.

5 Pour the batter into a large measuring cup or pitcher. Divide the batter evenly among 18 muffin papers. They'll be about half full.

6 Spoon about a measuring tablespoon of the peanut butter mixture into the center of each chocolate-filled muffin paper. Give the muffin tin a light rap on the counter to settle the filling mixture into the chocolate. Sprinkle the peanuts on top of the batter.

7 Bake for 25 to 27 minutes, until a toothpick inserted into the center pulls out moist, not wet, crumbs. Rotate the pans once, halfway through baking. Cool. The cupcakes will keep for 4 days.

Per serving: Calories 196 (From Fat 74); Fat 8g (Saturated 1g); Cholesterol 1mg; Sodium 146mg; Carbohydrate 28g (Dietary Fiber 1g); Protein 4g.

A Triumvirate of Chocolate Sauces — They Rule!

They say that good things come in threes. They, whoever *they* are, could be very right. In this section, you find three sauces — a sauce for every taste: milk chocolate, dark chocolate, and white chocolate. Instead of drawing straws to decide which sauce to give, how about giving all three? Let the recipient decide which to use first.

Malted Milk Chocolate Sauce

The crystal ball sees a banana split in your future. Malteds are nostalgic for some people and a new taste treat for others. Reminiscent of ice cream parlors or malted milk ball candies, this sauce is perfect for an old-fashioned ice cream social.

Preparation time: 10 minutes

Cooking time: 5 minutes

Yield: 1¾ cups

¾ cup heavy cream

½ cup malted milk powder

12 ounces good-quality milk chocolate, chopped

Heat the cream and malted milk powder in a medium saucepan over low heat. Add the chocolate, stirring constantly until melted. Store refrigerated in an airtight container for up to 2 weeks. Serve warm.

Per serving: Calories 186 (From Fat 113); Fat 13g (Saturated 8g); Cholesterol 24mg; Sodium 41mg; Carbohydrate18g (Dietary Fiber 1g); Protein 3g.

Deep Dark Chocolate Sauce

If your cravings run to the dark side, try this delectable sauce. The rich flavor of the dark chocolate is complemented by the buttery flavor of cane sugar syrup (sold in supermarkets under the brand name Lyle's).

Preparation time: 10 minutes

Cooking time: 5 minutes

Yield: 1½ cups

¾ cup heavy cream

4 ounces good-quality semisweet chocolate, chopped

2 ounces unsweetened chocolate, chopped

6 tablespoons cane sugar syrup

4 tablespoons (½ stick) butter

1½ teaspoons vanilla extract

Combine all the ingredients in a medium saucepan. Melt over low heat, stirring constantly until smooth. Store refrigerated in an airtight container for up to 2 weeks. Serve warm.

Per serving: Calories 183 (From Fat 141); Fat 16g (Saturated 9g); Cholesterol 31mg; Sodium 8mg; Carbohydrate 13g (Dietary Fiber 1g); Protein 2g.

Very Vanilla White Chocolate Sauce

In this recipe, little specks of vanilla seed float in an ethereal white chocolate sea. Set a slice of pound cake adrift in it, and you have an incredible dessert.

Preparation time: 15 minutes

Cooking time: 5 minutes

Yield: 1⅔ cups

¾ cup heavy cream

½ vanilla bean, split lengthwise

10 ounces good-quality white chocolate, chopped

1 teaspoon vanilla extract

1 Combine the heavy cream and vanilla bean in a medium saucepan. Gently bring to a simmer and remove from the heat. Allow to sit for 5 minutes.

2 Remove the vanilla bean from the cream. Scrape the seeds from the pod and return the seeds to the heavy cream.

3 Add the chocolate and stir. If is doesn't completely melt, return to very low heat until melted, stirring constantly. Add the vanilla extract.

4 Cool. Store refrigerated in an airtight container for up to 2 weeks. Serve warm.

Tip: *Recycle the vanilla bean to make vanilla sugar. Pat the bean dry and then submerge it in about 1 cup of sugar. Store it in an airtight container.*

Per serving: *Calories 166 (From Fat 109); Fat 12g (Saturated 7g); Cholesterol 23mg; Sodium 25mg; Carbohydrate 13g (Dietary Fiber 0g); Protein 2g.*

Desserts

Chocolate is never ordinary, but the recipes in this chapter give chocolate a chance to shine. If you want to go the extra mile and make something your friends will never forget, try one or more of the recipes in this section.

More than one way to skin a nut

Recipes often require nuts to be prepared in some way before using them. Here are some tips to help you out:

✔ **To skin hazelnuts:** Preheat the oven to 350 degrees. Spread the nuts out in a single layer in a pan with sides. Bake in the oven for about 8 to 10 minutes, until the skins start to crack and the nuts turn a light golden brown. Stir the nuts once about halfway through. Remove from the oven and place the nuts in a clean tea towel. Gather up the ends and twist closed in a bundle. Let them sit for about 15 minutes, until cool enough to handle. Hold the twisted end closed with one hand and vigorously rub back and forth with the other hand. Separate the toasted nuts from skins. Some skins will not come off totally — this is normal. It's usually okay to incorporate a small amount of the skin into the recipe. Or, if you have time and are so inclined, you can scrape off the remaining skin with a small sharp knife.

✔ **To blanch the skins off nuts (such as whole almonds and pistachios):** Dunk them in boiling water. Turn off the heat and let them sit about 3 minutes. Drain and rinse under cold water. The skins should slip off. Use a paring knife to remove stubborn skins.

✔ **To remove salt from salted nuts (if the recipe calls for unsalted, and salted are all you have):** Rinse under hot water. Pat dry. If still moist, put in a 350-degree oven for 2 to 3 minutes.

Freckled Chocolate, Cinnamon, and Hazelnut Biscotti

A generous dose of cinnamon in these biscotti gives off an aroma that alerts the whole household they're coming out of the oven. You just have to make everyone wait until they cool. Biscotti traditionally have no fat in them, but it won't be missed with the robust flavor of cinnamon, hazelnut, and chocolate. These crunchy slices can be dipped in chocolate (see Figure 5-3) to make an even tastier gift. Bring them along as treats for the people in your carpool — the traffic jam is an excuse to have one more. You can view the finished product in the color section of this book.

Special equipment: *Parchment paper*

Preparation time: *65 minutes*

Cooking time: *60 minutes*

Yield: *46 slices, plus the ends*

¾ cup hazelnuts, toasted and skins removed (see the sidebar "More than one way to skin a nut" in this chapter)

1¾ cups flour

1 teaspoon baking powder

½ teaspoon salt

2 teaspoons cinnamon

6 ounces good-quality semisweet or bittersweet chocolate, finely chopped

¾ cup sugar

2 whole eggs, at room temperature

3 egg yolks, at room temperature

1 teaspoon vanilla extract

7 ounces bittersweet chocolate, chopped, for dipping

1 Preheat the oven to 350 degrees. Line a baking sheet with parchment paper. Set aside.

2 While the hazelnuts are cooling, combine the flour, baking powder, salt, and cinnamon. Mix in the 6 ounces chocolate. Set aside.

3 Combine ½ cup of the hazelnuts and the sugar in the bowl of a food processor fitted with a metal blade. Process until the nuts are fairly well ground. Place in a medium bowl.

4 Add the whole eggs, yolks, and vanilla to the sugar mixture. With a mixer on medium-high, beat until the mixture begins to get lighter in color, about 1 minute. Add the flour mixture and beat until incorporated.

5 Turn the dough out onto a lightly floured surface. Divide into two equal parts. Roll each piece into a log 14 inches long, sprinkling the surface with more flour, if necessary Flatten the top to make it 2 inches wide. Place both logs on the baking sheet.

6 Bake for 30 minutes, rotating once during baking. Remove from the oven and gently place on a cooling rack for 15 minutes. Reduce the oven temperature to 325 degrees.

7 Carefully cut the logs on a diagonal with a serrated knife into ½-inch slices. Place the slices on their side on the baking sheet. (For a picture of this step, flip to the Almond and Date Mandelbrot recipe in Chapter 7.) Return to the oven.

8 Bake for 15 minutes. Remove from the oven and cool on a wire rack.

9 Finely chop the remaining ¼ cup hazelnuts. Set aside.

10 Melt the 7 ounces chocolate in a double boiler over, but not touching, simmering water. Remove from the heat.

11 Dip the rounded top third of each biscotti in the chocolate (as shown in Figure 5-3). Lightly scrape the biscotti across the edge of the bowl to remove the excess chocolate. Sprinkle with the chopped nuts. Place on a tray to set. The chocolate can be reheated gently if it becomes too thick. Store in an airtight container for up to 1 week.

Per serving: Calories 91 (From Fat 47); Fat 5g (Saturated 2g); Cholesterol 23mg; Sodium 37mg; Carbohydrate 11g (Dietary Fiber 1g); Protein 2g.

Cinnamon is actually the bark of a tree.

DIPPING BISCOTTI

1. DIP THE ROUNDED, TOP ⅓ OF THE BISCOTTI INTO THE MELTED CHOCOLATE. REMOVE EXCESS.

2. SPRINKLE WITH CHOPPED NUTS.

3. PLACE ON A TRAY TO SET.

Figure 5-3: Going for a dip with biscotti.

White Chocolate Coeur à la Crème with Fresh Strawberry Balsamic Sauce

Traditionally this delicate, heart-shaped, cheese dessert is served unsweetened. The addition of white chocolate adds just a light touch of sweetness. The heart mold is a deep ceramic dish with holes in the bottom to drain excess moisture. This dessert makes a self-contained gift — you may want to include the recipe. It makes a lovely dessert for a summer's eve or a tempting shape for someone you love.

Special equipment: *4 cup (7-inch) ceramic coeur à la crème mold, cheesecloth*

Preparation time: *40 minutes*

Cooking time: *5 minutes*

Yield: *Eight ½-cup servings*

4 ounces good-quality white chocolate, chopped

½ cup heavy cream

1 cup small-curd cottage cheese, at room temperature

8 ounces cream cheese, at room temperature

½ cup sour cream, at room temperature

Fresh Strawberry Balsamic Sauce (see the following recipe)

1 Gently melt the chocolate and heavy cream in a double boiler over, but not touching, simmering water. Set aside to cool slightly.

2 Press the cottage cheese through a strainer into a medium bowl. Add the cream cheese and sour cream. Beat until just blended. Add the melted chocolate mixture. Mix until just blended. Set aside.

3 Cut a double thickness of cheesecloth generous enough to fit into the mold and fold over itself when the mold is full. Wet the cheesecloth with cold water and squeeze out most of the moisture. Lay the cheesecloth in the mold. Ease out any wrinkles on the bottom — they'll leave indentations on the cheese. Let the excess hang over the edge.

4 Pour the cheese mixture into the mold. Gently overlap the cheesecloth on top. Cover the top with plastic wrap and place on a pan or plate with an edge. Refrigerate overnight to drain.

5 To unmold, gently pull the cheesecloth back off the top. Place a plate over the mold and invert onto the plate. Carefully remove the cheesecloth. Serve with the Fresh Strawberry Balsamic Sauce. This dessert keeps for 3 days.

Fresh Strawberry Balsamic Sauce

Preparation time: *15 minutes*

Yield: *2¼ cups*

16 ounces fresh strawberries

3 tablespoons balsamic vinegar

2 to 3 tablespoons sugar

1 Wash the strawberries. Remove the stems and hard core. Cut the strawberries in half and place them in a blender jar.

2 Add the balsamic vinegar and sugar. (The amount of sugar you need depends on how sweet the strawberries are.) Puree. This sauce keeps 4 days in the refrigerator.

Vary It! *Add cognac instead of balsamic vinegar.*

Tip: *Lacking the traditional heart mold, you can punch holes with a nail in 4-cup aluminum pan. (It won't look as pretty to give, but it will get the job done.) An uncoated breadbasket also works. Just wash thoroughly with water — but omit the soap. If you use one of these alternatives, you may want to unmold the coeur à la crème onto a plate and skip giving the mold as part of the gift.*

Per serving: Calories 320 (From Fat 218); Fat 24g (Saturated 15g); Cholesterol 65mg; Sodium 225mg; Carbohydrate 19g (Dietary Fiber 2g); Protein 8g.

Coeur à la crème is soft when unmolded, so a good way to give it is to put the mold (wipe the bottom first), with the crème still in it, on a plate and wrap the whole thing in cellophane and ribbon. Keep it refrigerated as long as possible before giving.

To determine the capacity of a mold, place a plastic bag inside the mold and fill with water one cup at a time, keeping track of how much you've added.

Alive-and-Kicking Chocolate Gateau

You've probably seen desserts named "Death by Chocolate." But who wants to *die* from eating chocolate? Living to eat *more* chocolate is a better option. This recipe, trufflelike in consistency, is a healthier variation of the popular chocolate cake known as gateau (pronounced ga-TOH). It's still mostly chocolate, but egg substitute replaces the eggs and the butter is swapped with puréed dried plums. You won't miss the butter, and everyone will wonder what that subtle flavor is.

Preparation time: 40 minutes

Cooking time: 25 minutes

Yield: 10 to 12 servings

½ cup water

½ cup dried plums (about 8 depending on size), halved

14 ounces good-quality semisweet chocolate, finely chopped

8-ounce container liquid egg substitute, at room temperature

1 teaspoon vanilla extract

Whipped cream (optional)

1 Bring the ½ cup water to a boil in a small saucepan. Remove from the heat and add the dried plums. Let sit for 20 minutes, until just warm.

2 Line an 8-inch round cake pan with wax paper or parchment paper. Grease lightly. (For easier removal of the cake, do not grease the pan bottom under the wax paper.) Start to prepare a bain marie by heating water to pour into a roasting pan that's large enough to hold the 8-inch cake pan with an inch all around it. (A *bain marie* is simply a hot water bath that coddles delicate ingredients from heat.) Preheat the oven to 400 degrees.

3 Meanwhile, melt the chocolate in a medium-size bowl over, but not touching, barely simmering water. Remove the bowl from the heat. Set aside.

4 Puree the plums in a blender until smooth and thick. Add the egg substitute and vanilla to the chocolate, stirring until blended. Scrape the pureed plums into the melted chocolate, stirring until blended.

5 Pour into the prepared cake pan. Place the cake pan in the roasting pan. Place on the oven rack. Carefully pour about ¾ inch boiling water into the roasting pan (to come halfway up the side of the cake pan).

6 Bake for 10 minutes. Loosely cover with a piece of aluminum foil. Bake for 15 minutes more.

7 Carefully remove from the oven. Remove the cake pan from the water and place on a cooling rack. Let cool for 1 hour. Refrigerate for 2 hours.

8 To turn the cake out, run a knife with a thin blade around the edge of the pan. Place a piece of wax paper on a cooling rack or plate. Invert the pan onto wax paper. Give the bottom a sharp tap. If the cake sticks, immerse the bottom of the pan in very hot water for a few seconds.

9 Reinvert the cake onto a serving plate. Bring to room temperature before serving. Serve with whipped cream, if desired. The cake will keep in the refrigerator for 1 week.

Tip: You can also release the cake from the pan by placing it on a cooktop burner over very low heat. Rotate the pan quickly in a circular motion for a few seconds. Invert onto a wax-paper-covered cooling rack. Repeat if necessary, in small increments. Don't get impatient, or else the cake will melt.

Note: This is a great cake that is kashrus (kosher) for a Passover Seder. Just omit the vanilla extract (the alcohol isn't kosher for Passover). It contains no dairy products, so it goes well with a meat or a dairy meal.

Per serving: Calories 182 (From Fat 119); Fat 13g (Saturated 7g); Cholesterol 0mg; Sodium 40mg; Carbohydrate 19g (Dietary Fiber 1g); Protein 5g.

Storing chocolate

In an earlier life, chocolate definitely was not a beach-goer. It hates excessive exposure to heat and has a major distaste for water. When you understand that about chocolate, you're pretty much home free.

Chocolate doesn't need to be refrigerated, but it should be kept in a cool, dry place. The ideal temperature is between 60 and 70 degrees, away from light and heat. If you choose to store it in the refrigerator, make sure that it's wrapped so it doesn't pick up the odors of the other foods in the fridge.

Chocolate Truffles

No chocolate confection has had quite the enduring love affair that truffles have had. The flavor of chocolate explodes in your mouth, followed by a divine sensation of smoothness. Truffles have been used as a canvas for every taste imaginable. Gourmet chocolate companies promote them at every season. They're the epitome of food gift giving. And they can be so simple to make. Use the best chocolate you can afford when making this recipe.

Special equipment: *#100 scoop*

Preparation time: *40 minutes, plus 2 hours chilling*

Cooking time: *10 minutes*

Yield: *Sixty-two 1-inch balls*

10 tablespoons (1¼ sticks) butter

⅔ cup heavy cream

12 ounces semisweet or bittersweet chocolate, chopped

1 egg yolk, at room temperature

2 tablespoons orange-flavored liqueur

Unsweetened cocoa, for rolling

1 Place the butter and heavy cream in a double boiler over, but not touching, hot water. Melt over medium heat. Turn the heat to low.

2 Add the chocolate, stirring until smooth. Remove from the heat. Whisk in the egg yolk and liqueur until smooth. (If the raw egg yolk is a health concern, replace it with 1 tablespoon pasteurized egg substitute product.)

3 Refrigerate the chocolate mixture for about 1½ hours, stirring occasionally.

4 When the chocolate mixture is very firm but not hard, scoop into 1-inch balls. Place on a tray or jelly roll pan lined with wax paper or parchment paper. Chill until firmed again, about 30 minutes.

5 With clean hands, roll the scooped chocolate into balls. Roll the balls in the cocoa. Refrigerate in an airtight container. Truffles can be rerolled in cocoa, if necessary, before giving or serving. They'll keep 2 weeks in the refrigerator.

Tip: *Although you store these truffles in the refrigerator, they're best enjoyed at room temperature. This is not to say you can't enjoy them cold from the fridge if you happen to be passing by and hear one call to you!*

Vary It! *Instead of rolling the truffles in cocoa, you can roll them in confectioners' sugar, a mixture of cocoa and confectioners' sugar, finely chopped nuts (including pistachios), chocolate or colored sprinkles, coconut, crushed peppermints, or crushed gingersnaps.*

Per serving: Calories 54 (From Fat 46); Fat 5g (Saturated 3g); Cholesterol 12mg; Sodium 2mg; Carbohydrate 3g (Dietary Fiber 0g); Protein 1g.

Chapter 6

Sweet Celebrations

In This Chapter

▶ Mastering the finer points of candy making

▶ Making candy to share with your friends

Recipes in This Chapter

▶ Piña Colada Candies

▶ Easy Alabaster Mints

▶ Microwave Kaffee Klatsch Nut Candy

▶ Benne Seed Candy

▶ Balsamic Vinegar Candy

▶ Toast-of-the-Town Big Apples on a Stick

▶ Candy Sushi

▶ Tea Party Sugar Cubes

Did you ever stand in front of a candy counter and try to decide what to do with your allowance? That was when you were 5 or 8 or 11 years old. Even now, as an adult, you probably have a secret favorite candy bar. (Mine's the caramel one rolled in salty peanuts.)

This chapter tells you how to create a candy store in your kitchen. It has all the information about thermometers, melting sugar, and testing doneness that you need to fulfill all your childhood dreams. It gives new meaning to the phrase "Home Sweet Home."

Visions of Sugar Plums: Getting Ready to Make Candy

The following sections fill you in on some guidelines you should pay attention to before jumping into making candy.

My best overall advice in the candy department is very simple but very important: Read all the directions carefully and know the steps. Sure, you know it's important to read and follow directions in any recipe. But it's even more important in candy making, because the candy can overcook in the blink of an eye. You need to know each step well enough that you don't have to stop and study it in the middle of things.

Would you believe that weather is a factor, too?

Paying attention to humidity

If today's the day you're going to make candy and you roll out of bed and feel your way down the hall to the bathroom, only to discover that your hair is frizzed beyond help, go back to bed. Today is not the day to make candy. No, you don't need picture-perfect hair in order to make good candy. But odds are, if your hair is frizzed, it's because of high humidity. And the first rule of candy making is never to make it on a humid or rainy day.

Why does weather play such a critical part in candy making? Because sugar — a main component of candy — loves to absorb water. It thinks it's helping by pulling water out of the atmosphere and keeping things moist. (You'll be grateful for this trait when you get to the cake chapter, but for candies, it's not much fun.) In order to keep the sugar in line, the ideal room temperature should be between 60 and 68 degrees, with low humidity. If the temperature or humidity is high, head to your local video store and rent *Willy Wonka and the Chocolate Factory* instead.

If you *must* make candy when the humidity is high, try cooking the candy 1 or 2 degrees higher than the recipe recommends.

Making the grade: Thermometers

What do doctors, weather forecasters, and candy makers have in common? They need accurate thermometers. Candy making is precise — there is no getting around that fact. So investing in a candy thermometer will make your results more satisfying.

Thermometers come in three basic varieties: metal, glass, and digital. Candy thermometers (or deep-fat thermometers, as they are sometimes called) have a range of 100 to 400 degrees. They should not be confused with meat thermometers, which go only to 220 degrees. Varying in price, candy thermometers are readily available, even in supermarkets.

When you're buying a candy thermometer, some of the features to look for include the following:

- ✔ **Increments of 2 degrees:** A glass thermometer with 1-degree increments is even better, but these are usually available only through catalogs and specialty stores. Plus, they cost more. Digitals, although a little more costly, read in 1-degree increments and are widely available.

- ✔ **A clip to attach to the pan side:** The tip of the thermometer should only be submerged in the liquid; it should never touch the bottom or sides of the pan — it will give an inaccurate reading. That's why a clip comes in handy.

▌ ✔ **Markings to indicate the various stages of hardness:** These markings are helpful, but they're not absolutely necessary.

Regardless of what kind of thermometer you purchase, you should test it before its first real use. Put the thermometer into a saucepan of boiling water and check, at eye level, what the thermometer is reading. Water boils at 212 degrees — at sea level. (And you thought you'd never use the information from that Earth Science class again.) If your thermometer reads 212 degrees, you're fine. If it reads something other than 212 degrees, you need to take that into consideration when you're following a recipe. If your thermometer reads 206 degrees in boiling water, then you know the actual temperature is always 6 degrees *higher* than what the thermometer says.

All the world's a stage: Paying attention to your candy's hardness

As sugar or sugar syrups get hotter, they boil away more and more water. The higher the temperature, the less water, and the more brittle the candy. Different candies require different temperatures or stages. Fudge, which requires one of the lowest stages, is obviously softer than a lollipop, which requires one of the highest stages.

Now is probably a good time for me to come clean: Despite what I said in the previous section, you actually *can* make candy without a thermometer. You may have figured out already that Fanny Farmer didn't have a shiny new digital thermometer. And you may remember seeing your grandmother perform strange rituals with a glass of water. Now you too can discover the voodoo of candy testing. If you're going to use this method, you may want to try it once or twice until you feel comfortable with the technique. (And if it seems too complicated, a thermometer is an easy fix.)

Each stage of candy temperature has a characteristic appearance. The age-old method of finding out the stage is to carefully dribble hot syrup into a glass of very cold water, as you can see in Figure 6-3, on the last page of this chapter. When you do, pay attention to the results and compare them to what you see in Table 6-1.

Table 6-1	Identifying the Stage of Your Candy	
Stage	**Temperature**	**Characteristic**
Thread	230 to 234 degrees	Soft 2- to 3-inch threads
Soft ball	235 to 240 degrees	A soft ball that will flatten when removed from the water

(continued)

Table 6-1 *(continued)*

Stage	Temperature	Characteristic
Firm ball	244 to 248 degrees	A pliable ball that will hold its shape when removed from the water
Hard ball	250 to 266 degrees	A firmer ball that can still be flattened between your fingers
Soft crack	270 to 290 degrees	Threads that are hard but still bendable
Hard crack	300 to 310 degrees	Hard, brittle threads
Caramel	320 degrees	Syrup that turns deep golden brown and will rapidly turn black

The major problem with this method of testing is that the candy continues to cook while you're squishing the syrup trying to determine its hardness. So start testing before the designated time period is up.

Sugar and spice and more candy advice

When you're ready to start the candy-making process, here are some hints to keep in mind:

- ✔ **Don't double a recipe unless the cookbook indicates that it's okay to do so.** Doubling is just a gamble that's not worth taking with recipes as precise as candy.

- ✔ **Use a burner wider than the bottom of the pan.** Doing so helps ensure more even heating.

- ✔ **Keep a cup of water and a pastry brush near the stove.** When the sugar has dissolved, "wash down" any crystals that remain (see Figure 6-1).

- ✔ **Be sure that when you clip the candy thermometer on the pan, the tip doesn't touch the side or the bottom.**

You're Ready to Roll: Candy Recipes

The recipes in this chapter vary in their degree of difficulty. If you're totally overwhelmed by thermometers and sugar syrup, start with Easy Alabaster Mints, which require basically no cooking. Move on to Kaffee Klatsch Nut Candy, which is done in the microwave. By then your cravings will lead you to the other sweet temptations that follow.

Piña Colada Candies

These little balls are rich morsels evoking dreams of the distant tropics. If you have friends in a northern climate, where a beach, palm trees, and poolside food service aren't available, try sending these candies instead.

Special equipment: *Candy thermometer*

Preparation time: *40 minutes*

Cooking time: *35 minutes, plus 45 minutes cooling time*

Yield: *About 3 dozen*

2 cups shredded sweetened coconut

8-ounce can crushed pineapple in its own juice, very well drained (about ½ cup)

1 cup sugar

¾ cup buttermilk

¼ cup light brown sugar (free of lumps)

2 tablespoons dark corn syrup

1 tablespoon butter

1 tablespoon dark rum

1 Preheat the oven to 350 degrees.

2 Toast 1½ cups of the coconut on a jelly roll pan in the oven for about 8 to 10 minutes, until golden. Set aside. The coconut on the outer edges of the pan will start toasting quickly, so check the progress and stir when needed.

3 Combine the pineapple, sugar, buttermilk, brown sugar, corn syrup, and butter in a saucepan. Dissolve over medium-low heat, stirring gently with a wooden spoon. Wash down any undissolved sugar crystals with a pasty brush dipped in cold water. (For more about this technique, see the section "Sugar and spice and more candy advice," earlier in this chapter.) Clip the candy thermometer on the inside of the pan.

4 Increase the heat to medium-high. Cook, stirring often, until the candy thermometer reaches 238 degrees. Remove from the heat. Gently stir in the remaining ½ cup coconut (untoasted) and the rum. Stir just until incorporated. Place on a cooling rack; let cool to 110 degrees, about 45 minutes.

5 Stir the candy mixture with a wooden spoon for about 5 minutes, until it starts to thicken.

6 Drop by slightly rounded measuring teaspoonfuls onto the toasted coconut. Roll in the coconut, shaping into a ball as you go. If the shape doesn't hold completely, pat the round again when cooler. Store in an airtight container for up to 1 week.

Vary It! *Substitute l teaspoon vanilla extract for rum, if you prefer. For a less sweet candy, stir ½ cup unsweetened coconut into the mixture instead of the sweetened coconut. You can place each coconut ball in a small foil cup (see Chapter 18 for resources) or a decorative petit four muffin paper, to dress it up for presenting it to your friends or family.*

Per serving: *Calories 64 (From Fat 20); Fat 2g (Saturated 2g); Cholesterol 1mg; Sodium 21mg; Carbohydrate 11g (Dietary Fiber 0g); Protein 0g.*

Easy Alabaster Mints

These bracing little candies (pictured in the color section of this book) are so simple to prepare — you'll want to give them to everyone. Try "dressing" them up with the decorating options, and then you can give them for different occasions.

Special equipment: #100 scoop (1⅛ inch), candy papers (optional)

Preparation time: 1 hour and 15 minutes, plus 3 hours drying time

Cooking time: 3 to 4 minutes for melting frosting

Yield: Fifty-four 1-inch balls or 1½-inch patties

8 tablespoons (1 stick) butter, softened

⅓ cup light corn syrup

1½ teaspoons peppermint extract

4¾ cups confectioners' sugar

16-ounce can basic vanilla frosting (not cream cheese or whipped frosting) (optional)

Food coloring

1 Using a mixer, cream the butter, corn syrup, and peppermint extract together in a medium bowl.

2 Add about half the confectioners' sugar and mix until smooth. Continue adding the sugar until the mixture is too thick to beat. Knead any of the remaining sugar into the mixture by hand until a smooth ball forms.

3 Scoop the mixture, leveling across the top of the scoop with a knife. You can also use a slightly rounded teaspoon if you don't have a scoop. Roll the mixture between your palms to form into 1-inch balls. If not using the scoop, take a rounded teaspoonful and roll into 1-inch balls. If you prefer, flatten into 1½-inch disks or patties.

4 Place the balls or patties on wax paper and allow to air dry for about 2 hours, until a slight crust forms. You can stop here and leave the dried mints in their "birthday suits" to be packaged later in colorful candy cups. Or you can continue on to Step 5 and dress them up with colored sugar, crushed peppermints, or icing.

5 Line 2 jelly roll pans or trays with wax or parchment paper. Place cooling racks on top.

6 If decorating with a drizzle (see Step 7), remove ⅓ cup of the frosting and set aside. Place the remaining frosting in a double boiler over medium-low heat. Melt just until thin enough to pour easily off a spoon. Do not heat too much or the icing will be too thin to coat the mints. Remove from the heat but keep the frosting over hot water. Add the food coloring to achieve the desired tint.

7 Place one ball or patty at a time on a fork. Dip into the melted icing and coat. Let as much excess frosting as possible run off. If necessary, scrape off additional drippings on the edge of the double boiler. Place the candy on the cooling racks, allowing about 1 inch between candies. Let dry about 1 hour. You can reheat the frosting in the double boiler if it starts to thicken.

8 Put the remaining frosting in a small resealable plastic bag. Partially close the bag and place it upright in a measuring cup or small microwaveable bowl. Place in the microwave and heat until just softened, in small increments, 5 seconds at a time.

9 Squish the frosting gently in the bag to ensure even melting. (You can also add a drop of different food coloring before squishing.) Make a tiny cut off the corner of the bag. Before decorating, gently loosen the mints from the rack with a metal spatula. Gently squeeze stripes or squiggles across the top of the mints. Let dry. Place in candy papers, if desired. Store in an airtight container for up to 1 week.

Tip: *The closer the bars are on the cooling rack, the better it will work. The cooling racks that have crisscross bars forming a square actually are the best.*

Vary It! *If you don't want to leave the mints plain but you don't want to dip them in icing either, no problem! After you've shaped the balls, while they're still soft, roll them in colored sugar or crushed peppermints. You can also roll the candy into egg shapes for Easter.*

Per serving: *Calories 92 (From Fat 29); Fat 3g (Saturated 1g); Cholesterol 5mg; Sodium 20mg; Carbohydrate 16g (Dietary Fiber 0g); Protein 0g.*

You can easily make your own colored sugar. Put about a cup of sugar in a small plastic bag. Add a few drops of food coloring and work into the sugar. Keep adding a drop of coloring at a time until you reach a color you like.

Figure 6-1: The "wash down" process.

WASHING DOWN SUGAR

☆ KEEP A CUP OF WATER + A PASTRY BRUSH NEAR THE STOVE.

1. WHEN THE SUGAR HAS DISSOLVED, 'WASH DOWN' ANY CRYSTALS THAT REMAIN DIP THE BRUSH IN WATER.

2. PLACE ON THE SIDE OF THE PAN JUST ABOVE SYRUP AND GENTLY 'PUSH' CRYSTALS DOWN ↓ WITH WATER.

3. WET BRUSH AS NEEDED. CONTINUE ALL THE WAY AROUND THE PAN.

Microwave Kaffee Klatsch Nut Candy

What could be better than having a few friends over for coffee? It's better if the few friends are three of your favorite nuts and they're surrounded by coffee, cream, and sugar coating.

Preparation time: *15 minutes*

Cooking time: *17 minutes (in a 700-watt microwave oven)*

Yield: *5 loosely packed cups*

1 cup pecans	½ cup sour cream (measured in a dry measuring cup)
1 cup walnuts	
1 cup whole blanched almonds	1 tablespoon instant espresso granules
¾ cup light brown sugar (free of lumps)	1 teaspoon vanilla extract
½ cup sugar	

1 Preheat the oven to 350 degrees. Spread the pecans, walnuts, and almonds on a jelly roll pan or baking sheet. Bake for about 10 minutes, tossing once halfway through. Turn off the oven and open the door. Leave the nuts in the oven to keep them warm.

2 Carefully combine the sugars, sour cream, and espresso granules in an 8-cup glass measuring cup or an 8-cup glass bowl. (Don't use a smaller size measuring cup. Trust me on this one.) Try not to slosh any mixture up the sides. (If it happens, scrape down the sides with a rubber spatula. Wipe any remaining residue off with a damp paper towel.)

3 Place in the microwave, uncovered, and cook on high for 3 minutes. Remove the measuring cup and stir with a rubber spatula. Leave as little of the sugar mixture on the sides as possible (but you don't have to wipe with a damp towel again). Microwave on high for 3 more minutes. Stir again. Microwave on high for 1 more minute. Remove from the microwave.

4 Line a second jelly roll pan or baking sheet with parchment paper. Set aside.

5 Carefully stir the warm nuts into the sugar mixture. Add the vanilla. Stir continually until the sugar mixture starts to thicken and coats the nuts.

6 Turn out the nut mixture onto the parchment-paper-lined baking sheet or jelly roll pan. Spread the mixture out, separating the nuts. Let cool. Break into smaller clusters if necessary. Store in an airtight container in the refrigerator for up to 4 days.

Per serving: Calories 175 (From Fat 107); Fat 12g (Saturated 2g); Cholesterol 3mg; Sodium 7mg; Carbohydrate 16g (Dietary Fiber 1g); Protein 3g. (per 1/4 cup).

If you're looking for a great way to present candies such as the Microwave Kaffee Klatsch Nut Candy to your family or friends, pile matching coffee mugs full of candy. Wrap them in cellophane and ribbon.

Benne Seed Candy

These crispy candies are loaded with intensely-flavored sesame seeds. (*Benne* is from a West African dialect and means "sesame.") Their preparation doesn't require a thermometer but does require a great deal of care, because the sugar syrup gets incredibly hot. Sesame seeds supposedly bring luck, so this is a nice gift for someone starting a new job, celebrating a graduation, or beginning any other grand endeavor. (But they taste equally wonderful for those whose lives aren't changing in the slightest.)

Preparation time: *20 minutes*

Cooking time: *15 minutes*

Yield: *2½ cups*

1¼ cup sesame seeds, toasted (see the sidebar "Toasting nuts and seeds" in this chapter)

2 teaspoons grated lemon zest

¾ teaspoon ginger

1½ cups sugar

2 tablespoons light corn syrup

1 teaspoon vanilla extract

1 Lightly grease a jelly roll pan and the back of a large metal spoon.

2 Combine the cooled sesame seeds, lemon zest, and ginger in a small bowl.

3 Heat the sugar and corn syrup in a skillet over medium heat. Stir gently and often with a wooden spoon or a squared-off wooden spatula. The sugar melts slowly and most of the time looks like what the snowplow has left on the side of the road. Watch the sugar carefully. As it melts, it changes from clear to pale yellow to rich golden. When it is golden, remove it from the heat.

4 Working quickly but with extreme care — this is as hot as it gets — add the sesame seed mixture and the vanilla to the melted sugar. Stir thoroughly. Pour into the greased pan. Smooth out with the back of the metal spoon.

5 Allow to cool totally. Remove the candy from the pan and break into pieces. Store in an airtight container for up to 2 weeks.

Tip: *Using a flat baking pan helps ensure that the candy thickness will be more even.*

Tip: *Sesame seeds burn easily when toasting. Keep your eye on them and stir often. The seeds have a mind of their own. After toasting them, place them on parchment paper or even a paper towel. Use the parchment paper or paper towel to "funnel" the seeds into the bowl.*

Per serving (¼ cup): *Calories 253 (From Fat 79); Fat 9g (Saturated 0g); Cholesterol 1mg; Sodium 5mg; Carbohydrate 37g (Dietary Fiber 0g); Protein 3g.*

Buy large quantities of sesame seed at a health food store or in bulk from a catalog. (See Chapter 17 for a list of resources.) That's cheaper than buying sesame seed in a supermarket.

TIP

Toasting nuts and seeds

You can toast nuts and seeds in the oven, in a skillet on the stove, or in the microwave. To toast them in the oven, preheat the oven to 350 degrees. Toast the seeds or nuts in a single layer on a jelly roll pan for about 8 to 10 minutes. Stir large nuts once while toasting. Small nuts and seeds may need more frequent attention. Watch seeds carefully to keep them from burning.

To toast them in the skillet, cook the seeds or nuts in a single layer over medium heat until lightly golden. Times will vary. Stir often. Skillet-toasting works best for seeds and flat nuts such as slivered and sliced almonds or pignoli.

To toast nuts and seeds in the microwave, place them on a plate in a single layer. Microwave on high for 3 to 5 minutes. Stir. Repeat, if necessary. Some nuts will not look toasted, but they will have a nice aroma.

Balsamic Vinegar Candy

Not anywhere as unappealing as it sounds, the vinegar in this candy takes the edge off the overwhelming sweetness that most hard candies have. These candies make a great gift for a friend with a lingering cough.

The balsamic-style vinegar found in supermarkets is okay here as long as the label indicates that the product actually contains some *must,* or fermented vinegar. You're just getting the flavor of vinegar in this recipe. Cask masters would be aghast if the expensive vinegars were recommended here. But do take the opportunity sometime to sample the true elixir (which I describe in the sidebar "Nectar of Modena: Balsamic vinegar," elsewhere in this chapter); you'll be delighted.

Special equipment: *Candy thermometer*

Preparation time: *10 minutes*

Cooking time: *35 minutes*

Yield: *2¼ cups*

1 tablespoon butter	*¼ cup light brown sugar (free of lumps)*
1⅔ cup sugar	*⅔ cup balsamic vinegar*

1 Lightly grease a jelly roll pan. (Don't use a warped one.) Set aside.

2 Melt the butter in a saucepan, swirling up the sides about 2 inches.

3 Add the sugar, brown sugar, and vinegar. Cook over medium-low heat, gently stirring with a wooden spoon until the sugar dissolves.

4 Wash down the sugar crystals from the sides of the pan with a brush dipped in water. (For more on this technique, see the section "Sugar and spice and more candy advice," earlier in this chapter.) Clip a candy thermometer to the side of the pan, making sure that the tip doesn't touch the bottom of the pan. Increase the heat to medium-high. Boil, without stirring, to 310 degrees. (Be careful — the fumes from this process will really clear your sinuses.)

5 Carefully pour the candy into the prepared pan. (Remember to pour away from you.) Let as much flow out as possible. Do not scrape the pan.

6 When cool, break into individual candies. Layer between wax paper in an airtight container.

Tip: *Pouring the syrup into hard candy or lollipop molds gives a fancier, more uniform presentation. See Chapter 18 for a list of equipment resources such as lollipop molds.*

Tip: *To remove stuck-on candy faster, fill the saucepan with hot water and return to the stove. Bring to a boil with the wooden spoon and thermometer in it.*

Per serving (¼ cup): Calories 170 (From Fat 11); Fat 1g (Saturated 1g); Cholesterol 3mg; Sodium 7mg; Carbohydrate 41g (Dietary Fiber 0g); Protein 0g.

Nectar of Modena: Balsamic vinegar

Balsamic vinegar is the pampered queen of vinegars whose lineage shines through in every drop. Do not judge this mahogany liquid by the acrid, watery substance found in the supermarket aisles. The true ruler of vinegars is produced in Modena, Italy, where it goes through a long process before claiming the crown.

Balsamic vinegar is sort of like a wine that took a different fork in the road. The method is similar to that of winemaking. And like a Bordeaux or even a Champagne that can come only from its assigned region of France, balsamic vinegar has the equivalent *denomination of controlled origin.* That is, only the area of Modena, Italy, is allowed to produce the vinegar. The label must have the words *Aceto Balsamico Tradizionzle di Modena* on the package to warrant the price tag that goes along with it.

Wines have preferred grapes, and so do balsamic vinegars. The grapes — skin, seed, pulp, and all — are slowly cooked down and then fermented for a year. Not satisfied, balsamic vinegar requires more attention. It is then stored, not in one wooden cask, but in a succession of at least five wooden casks — each from different woods, traditionally ones such as juniper, oak, chestnut, ash, cherry, or mulberry. Each wooden cask gives it own special flavor to the vinegar. The barrels are then stored in attics in the village for several years. The longer it stays in a barrel, the higher the price. Some vinegars are aged 100 years. Modena can barely keep up with the production of real balsamic.

The more expensive the vinegar gets, the simpler the serving of it should be. You can drizzle balsamic vinegar over strawberries or ice cream, toss it with simple salads, or serve it straight up, as an after-dinner digestive. After all, *balsamic* means "health giving."

Toast-of-the-Town Big Apples on a Stick

Plain caramel apples won't be the same after you try these treats. Granny Smith apples make a nice contrast to the sweet coating. Just dispel any notion that these apples are even remotely healthy. If Adam and Eve got thrown out of Eden because of these apples, they would've left happy. These treats make great gifts in the fall. Bring them to a Halloween party or give them as a back-to-school treat, and you're sure to be a hit.

Special equipment: *Three or four 7-inch dowels about ³⁄₁₆ inch thick; candy thermometer; parchment paper*

Preparation time: *30 minutes, plus 1 hour drying time*

Cooking time: *30 minutes*

Yield: *3 large apples or 4 medium apples*

3 large apples or 4 medium apples (about 1½ pounds)

¾ cup sugar

½ cup light brown sugar (free of lumps)

½ cup dark corn syrup

½ cup sweetened condensed milk (not evaporated milk)

½ cup heavy cream

3 tablespoons butter, softened

1 teaspoon vanilla extract

¼ teaspoon cinnamon

Toppings:

8 ounces semisweet chocolate, finely chopped

1 tablespoon solid vegetable shortening

1 cup chopped pecans

2 ounces white chocolate, finely chopped

1 Wash and dry the apples thoroughly. Remove the stems, if necessary. Push the dowel into the stem end about three-fourths of the way into the apple. If this is difficult, tap with a hammer or the end of your trusty rolling pin. Dry any apple juice that seeps out.

2 Line a jelly roll pan or tray with parchment paper. Grease and set aside.

3 Combine the sugar, brown sugar, corn syrup, sweetened condensed milk, cream, and butter in a saucepan over medium-low heat. Stir gently until the sugar dissolves. Wash down the sugar crystals with a brush dipped in water. (For more on this technique, see the Figure 6-1 earlier in this chapter.) Insert the candy thermometer.

4 Increase the heat to medium-high. Clip on the candy thermometer. Bring to a boil. Stir constantly until the temperature reaches 242 degrees. Remove from the heat. Add the vanilla and cinnamon. Cool to 200 degrees. Remove the thermometer.

5 Dip the apple in the caramel mixture and spoon completely over the apple. (It doesn't matter how messy it is — it's going to be covered with chocolate.) Scrape off the excess drips; place on the jelly roll pan. Repeat with the remaining apples. You can return the caramel to low heat if it gets too thick. Let dry about 30 minutes. As you finish each stage of the dipping process, pour out any excess onto greased wax paper. Layer it, starting with caramel and ending with white chocolate.

6 Melt the semisweet chocolate and vegetable shortening over low heat in a double boiler. The top of the double boiler should be over but not touching the hot water. Remove from the heat, but keep the chocolate over hot water.

7 Working quickly, hold the caramel apple over the chocolate and spoon over to completely cover. Wipe off excess drips. Place on the jelly roll pan. Repeat with the remaining apples.

8 While the chocolate is still wet, sprinkle with the chopped pecans. Let dry about 30 minutes.

9 Melt the white chocolate over low heat in a double boiler. With a spoon, drizzle the chocolate back and forth across the tops and sides of the apples. Let dry.

Simplify: Instead of making the caramel topping, melt a package of caramel candies according to package instructions. Add ½ teaspoon cinnamon.

Tip: Sharpen the dowels in a pencil sharpener to make pushing them through the apples easier. Wrap the dowels tightly in foil to help keep them clean while working with the sticky, gooey stuff. You can also use a chopstick instead of a dowel.

Tip: Instead of drizzling the white chocolate with a spoon, scrape the melted chocolate into a small resealable plastic bag. Close the bag; cut a very small corner off the bag. Drizzle over the top and sides of the apples.

Per serving: Calories 1,323 (From Fat 664); Fat 74g (Saturated 32g); Cholesterol 80mg; Sodium 151mg; Carbohydrate 179g (Dietary Fiber 8g); Protein 12g.

 For individual treats such as caramel apples, find a few little saucers or dessert plates at a flea market or tag sale. Place one apple in the center of each plate and wrap with cellophane and a ribbon. Attach a tag suggesting it be cut with a knife and served in slices.

Candy Sushi

No, this Candy Sushi (SOO-she) isn't the raw fish so popular today. Call it faux food. It's a fun roll full of nuts and candy wrapped in chocolate *nori* (seaweed). Amaze and amuse your friends with it — it's a treat they'll never forget.

Preparation time: *1 hour and 15 minutes, plus overnight to thicken and firm up*

Cooking time: *15 minutes*

Yield: *Fifty-four ½-inch sushi rolls*

Chocolate nori wrapper:

5 ounces semisweet chocolate, finely chopped

2 tablespoons light corn syrup

¼ teaspoon vanilla extract

Filling:

1 tablespoon butter

10 regular marshmallows

3 tablespoons light corn syrup

4 tablespoons superfine sugar

¼ teaspoon vanilla

Pinch of salt

2 cups (8 ounces) slivered almonds, finely chopped (can be done in a food processor)

Confectioners' sugar, for dusting

Pistachios, dried apricots, gumdrops, or red licorice

1 The day before, make the chocolate nori wrapper: Melt the chocolate in a double boiler over, but not touching, hot water, over medium-low heat. Remove from the heat. Stir in the 2 tablespoons corn syrup and ¼ teaspoon vanilla. With a rubber spatula, scrape the chocolate mixture onto a piece of plastic wrap. Wrap up and allow to sit overnight at room temperature.

2 To start making the filling, melt the butter in a medium saucepan over low heat. Add the marshmallows and 3 tablespoons corn syrup. Stir constantly until melted. Add the sugar, ¼ teaspoon vanilla, and salt and stir. Add the almonds and stir. Remove from the heat. Turn out onto greased parchment paper.

3 Divide the nut mixture into 3 equal parts. Sprinkle a surface with confectioners' sugar. Roll one part into a 9-inch-long log. Repeat with the remaining two parts. (Please note that Figure 6-2 is an illustrated tour of the whole rolling process.)

4 Lightly grease a knife blade. Cutting lengthwise, butterfly the log by making a slit three-fourths of the way through one log. This slit creates a trough in which to place a line of pistachio nuts end to end. You can also use thinly sliced dried apricots, for adults. For kids, dice gumdrops or slice licorice, any color but black, lengthwise. Ease the split sides of the log up and over the filling, enclosing it with the nut mixture. Gently roll to reshape. Repeat with the remaining logs. Set aside.

5 Divide the chocolate nori wrapper into 3 equal pieces. Knead to soften slightly. If necessary, microwave on 70 percent (medium-high) power in very small increments, 5 to 8 seconds at a time. Roll out to a 9½-x-4½-inch rectangle. Loosen from the surface every few rolls. Trim with a sharp knife to a 9-x-4-inch rectangle.

6 Place one nut log on the chocolate and bring the sides up to meet each other. Press together to form the seam. Roll over, seam side down, and gently rock to seal. Repeat with the remaining pieces of chocolate and nut logs. Wrap each log in plastic wrap.

7 Just before giving, unwrap the logs and slice into ½-inch rounds. If necessary, chill 20 minutes for easier slicing. This candy keeps at room temperature about 1 week.

Per serving: Calories 53 (From Fat 31); Fat 4g (Saturated 1g); Cholesterol 1mg; Sodium 6mg; Carbohydrate 6g (Dietary Fiber 1g); Protein 1g.

ROLLING A CANDY/NUT SUSHI

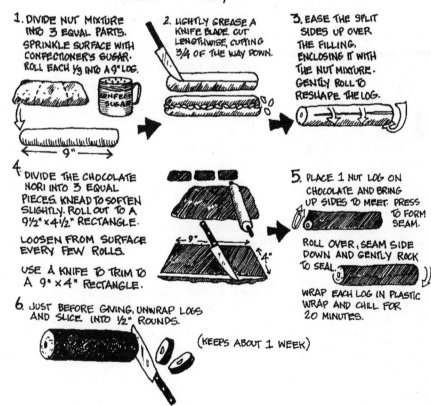

1. DIVIDE NUT MIXTURE INTO 3 EQUAL PARTS. SPRINKLE SURFACE WITH CONFECTIONER'S SUGAR. ROLL EACH ⅓ INTO A 9" LOG.

2. LIGHTLY GREASE A KNIFE BLADE. CUT LENGTHWISE, CUTTING ¾ OF THE WAY DOWN.

3. EASE THE SPLIT SIDES UP OVER THE FILLING, ENCLOSING IT WITH THE NUT MIXTURE. GENTLY ROLL TO RESHAPE THE LOG.

4. DIVIDE THE CHOCOLATE NORI INTO 3 EQUAL PIECES. KNEAD TO SOFTEN SLIGHTLY. ROLL OUT TO A 9½" x 4½" RECTANGLE.

LOOSEN FROM SURFACE EVERY FEW ROLLS.

USE A KNIFE TO TRIM TO A 9" x 4" RECTANGLE.

5. PLACE 1 NUT LOG ON CHOCOLATE AND BRING UP SIDES TO MEET. PRESS TO FORM SEAM.

ROLL OVER, SEAM SIDE DOWN AND GENTLY ROCK TO SEAL.

WRAP EACH LOG IN PLASTIC WRAP AND CHILL FOR 20 MINUTES.

6. JUST BEFORE GIVING, UNWRAP LOGS AND SLICE INTO ½" ROUNDS.

(KEEPS ABOUT 1 WEEK)

Figure 6-2: Log rolling, step by step.

Tea Party Sugar Cubes

Not exactly a candy but certainly a sweet, these decorated sugar cubes are available in all the trendy food shops. They look so pretty that you won't want to put the pastry bag down. Royal icing is piped separately and later applied to the cubes. And the really good part is that if your results are less than perfect, the cubes will dissolve in a cup of coffee. They dress up a holiday buffet table (see the color section of this book for a preview), or you may want to bring them to your bridge club hostess.

Special equipment: *Two 10-inch pastry bags; 1 plain #2 pastry tip; 1 #106, #18, or #27 pastry tip (Wilton); and 2 couplers*

Preparation time: *About 2 hours*

Yield: *Approximately 100 cubes*

1⅓ cups confectioners' sugar

1 tablespoon meringue powder (Wilton)

2½ tablespoons warm water (more if needed)

Liquid food coloring or paste food coloring

About 100 sugar cubes (from a 1-pound box of sugar cubes or half cubes)

1 Place the threaded half of the couplers in the pastry bags. Attach the plain tip to one bag and the fancy tip to the other. Screw on the outside piece of the coupler. (The first time you make this recipe, start with two bags. You can add more colors and tips later.) Set aside. Line a tray or baking sheet with parchment or wax paper.

2 Combine the confectioners' sugar, meringue powder, and water in a small bowl. Beat with an electric mixer until the mixture is thick and just holds a stiff peak, about 5 minutes. The icing is very accommodating. If the icing is too thick, just add a little water a few drops at a time. If it's too thin, add a teaspoon of confectioners' sugar at a time. The icing should flow smoothly and be easy to squeeze but not so thin that it doesn't hold its shape.

3 Divide the icing into two smaller bowls. Keep covered with a damp (not wet) paper towel or plastic wrap. The cover should touch the surface of the icing, because royal icing wants to dry out. Add a few drops of food coloring, one bowl at a time, and blend well. If using paste food coloring, start with a very small amount; because this type of coloring is so concentrated, the very intense colors may make coffee or tea somewhat unappealing. Re-cover the bowls.

4 Stand the pastry bag in a measuring cup or glass; fold the top of the bag over the edge of the glass. Filling the bag is easier with two hands free. Spoon one color of icing into each bag. Squeeze all the icing toward the tip to remove all air pockets. Gently twist the open end of the bag and fold over to keep the icing from leaking out or drying. (I sometimes secure the ends with a long twist tie.) Keep the tips covered with plastic wrap or aluminum foil or stick a toothpick into the tip opening when not in use. Repeat with the other bag.

5 Hold one bag in your preferred hand. Grasp at the twist. This hand controls the pressure. Use your other hand to guide the tip. Double-check to make sure that no icing has dried and clogged the tip. Place the bag perpendicular to the parchment, hovering barely above the paper. Give a gentle squeeze. Let up on the pressure when you start to see the icing emerging. Repeat. Do a few practice flowers.

6 Re-cover the tip you just used. Using the other color icing with the plain tip, follow the same piping procedure and pipe a small dot in the center of the flower. (This would be the "eye" if you were making a black-eyed Susan.) If you have any odd little peaks, just push them down with a toothpick before they dry. Because the icing dries fairly quickly, pipe a few of the flowers and then switch to filling in the center dot. The flowers should be small and not exceed the narrow dimension of the sugar cube. Keep a cube handy for reference or draw squares the size of the sugar cubes on the parchment paper. Otherwise, you will not be able to pack the sugar cubes side by side in a container later.

7 When you're halfway done, switch tips on the pastry bags and reverse the colors. Let all the flowers dry for an hour.

8 Line up as many sugar cubes as there are flowers on a tray. Very gently loosen all the flowers from the parchment with a small, flat metal spatula or the tip of a small knife. Using the plain pastry tip (the color doesn't matter as long as you're neat), apply a small dab of icing to the bottom of the flower. Attach to a sugar cube. Repeat with the remaining flowers. Allow to dry for about 1 hour. When you feel comfortable with the piping techniques, you can skip this step entirely and just pipe directly onto the sugar cubes.

9 Store in an airtight container for up to 3 months.

Tip: *If you have extra flowers or want to make extras, you can also use them as a beautiful decoration on the iced Easy Alabaster Mints. The dried icing flowers will keep for many months. (See the recipe earlier in this chapter.) Just plunk one, or two, or three on each mint while the icing is still soft.*

Per serving: *Calories 15 (From Fat 0); Fat 0g (Saturated 0g); Cholesterol 0mg; Sodium 1mg; Carbohydrate 0g (Dietary Fiber 0g); Protein 0g.*

In 1878 Henry Tate, the namesake and founder of the famous Tate Gallery in London, made his millions by introducing sugar cubes. Until he patented the process, sugar was snipped off a big cone or loaf of sugar with metal tongs.

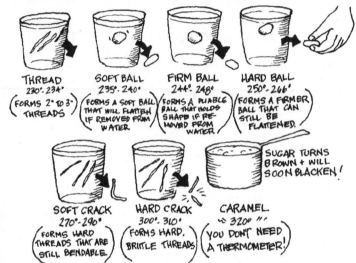

TESTING CANDY SYRUP STAGES

USE A GLASS OF VERY COLD WATER AND DRIBBLE HOT SYRUP INTO THE GLASS TO FIND OUT WHAT STAGE IT IS IN!

THREAD
230°-234°
(FORMS 2" TO 3" THREADS)

SOFT BALL
235°-240°
(FORMS A SOFT BALL THAT WILL FLATTEN IF REMOVED FROM WATER)

FIRM BALL
244°-248°
(FORMS A PLIABLE BALL THAT HOLDS SHAPE IF REMOVED FROM WATER)

HARD BALL
250°-266°
(FORMS A FIRMER BALL THAT CAN STILL BE FLATTENED.)

SOFT CRACK
270°-290°
(FORMS HARD THREADS THAT ARE STILL BENDABLE.)

HARD CRACK
300°-310°
(FORMS HARD, BRITTLE THREADS.)

CARAMEL
320°
SUGAR TURNS BROWN + WILL SOON BLACKEN!
(YOU DON'T NEED A THERMOMETER!)

Figure 6-3:
The good
old cold
water test.

Orchard outings

Just as people have different personalities and characteristic strengths, so do apples. And with over 7,000 named varieties in existence, you could spend as much time looking for the perfect apple as you do for the perfect spouse.

Few apple varieties are used solely for baking or eating; most have dual purposes. You may want to try out a few to see which suit your taste buds. Some good all-purpose eating apples are Jonathan, Braeburn, Baldwin, Cortland, Winesap, Empire, Northern Spy, Gravenstein, Granny Smith, and Mutsu. Good pie apples (because the slices tend to hold their shape during baking) are Stayman, Braeburn, Pippin, Ida Red, and Northern Spy.

Although apples are in the market all the time, prime munching season is late summer through winter. Availability varies from region to region, so visit local growers, who will be more than happy to guide you. And keep in mind that apples are one of the few fruits that get sweeter after being picked. Plus, ancient wisdom extols the healthy properties of apples. Guess what? Scientists are finding that apples help digestive juices kill germs in the stomach. All the more reason to eat one a day!

Chapter 7

Cookies and Their Cousins

• •

In This Chapter

▶ Baking cookies of assorted textures

▶ Shaping mandelbrot

▶ Making "cookies" that aren't sweet

▶ Folding fortune cookies

▶ Preparing treats for Fido

• •

*W*ebster defines a cookie as a "thin, crisp cake, usually sugared or spiced and cut in fancy or circular shapes before baking." But this chapter stretches Mr. Webster's words a bit. Perhaps "self-contained unit of joy" is a more accurate definition of the recipes.

Cookies and their cousins, such as cheesy crisps and crackers, are one of America's largest food groups — just look at the runway-length supermarket aisles stacked with all those tempting boxes and bags. But leave the commercial packages on the shelves and indulge your friends with homemade delights from this chapter.

Presenting Crispy Froths, Granola Bars, and Shortbread

Some people like crispy cookies. Some like chunky. Some like delicate. They're all here. This section includes the almost lighter-than-air, coffee-flavored meringue cookies. Pop them in your mouth and don't even chew them — just let them melt. Others will enjoy the chunkiness of the ingredient-laden Anzac bars, which have nuts, fruit, and seeds to steel hikers who need energy to complete the trail. Others may prefer the buttery cardamom-scented shortbread that delights the mouth with richness.

Crispy Cappuccino Froths

Crispy Cappuccino Froths are a perfect example of how less is more — coffee flavor surrounded by crispy air. You don't believe me? Just try one: a loud crunch, a taste of coffee, and it's gone, leaving sheer delight but not one iota of cholesterol behind. This is a great gift for someone on a lowfat diet.

Special equipment: *Parchment paper*

Preparation time: *20 minutes*

Cooking time: *l hour, plus l hour drying time*

Yield: *About sixty-four 1¼-inch pieces*

½ cup egg whites (from about 4 eggs), at room temperature

Pinch of salt

¼ teaspoon cream of tartar

¾ cup sugar

4 teaspoons instant espresso granules

Cinnamon or cocoa

1 Preheat the oven to 225 degrees. Line 2 baking sheets with parchment paper. Set aside.

2 Using an electric mixer with grease-free beaters, and a grease-free medium bowl, beat the egg whites on low for about l minute, until frothy. Add the salt. Beat for another minute and add the cream of tartar. Continue beating on low for 1 more minute.

3 Increase the mixer speed to medium and beat for l minute. Start adding about a tablespoon of sugar every 30 seconds. After incorporating about half of the sugar, add the espresso. Continue adding the remaining sugar. Increase the mixer speed to high and beat 4 more minutes. The meringue will be very stiff.

4 Dollop (loosely translated as "plop") tablespoons of meringue about 1 inch apart on the prepared baking sheets. Sprinkle each lightly with cinnamon or cocoa (or both).

5 Bake for l hour. Rotate the baking sheets once during baking. After l hour, turn off the oven, leaving the door closed for 1 hour. Remove the meringues from the oven. Cool completely on the baking sheets on a wire rack. Store in an airtight container for up to 3 weeks.

Tip: You can practice your piping here without trepidation. (See Chapter 6 for more on this technique.) Just fit a 14-inch pastry bag with a ½-inch #7 Ateco tip and fill the bag with meringue. Hold the tip a little above the parchment paper and squeeze out a 1¼-inch mound. For a really pretty presentation, fit the bag with a ½-inch #6 star tip from Ateco instead.

Per serving: Calories 10 (From Fat 0); Fat 0g (Saturated 0g); Cholesterol 0mg; Sodium 6mg; Carbohydrate 2g (Dietary Fiber 0g); Protein 0g.

Anzac Granola Bars

Here's a cookie with a past. It's based on an Australian recipe called Anzac that is an abbreviation for Australian and New Zealand Army Corps. It's a sturdy, dried-fruit cookie that was shipped to troops in humid Gallipoli during World War I. It apparently was the only cookie that didn't get moldy. All kinds of weekend warriors can enjoy this softer, bar-cookie version, with dried fruit, nuts, and honey.

Special equipment: *Parchment paper*

Preparation time: *20 minutes*

Cooking time: *25 to 28 minutes*

Yield: *24 bars, each about 1¼ x 3 inches*

2 cups fruit bits (about 10 ounces) (I used Sun-Maid)

¾ cup uncooked old-fashioned oats (not quick-cooking oats)

1 cup coarsely chopped unsalted cashews

½ cup all-purpose flour

½ cup shelled sunflower seeds

⅓ cup whole-wheat flour

⅓ cup packed light brown sugar

½ teaspoon salt

¼ teaspoon baking soda

½ cup vegetable oil

⅓ cup honey

1 egg

1 Preheat the oven to 350 degrees. Line a 9-x-13-inch baking pan with parchment paper. Grease lightly.

2 Combine the fruit bits, oats, cashews, all-purpose flour, sunflower seeds, whole-wheat flour, brown sugar, salt, and baking soda in a medium bowl. Toss until well combined.

3 Add the oil, honey, and egg and toss until well combined. The ingredients will be just moistened by the liquids and will look like wet granola. Spread the batter evenly in the prepared pan. Press down the ingredients with the back of a spoon or spatula.

4 Bake for 25 to 28 minutes, rotating the pan 180 degrees once if necessary. Remove from the oven and cool on a wire rack for 15 minutes. Run a knife around the edge of the pan to loosen the cookies. Invert the pan and remove the cookies. Carefully peel off the parchment paper. Reinvert the cookies and cool completely on a wire rack. Cut into 24 bars. Store in an airtight container. These bar cookies keep for 5 days.

Tip: *To decrystalize honey, remove the cap and microwave it on high for 30 to 40 seconds.*

Per serving: *Calories 153 (From Fat 66); Fat 7g (Saturated 1g); Cholesterol 0mg; Sodium 99mg; Carbohydrate 21g (Dietary Fiber 2g); Protein 3g.*

Lemon-Cardamom Shortbread

A classic Scottish shortbread relies on the purity of the ingredients, because the short-bread usually doesn't have any additional flavoring. Here, the Swedish half of me got the better of the Scottish half of me and added the deliciously perfumed spice of cardamom for an extra teatime treat. (Forgive me, Robert Burns.) See the color section of this book for a preview of Lemon-Cardamom Shortbread.

Special equipment: *Two 8-inch tart pans with removable bottoms (or two 8½-inch round disposable aluminum foil pans, which are cheaper and easier to find)*

Preparation time: *25 minutes*

Cooking time: *60 minutes*

Yield: *24 cookies*

2¾ cups flour

½ cup cornstarch

1½ cups (3 sticks) butter, at room temperature

¾ cup superfine sugar

¾ teaspoon lemon zest (see Chapter 8 for more on zest)

½ teaspoon ground cardamom (freshly ground if possible)

1 Preheat the oven to 300 degrees. Sift together the flour and cornstarch. Set aside.

2 Cream the butter and sugar together in a medium bowl. With an electric mixer on medium-high, beat until light and fluffy, about 1 minute. Add the lemon zest and cardamom. Scrape down the sides of the bowl.

3 Add the flour mixture until just incorporated. It will look crumbly. Turn out onto a surface and gather up into a ball. Knead gently a few times.

4 Divide the dough in half and shape each half into a 6-inch disk. Place each disk in a pan and, with your fingers, pat the dough to the edges of the pan.

5 Score the dough in each pan into 12 even wedges. Prick the dough with a fork in 2 to 3 places on each wedge. Prick so that you form a pattern on the dough, rather than a random design. Bake for 60 minutes, until very lightly golden. Rotate the pans once during baking. Cool for 15 minutes. Gently turn out of the pans and cool for 15 minutes more. Carefully cut into wedges, using a serrated or sharp knife. Store in an airtight container for up to 1 week.

Tip: *To cut into wedges, don't try to cut all the way through the baked shortbread all at once. Make a few light passes, pulling the knife toward you instead of sawing back and forth.*

Tip: Cardamom is a member of the ginger family. It is highly regarded in Scandinavian and Indian cuisine. Try and find the green pods, which are usually used in desserts and are more flavorful.

Per serving: Calories 185 (From Fat 104); Fat 12g (Saturated 7g); Cholesterol 31mg; Sodium 2mg; Carbohydrate 19g (Dietary Fiber 0g); Protein 2g.

You may want to consider decorating cookies such as the Lemon-Cardamon Shortbread in this chapter with small candied violets or rose petals. Lightly press the flowers into the dough just before baking. Or sprinkle the dough with colored sugar just before baking. (See Chapter 17 for a list of food resources.)

Round shortbread like the recipe in this chapter is also called "petticoat tails" because it is believed to look like ladies' full hoop skirts. Lore also credits a similar cookie being used in ancient rites because it resembled the sun.

Moving On: Mandelbrot and Eggnog Cookies

Many cultures have their own versions of twice-baked goods, each slightly different. But they all have low water content, so originally they sustained marching armies and sailors at sea. Examples include rusks and zwieback, which are yeast based and usually have little or no sweetening, and mandelbrot and biscotti, which are sweeter and can contain nuts and dried fruit. (See Chapter 5 for the Freckled Chocolate, Cinnamon, and Hazelnut Biscotti recipe.) Babies have teethed on zwieback while adults have dunked biscotti in wine. Everyone's happy.

This section includes my favorite recipe for mandelbrot, one of those crunchy, twice-baked cookies. It keeps for 2 weeks, so it's perfect for gift giving because you don't have to make it at the last minute. If you prefer quieter cookies, the other recipe in the section goes for the softer side — eggnog cookies. You can enjoy them by themselves or as an accompaniment to a dish of ice cream.

Almond and Date Mandelbrot

A traditional twice-baked biscuit, this Jewish treat actually means "almond bread." It's baked in a loaf, sliced, and baked again, giving it a crunchy texture. Sweet dates and chunky almonds make it a satisfying combination for dessert. It's also great for midnight munching (although you may want to dunk it in your milk so the crunch doesn't wake anyone).

Special equipment: *Parchment paper*

Preparation time: *25 minutes, plus 15 minutes resting*

Cooking time: *40 minutes*

Yield: *About 68 slices plus ends*

3½ cups flour

2 teaspoons baking powder

½ teaspoon baking soda

½ teaspoon salt

1 cup vegetable oil

3 eggs, at room temperature

⅔ cup sugar

½ cup light brown sugar

1 teaspoon grated orange zest

1 teaspoon vanilla extract

8-ounce box chopped dates

1 cup natural whole almonds, coarsely chopped

1 Preheat the oven to 350 degrees. Line 2 baking sheets with parchment paper.

2 Combine the flour, baking powder, baking soda, and salt. Blend thoroughly. Set aside.

3 Combine the oil, eggs, sugar, brown sugar, orange zest, and vanilla extract in a medium bowl. Beat with an electric mixer until smooth. Add the flour mixture to the oil mixture. Mix with a spatula until partially blended. Mix in the dates and almonds. Continue mixing until just blended.

4 Turn out the dough onto a lightly floured surface. Divide into 4 equal parts. With lightly floured hands, shape each quarter into a log 10 inches long. Place all 4 logs on one baking sheet. (Save the second one for later.) Gently flatten each log to measure 2 inches wide.

5 Bake for 30 minutes, rotating the baking sheet 180 degrees halfway through the baking time. The top will be firm to the touch and slightly cracked down the center.

6 Remove the baking sheet from the oven. Reduce the oven temperature to 325 degrees. Gently remove the logs with a metal spatula to a cooling rack for 15 minutes.

7 Carefully cut ½-inch-thick slices on the bias with a serrated bread knife. (See Figure 7-1.) Place the slices, cut side down, on both baking sheets. Repeat with the remaining 3 logs.

8 Return the baking sheets to the oven and bake for 10 minutes, rotating the sheets once during baking.

9 Remove the baking sheets from the oven. Set on cooling racks for 5 minutes. Remove the cookies to the cooling rack and cool completely. The cookies can be stored at room temperature in an airtight container for 2 weeks.

Per serving: Calories 194 (From Fat 90); Fat 10g (Saturated 1g); Cholesterol 20mg; Sodium 88mg; Carbohydrate 24g (Dietary Fiber 1g); Protein 3g.

CUTTING UP AND LAYING OUT MANDELBROT

Figure 7-1: Giving mandelbrot its crunch.

1. FLATTEN THE TOP OF EACH LOG OF DOUGH SO ITS 2" WIDE. BAKE FOR 30 MINUTES (ROTATE ONCE) PLACE ON A COOLING RACK FOR 15 MINUTES.

☆ REDUCE THE OVEN TEMPERATURE TO 325°

2. CUT THE LOGS ON A DIAGONAL WITH A SERRATED KNIFE, INTO ½" SLICES.

3. PLACE SLICES ON THEIR SIDE ON A BAKING SHEET. RETURN TO THE OVEN.

RETURN TO THE OVEN AND BAKE FOR 10 MINUTES. REMOVE THEM AND COOL.

Eggnog Cookies

Nutmeg sprinkled on top of eggnog seems to be synonymous with winter holidays. But this combination of eggs and nutmeg comes in the form of a rich cookie that's perfect any time of year. Especially if you leave out the nutmeg, you'll have a delicate, all-purpose, anytime cookie. Serve it with ice cream or apple cider.

Preparation time: *45 minutes, plus 1 hour chilling*

Cooking time: *6 to 7 minutes*

Yield: *4 dozen 3-inch cookies*

2 cups flour	½ cup (1 stick) butter, at room temperature
½ teaspoon baking soda	¾ cup sugar
¼ teaspoon ground nutmeg (freshly grated, if possible)	2 egg yolks
	¼ cup sour cream
Pinch of salt	½ teaspoon vanilla extract

1 Sift together the flour, baking soda, nutmeg, and salt. Set aside.

2 With an electric mixer on medium, cream together the butter and sugar in a medium bowl until light in color. Add the yolks and beat until incorporated. Beat in the sour cream and vanilla extract.

3 With the mixer on low speed, beat the flour mixture into the butter mixture just until incorporated. Divide the dough into 3 parts. Shape into 5-inch disks and cover with plastic wrap. Refrigerate until firm, about 1 hour.

4 Preheat the oven to 350 degrees.

5 Roll one section of dough between 2 sheets of wax paper to a ⅛-inch thickness. Chill again in the refrigerator if the dough has gotten too soft. Cut out stars, or any other desired shape, and place on an ungreased baking sheet, 1 inch apart. Save the scraps. Repeat with the remaining disks. Combine the scraps and chill them. Roll out this dough and cut out the cookies. Do not reroll again or the cookies will be tough.

6 Bake for 6 to 7 minutes, rotating the baking sheet 180 degrees once during baking, if necessary, until the edges are just turning golden. Remove to a cooling rack. Store in an airtight container up to 1 week.

Tip: *If you're using only one baking sheet, make sure that it's completely cool before placing another batch of cut-out dough on it.*

Vary It! *Omit the nutmeg and try cinnamon or ginger instead.*

Vary It! *Decorate the cookies with colored sugar or finely chopped nuts.*

Per serving: *Calories 63 (From Fat 22); Fat 2g (Saturated 1g); Cholesterol 15mg; Sodium 17mg; Carbohydrate 9g (Dietary Fiber 0g); Protein 1g.*

Merrily, we roll along

Drop cookies are easier to make than rolled cookies. But there's something engaging about picking up a fancifully shaped rolled cookie, admiring it as it approaches your mouth, and then biting down on it with delicate intent. So why then should December be the only month that you drag out the rolling pins and cookie cutters and sprinkles? The month is so full of frenzy and stress that it's hard to fully appreciate the rewards of a rolled cookie during the holidays. And if you need further reason to bake rolled cookies other times of the year, the cookie cutter kingdom abounds. Busy little elves have created cutters in so many shapes that you'll be planning your gift-giving occasions around your cookie cutter collection. (See Chapter 18 for cookie-cutter suppliers.) Here are some tips to get you rolling:

- Make sure that your kitchen isn't too warm.

- If called for in the recipe, chill the dough before rolling it out.

- Divide the dough into portions and wrap well. Roll out one portion at a time and keep the remaining portions refrigerated.

- Roll out the dough using as little flour as possible. Try using a rolling pin cover. Or roll out the dough between two pieces of wax paper or parchment paper.

- Place the dough in the refrigerator (or even briefly in the freezer) if it gets too soft to handle.

- Dip the cookie cutter in flour if the dough sticks to it.

- Roll from the center outward. Don't roll over the edges, or they'll get too thin.

- Before cutting, gently loosen the dough from the surface or wax paper with your fingers or a metal spatula.

ROLLING COOKIE DOUGH IN WAXED PAPER

1.
CUT 2 PIECES OF WAXED PAPER.

2. SHAPE THE DOUGH INTO A 5" DISC AND PLACE BETWEEN THE SHEETS OF PAPER.

3. ROLL OUT THE DOUGH INTO A 1/8" THICKNESS.

REMOVE TOP LAYER. LOOSEN DOUGH AND CUT OUT SHAPES

Don't Overlook Two Party-Going Wafers

One wafer in this section is made from cheese; the other loves to escort cheese. Those attributes alone make these two wafers welcome at any gathering. Frico Cheese Crisps are delicate cheesy wafers that are a perfect complement to sipping wine and looking at the mountains from a porch. The Savory Walnut-Pepper Digestives are scrumptious by themselves but get even better with a wedge of cheese on top. They're not bad with Pâté 101 either! (See Chapter 12.)

Frico Cheese Crisps

Frico (FREE-koh) or "little trifles" look like brittle lace, but don't let that fool you. Intensely cheesy and immensely crisp, they go like hotcakes. The good news is that they're easy to make. They're quite fragile, but any broken ones go nicely on top of a salad. They're traditionally made with Montasio cheese. If you can find it, use it. Otherwise, experiment with more readily available hard cheeses, which I list in the variation at the end of the recipe. If you have a nonstick baking sheet or a silpat (a flexible, silicone-coated, nonstick mat meant for baking), these are easier to bake.

Preparation time: *10 minutes*

Cooking time: *5 to 6 minutes*

Yield: *Twenty-four 2-inch crisps*

1 cup shredded Asiago cheese

1 tablespoon finely ground cornmeal

½ teaspoon dried Italian seasoning

1 Preheat the oven to 400 degrees.

2 Combine the cheese, cornmeal, and Italian seasoning on a piece of wax paper. Using a measuring teaspoon, place spoonfuls of the mixture on the baking sheet about 3 inches apart. Toss the mixture after every teaspoon so that the cornmeal and seasoning are evenly mixed. Sprinkle any remaining cornmeal-seasoning blend over the shredded cheese. Spread each mound into an even 2-inch round. You can get about 12 spoonfuls of cheese on a baking sheet.

3 Bake only one sheet at a time. Check after 5 minutes. The wafers should be a medium golden color. Carefully remove them from the baking sheet with a thin metal spatula.

Vary It! *This recipe works with other hard, well-aged cheeses like Manchego and Parmesan. Mix and match with seasonings like thyme, cracked black pepper, caraway, fennel seed, crushed rosemary, and chili powder. Baking times may vary with different cheeses, so watch carefully during baking.*

Per serving: *Calories 18 (From Fat 11); Fat 1g (Saturated 1g); Cholesterol 4mg; Sodium 12mg; Carbohydrate 0g (Dietary Fiber 0g); Protein 1g.*

Savory Walnut-Pepper Digestives

A digestive is really a cracker — honest. It's just not the thin, crispy ones Americans get out of a box. Instead, it's a lovely English cracker. A bit thicker, a digestive is made with whole-wheat flour and is just a tad sweet. But don't let this plain Jane fool you. The white pepper gives this cracker just enough bite to make you sit up and take notice. Pair this cracker up with a triple cream cheese, such as Explorateur or Saint Andre, and a robust wine.

Special equipment: *Parchment paper*

Preparation time: *30 minutes, plus 2 hours for chilling*

Cooking time: *12 minutes*

Yield: *64 slices*

1 cup all-purpose flour	½ cup solid vegetable shortening
1 cup whole-wheat flour	4 tablespoons (½ stick) butter, at room temperature
1½ teaspoons ground white pepper (preferably freshly ground)	
	¼ cup sugar
1 teaspoon salt	1 egg
½ teaspoon baking powder	¾ cup walnuts, very finely chopped

1 Sift together the all-purpose flour, the whole-wheat flour, pepper, salt, and baking powder. Set aside.

2 With an electric mixer, cream together the vegetable shortening, butter, and sugar in a medium bowl. Scrape down the sides of the bowl with a rubber spatula. Add the egg. Beat until smooth.

3 Add the flour mixture and beat until incorporated. Stir in the nuts.

4 Divide the dough in half. Roll each half into a log that measures 8 inches by about 1¼-inches. Press back together if any separation occurs. (This is a sturdy dough.) Roll wax paper or plastic wrap around the dough and chill for 2 hours.

5 Preheat the oven to 350 degrees. Line 2 baking sheets with parchment paper.

6 Unwrap and carefully slice the dough into ¼-inch rounds. Use a serrated knife if necessary. Place about ¾ inch apart on the baking sheets.

7 Bake for 12 minutes, until lightly golden on the bottom. Cool. Store in an airtight container for up to 1 week.

Tip: Food stylists have a simple secret to making an attractive cookie: They take an extra minute or two to reshape the cookie dough into a more symmetrical round before baking.

Per serving: *Calories 44 (From Fat 30); Fat 3g (Saturated 1g); Cholesterol 5mg; Sodium 41mg; Carbohydrate 3g (Dietary Fiber 0g); Protein 1g.*

Fortunate Choices for You and Fido

Here are two distinctive cookies that will receive special notice. The first recipe is a Fortune Cookie that bears no resemblance to the hard, tasteless cookies brought to you in most Chinese restaurants. Charm your friends by tailoring the fortunes for a special event. Then give "paws" to the final recipe in this chapter for it acknowledges man's best friend. Unconditional love deserves unbeatable treats.

Fortune Cookies

Now you can have the power to control man's fortunes. Well, okay, maybe not his fortunes, but at least his fortune cookies. These delicate, edible oracles are great fun to open and to eat. You can customize the words of wisdom to suit the event, whether it's New Year's Eve or a Sweet 16 party. The cookies are a little tricky to make until you get the hang of them. Be sure and read the directions all the way through and have your fortunes all lined up before you start.

Special equipment: *Nonstick baking sheets, or a silpat (flexible, silicone-coated nonstick mat)*

Preparation time: *15 minutes*

Cooking time: *6 to 7 minutes per batch*

Yield: *12 cookies*

12 fortunes	*3 tablespoons flour*
1 egg white, at room temperature	*½ teaspoon almond extract*
¼ cup sugar	*Pinch of salt*
3 tablespoons butter, melted and cooled slightly	

1 Write with permanent ink, type, or print from the computer 12 fortunes on strips of paper that are about 2 inches x ½ inch. Have them ready when the cookies come out of the oven. Also have a few glasses or small bowls on hand. You hang the cookies on the edges of them to harden.

2 Preheat the oven to 350 degrees.

3 Whisk the egg white and sugar in a small bowl. Add the butter, flour, extract, and salt.

4 Pour a teaspoonful, forming a neat circle, 3 inches in from the corners of a baking sheet. Don't use a warped baking sheet, or the batter will run and the cookies will not be round. Prepare only four cookies at a time and space them an equal distance apart. (You may want to do the first batch with only 2 cookies to get the timing down.) With the back of the spoon, start in the center of the batter and spiral outward, evenly spreading the batter into a 3-inch circle of even thickness. If the batter starts to solidify between batches, place the bowl in very hot water and stir until it flows again.

5 Bake for 5 minutes. Rotate the pan 180 degrees, if necessary, and start watching the cookies. In another minute or so, the edges will have turned a light golden brown, but the center will still be pale. Here's where you have to work quickly. Carefully loosen the cookies and flip them over. Pick one up and start folding in half. Insert a fortune strip and finish folding in half to form a semicircle. Hold the curved edges closed while bringing the two ends together, folding in half again to form a quarter-circle shape. Hang over the edge of a glass or bowl to harden. (Figure 7-2 shows you this whole process in summary form.) Repeat with the remaining batter. If the batter starts to solidify between batches, place the bowl in very hot water and stir until it flows again.

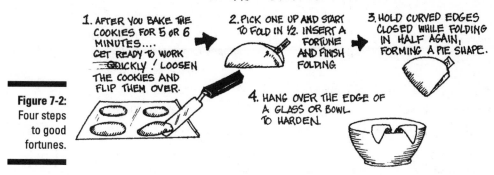

Figure 7-2: Four steps to good fortunes.

Tip: *If any remaining cookies get too hard to fold, return them to the oven for a few seconds to soften them.*

Per serving: *Calories 51 (From Fat 26); Fat 3g (Saturated 2g); Cholesterol 8mg; Sodium 17mg; Carbohydrate 6g (Dietary Fiber 0g); Protein 1g.*

Fido's Fetching Bones

It's payback time. For all those wet-tongue slobbers and obedient handshakes, and for patiently listening to your rantings, here's a sweet return for your canine friend. Grains, milk powder, and molasses make a nourishing cookie. (If you have any concerns about the ingredients in this recipe, consult your veterinarian.) The carob chips (found in health food stores) only make it seem like human food. Because chocolate is toxic to dogs, do not replace the carob chips with real chocolate chips. If you can't find carob chips, omit them.

The reports on this dog snack are in: The treats have been "Lab" tested by Flossy, the chocolate Labrador; field tested by Miss Eleanor, the wire-haired Dachshund; and of course, vet-approved by Doc Schimmelman, our loving caregiver. And, in late-breaking news, Rusty the quarter horse didn't think they were too bad either.

Special equipment: *4-inch dog-bone-shaped cookie cutter*

Preparation time: *40 minutes*

Baking time: *45 minutes*

Yield: *48 bones*

2 cups whole-wheat flour	*½ teaspoon baking soda*
1 cup all-purpose flour	*1 cup carob chips (do not substitute real chocolate chips)*
¾ cup quick-cooking oats (not the old-fashioned kind)	
	1 cup beef, chicken, or vegetable broth
¾ cup wheat germ, plus extra for rolling	*⅓ cup molasses*
¾ cup powdered milk	*2 tablespoons vegetable oil*

1 Preheat the oven to 300 degrees.

2 Thoroughly mix the whole-wheat flour, all-purpose flour, oats, wheat germ, powdered milk, and baking soda in a large bowl. Mix in the carob chips. Set aside.

3 Whisk the broth, molasses, and oil in a small bowl. Add to the flour mixture and stir as much as possible. The mixture will be somewhat dry. Knead a few times into a ball. Divide the ball in half and wrap one-half in plastic.

4 Working with one of the balls of dough, sprinkle the surface with a little wheat germ and roll the dough out to ¼ inch. Cut out as many bones as possible and place on one ungreased baking sheet. You can place them as close as ½ inch apart because they don't spread during baking. Save the scraps of dough. Repeat the steps with the remaining ball of dough and place on a second ungreased baking sheet. Combine the scraps and reroll the dough. Cut out as many bones as possible and place on a baking sheet.

5 Bake for 45 minutes, rotating once halfway through the baking time. Cool completely on a rack. Store in an airtight container at room temperature for up to 2 months.

Per serving: *Calories 79 (From Fat 24); Fat 3g (Saturated 2g); Cholesterol 2mg; Sodium 46mg; Carbohydrate 12g (Dietary Fiber 1g); Protein 3g.*

Part III

Over the Top: Flavorful Sauces and Spreads

The 5th Wave   By Rich Tennant

"Hand me that mallet and a box of chocolate chip cookies. The kids want to make up aroma sachets for their teacher."

In this part . . .

Spread good wishes to everyone you know with recipes in this part, including sauces for meat and poultry, and toppings for waffles and ice cream, all in Chapter 8. You can indulge in a bit of old-fashioned kitchen craft with gifts such as jam, mustard, relish, and flavored oil and flavored vinegar, all in Chapter 9.

Chapter 8

We've Got You Covered: Sauces, Syrups, and Flavored Butters and Sugar

- -

In This Chapter

▶ Making sauces to accent steak

▶ Capturing seasonal fruit in toppings

▶ Spicing up your butters and sugars

- -

It's the little things that make your day. Gas prices went down a nickel. The new puppy hasn't chewed up your favorite pair of shoes. Your child actually said thank you to a neighbor — without prompting. Happiness is spread in various and sundry forms. You can pay forward some of this happiness with a random act of kindness, such as giving someone a homemade gift from your kitchen. Does your brother-in-law gripe about your sister's dry fish? Give him an assortment of flavored butters. Does your sister complain about your brother-in-law's overdone steak? Give her a bottle of steak sauce. Flavor is spread in different forms. It's a welcome guest that brings a little something extra to the party. Some hosts may appreciate a sweet touch like blueberry sauce. Other hosts may prefer a rowdy steak sauce. Everything has its place, and foods work together to keep the party interesting.

The Bold and the Beautiful: Sauces with Attitude

The French seem to have staked a claim on sauces for centuries. Perhaps some smart chef way back when was a little short on refrigeration and very overstocked with near-rancid meat. So he added a pinch of this and a dab of that and — voilà! — he ended up with an edible camouflage that probably saved his job . . . and his life. With leaps and bounds in the technology of refrigeration, freezing, and irradiation, sauces needed a new career. They have finally come into their own. They still do some charitable work, such as helping a tough chuck roast achieve respectability. But now sauces are complements rather than disguises. For example, Happy Hubby Steak Sauce can happily accompany any steak. It has many of the ingredients of a barbecue sauce but a more sophisticated flavor.

Happy Hubby Steak Sauce

All husbands have lovable affectations — mine hums when he eats. He hums even louder when he eats steak, especially when this steak sauce recipe accompanies it. It's a little bit of liquid love to spread around. And while you're spreading, don't stop at steak. Use it straight out of the fridge or at room temperature on a burger.

Preparation time: *15 minutes*

Cooking time: *30 minutes*

Yield: *3¾ cups*

29-ounce can tomato puree	*1 tablespoon liquid beef bouillon concentrate*
5 tablespoons orange juice concentrate	*2 teaspoons dried onion powder*
5 tablespoons honey Dijon mustard	*1 teaspoon dried garlic powder*
4 tablespoons balsamic vinegar	*½ teaspoon black pepper*
2 tablespoons dark corn syrup	*¼ teaspoon cayenne*
1 tablespoon salt	*2 tablespoons prepared horseradish*

Combine all ingredients except the horseradish in a heavy saucepan. Bring to a simmer over medium heat, stirring occasionally, for 30 minutes. Cool slightly. Stir in the horseradish and refrigerate. Store in an airtight container in the refrigerator for up to 10 days.

Per serving: *Calories 16 (From Fat 2); Fat 0g (Saturated 0g); Cholesterol 0mg; Sodium 202mg; Carbohydrate 3g (Dietary Fiber 0g); Protein 0g.*

Cayenne is also labeled as ground red pepper.

If a recipe calls for a sticky ingredient such as honey, molasses, or syrup, lightly coat the measuring spoon or measuring cup with mild vegetable oil or nonstick cooking spray before pouring in the sticky substance.

Chimichurri Steak Sauce

Rustle up a steak dinner the Argentinean way. This herb and garlic vinaigrette sauce is the complement to beef of the Pampas. The red pepper flakes give it a little bit of gaucho flair. Of course, it goes equally well with poultry or fish.

Preparation time: *25 minutes*

Yield: *1⅔ cups*

2 bunches Italian parsley (enough to yield 2 cups packed leaves)

3 cloves garlic, coarsely chopped

1 teaspoon dried oregano

1 cup olive oil

½ cup white wine vinegar

½ to ¾ teaspoon red pepper flakes

½ teaspoon salt

¼ teaspoon pepper

1 Wash the parsley and dry thoroughly. Remove enough leaves to yield 2 packed cups. Set aside.

2 Place the garlic in the bowl of a food processor fitted with the metal blade. Process on and off until finely chopped. Add the parsley and oregano. Process on and off 6 to 8 times until coarsely chopped. Remove from the processor to a small bowl or container.

3 Add the oil, vinegar, red pepper flakes, salt, and pepper. You can store this in the refrigerator for 2 to 3 days.

Per serving: Calories 78 (From Fat 75); Fat 8g (Saturated 1g); Cholesterol 0mg; Sodium 48mg; Carbohydrate 1g (Dietary Fiber 0g); Protein 0g.

Using Fruit to Flavor Syrups

Although sauces appear in every form (savory, sweet, thick, thin), syrups are almost always sweet — not that this is a bad thing. Ranging in flavor from simple sugar to maple and chocolate, syrups make their presence known on ice cream, pancakes, waffles, cakes, and meringues and in beverages.

Pear-Cranberry Compote

Compote is traditionally a dish of fresh or dried fruits that are cooked in light syrup. The fruits can be greatly varied and are left whole or cut into pieces. It can have any number of spices and seasonings, including brandy and curry. Although compote is most often thought of as a dessert, it can make an appearance earlier in the meal as a complement to meats. See the color section of this book for a picture of Pear-Cranberry Compote.

Take advantage of pears' sweet nature for this compote. This recipe is meant to be spread around — into places such as the crannies of waffles and across the splendid domes of ice cream and pound cake. And yes, you can serve it hot or cold.

Choose pears that are somewhat firm but not hard. If necessary, ripen them at room temperature. Ripe pears should give to slight pressure at the stem end. As with all fruit, choose unblemished ones.

Preparation time: *20 minutes*

Cooking time: *25 to 30 minutes*

Yield: *4 cups*

1 cup fresh cranberries, coarsely chopped	*1 tablespoon lime juice*
½ cup real maple syrup	*3 pounds pears, about 7 medium*
½ cup water	*1 teaspoon grated lime zest*
1 cup cranberry juice	*¾ cup chopped walnuts*

1 Combine the cranberries, maple syrup, and water in a saucepan. Simmer for 5 to 10 minutes over low heat. Remove from the stove.

2 Combine the cranberry juice and lime juice in a medium bowl. Peel the pears and cut them into quarters lengthwise. Core the pears and cut into 1-inch cubes. Add the pears to the cranberry juice until ready to use.

3 Add the pears and cranberry juice to the saucepan with the cranberry mixture. Cover and cook over medium heat until the pears are just tender (soft but not mushy), about 5 minutes. (The cooking time will depend on how ripe the pears were to start out.)

4 Remove the pears and cranberries from the liquid with a slotted spoon. Set aside.

5 Increase the heat to medium-high for about 15 minutes, reducing the pear liquid to 1 cup. Add the lime zest. Pour over the reserved pears and cranberries. Add the walnuts. Cover and chill. Store in an airtight container in the refrigerator for up to 4 days.

Tip: Pears (as well as apples) are embarrassed by being peeled and tend to turn brown quickly. To help slow this process, lightly brush pears with lemon juice for immediate use. You also can toss sliced pears with orange juice for a slightly different taste sensation. Or you can hold pears for a slightly longer time in acidulated water, which is a mixture of about 4 tablespoons of lemon juice to 4 cups of water.

Per serving: Calories 30 (From Fat 9); Fat 1g (Saturated 0g); Cholesterol 0mg; Sodium 0mg; Carbohydrate 6g (Dietary Fiber 1g); Protein 0g.

Pears don't mind their shape

Pear-shaped may be an unfortunate contour for the human body, but Mother Nature thinks this is a wonderful form and has imbued the pear with one of the sweetest ambrosias known to man. And what timing she has. Your tan lines have faded, your tennis elbow has healed, and there is no more sand in the doormat. All the bountiful fruits of summer are just a lip-smacking memory. Then pears arrive.

Here are the ones you'll see most often:

- **Yellow Bartlett:** Available from August through December, this is the quintessential pear in your mind's eye. They're great for eating and excellent for cooking.

- **Red Bartlett:** This pear is similar to the Yellow Bartlett, but it prefers to wear red.

- **Bosc:** Available from August through April, this variety has brownish skin and is perfect for baking.

- **Green Anjou:** Available from October through June, these pears are wonderful in a salad.

- **Red Anjou:** You can find these pears from October through May. These can go anywhere the green Anjou goes, but you may prefer them for the contrast of their red skin.

- **Comice:** Available from August through February, the Comice is the juiciest, sweetest of all pears. Be sure to serve these pears with several napkins. Enjoy a Comice just by itself or with cheese.

- **Seckel:** Available from August through February, this pear proves that good things do come in small packages. It's very sweet and makes a great treat in a lunch box.

Just blend it

Blenders are one of the indispensable mainstays of the kitchen, but you don't need the one with 20 buttons. Financed in the 1930s by Fred Waring — yes, the band leader — the Waring Blendor (yes, that was the correct spelling) had a simple on/off switch. This was sufficient at the time to blend drinks — its main purpose. Now you need a few more speeds, but the standard eight or so should suffice.

Blissful Blueberry Citrus Syrup

Blueberries abound in the lazy summer months of late May to mid-August. If you're tired of having blue fingers from popping these little fruits in your mouth, make this syrup and pour summer flavor over hearty French toast in the morning or over ice cream and pound cake at night.

Blueberries should have a deep blue-purple skin with a powdery appearance. Discard any green, shriveled, or smashed berries. Blueberries, as with all berries, like a bath only right before you use them. Store them in the refrigerator until that time. They'll keep for a week to 10 days.

Preparation time: *15 minutes*

Cooking time: *10 minutes*

Yield: *4 cups*

2 pints fresh blueberries	*1 teaspoon grated lemon zest*
12-ounce jar orange marmalade	*¼ teaspoon cinnamon*
¼ cup water	*Pinch of cloves*

1 Wash and pick over the blueberries. Remove any stems or bruised berries.

2 Combine the blueberries, marmalade, water, lemon zest, cinnamon, and cloves in a saucepan. Cook over medium heat for 10 minutes. Remove from the heat.

3 Carefully ladle about 2 cups of the cooked blueberry mixture into a blender. Puree until smooth. Add the puree to the remaining blueberry mixture. Cool and refrigerate in an airtight container for up to 5 days.

Tip: July is National Blueberry Month. So if you get a little overenthusiastic at the farmers market and come home with more blueberries than you know what to do with, you're in luck. Wash the berries and dry very thoroughly. Place them in a single layer on a baking sheet with sides and put them in the freezer. When frozen, put the blueberries in a resealable plastic bag and return them to the freezer. They'll keep for 6 to 8 months.

Per serving: Calories 18 (From Fat 0); Fat 0g (Saturated 0g); Cholesterol 0mg; Sodium 4mg; Carbohydrate 5g (Dietary Fiber 0g); Protein 0g.

Customizing Your Sugar and Butter Stash

The average American eats 43 pounds of sugar a year. Oh my! Despite what nutritionists tell us, we keep soothing our souls and bribing our children with it. Sugar has, for generations, hidden tastes we can't abide — like medicine. *Sugar-coated* has become part of the vernacular. Now we unabashedly gobble it down for the pure sugar high. So you're going to love the flavored sugar recipes in this section.

Butter is one of the workhorses of the kitchen. Few ingredients contribute as much as this golden substance. It gives texture to pound cakes, binds sauces, and makes pie crusts tender. But butter is also fickle. It just loves the strongest odor in the refrigerator — and like a sponge, it sops it up. But these recipes are going to take full advantage of that character flaw. The butter will adore the seasonings added to it.

Vanilla-Flavored Sugar

Remember that cup of sugar your neighbor borrowed? Get it back. You're going to want all the sugar you can get to experiment with these flavors and then create some of your own. Start with vanilla sugar. Its flavor goes well with just about anything. Use it in coffee or baked in cookies. Combine that basic vanilla sugar with other flavors, such as cinnamon or orange. It can make friends with anyone.

Preparation time: *5 minutes*

Yield: *2 cups*

2 cups granulated sugar   1 vanilla bean

Combine the sugar and the vanilla bean in an airtight jar. Stir occasionally. Allow to sit for 2 weeks before using.

Vary It! *If you want to try another flavor, experiment with other ingredients. You can even add more than one ingredient if you want. Here are some ideas to get you started. Simply add one or more of the following ingredients to 2 cups of sugar: 4 teaspoons ground cinnamon; the zest of 2 large oranges, cut with a vegetable peeler; the zest of 2 lemons and the zest of l lime, cut with a vegetable peeler; 2 teaspoons ground cardamom; ¼ cup mint leaves. If you're combining two flavors, halve each amount.*

Tip: *If you're making orange zest sugar, place strips of orange zest in the microwave on high for 2 to 3 minutes, depending on the size and moisture content of the strip, to dry it out. You don't have to do this with lemon or lime zest. For tips on ways to remove zest from citrus fruits, see the sidebar "More than one way to skin an orange" in this chapter.*

Per serving: *Calories 48 (From Fat 0); Fat 0g (Saturated 0g); Cholesterol 0mg; Sodium 0mg; Carbohydrate 13g (Dietary Fiber 0g); Protein 0g.*

Vanilla beans are a little like old jalopies: They just keep racking up the miles. If you can't bear to throw away that vanilla bean you just fished out of a custard (and who can at those prices?), then just pat it dry and toss it in with a few cups of sugar. Stir it once in a while and taste it. You'll get delicious vanilla sugar; it may just take a little longer than it would if you had an unused bean (because the flavor will be a little weaker than it is when the bean is fresh).

Diner slang for sugar is yummy. Yummy!

More than one way to skin an orange

When it comes to citrus fruit, zest and peel, although often used interchangeably, are not the same thing. *Zest* is the beautifully colored, tasty skin of the fruit. *Peel* includes the very bitter white pith underneath and is very definitely "un-a-peeling." Here are some ways to best prepare zest for cooking. The way you do it may vary according to recipe directions or the tools you have on hand.

- **Chopping:** Use a vegetable peeler to remove the zest. Cut into thin strips with a chef's knife and then very finely chop. This method results in a slightly coarser texture than grating.

- **Zesting:** A zester is a tool that lives solely for the purpose of removing thin strips of zest from citrus fruit. Use this tool and then chop the strips very finely with a chef's knife.

- **Grating:** Grate citrus fruit on the finest hole of a box or flat grater. This gives you the best zest, but it is hard to clean out of the grater. A stiff toothbrush (bought specifically for this purpose only) is a nifty tool to get stubborn zest off the teeth of a grater. But a greater grater idea is to place a piece of wax paper over the teeth of the grater, push down slightly, and proceed to grate. Then just lift off the paper and the zest. This technique makes the task downright pleasant.

The Microplane grater/zester is a relatively new product on the market. It looks likes a rasp (a coarse metal file). As a matter of fact, that's where the inventor (a woman) got the idea. It is the easiest, cleanest way to grate an orange. Just know that it makes a fluffier zest, so you should press it down into the measuring spoon to get an accurate measurement.

You have a couple options when giving flavored sugars as gifts. Package a sampling of sugars in glass vials or test tubes sealed with a cork. Dip the ends of the cork into melted colored wax to keep them secure. Or you can present the sugars in an inexpensive *dredger tin,* which is a metal can with a handle and perforated lid. Dredgers are ideal containers for cinnamon sugar. But do place a piece of plastic wrap or thin material across the can before screwing the lid back on so that the sugar doesn't spill out before you have a chance to give your food gift.

If you're looking for places to use flavored sugars, try them on toast and English muffins, cereal, tea, meringues, whipped cream, dessert sauces, pancakes, fruit, and cookies.

The famous insurance company, Lloyds of London, began in 1688 as a coffeehouse.

Coffee break!

If you've just made some of the flavored sugars in this chapter, you may want to decide just whom to give them to over a cuppa joe (that's coffee to all you tea drinkers). Here are a few hints on brewing a cup of coffee that your guests will consider a true gift:

✔ The recommended measurement for the perfect brew is 2 tablespoons of ground coffee per 6 ounces of water. (Use more or less depending on your taste.)

✔ Water affects the taste of coffee. Coffee is basically flavored water. If your water tastes like chlorine or sulfur, so will your coffee.

✔ Nature abhors vacuums, but coffee prefers them. Use a vacuum carafe to keep coffee tasting fresh longer. Coffee naturally deteriorates after about 20 minutes, so continuous heating on a warmer plate gives you swill.

✔ Ground coffee will last longer if stored in the refrigerator. You can store it for an even longer period in the freezer, but you should wrap it in plastic. Don't take coffee in and out of the freezer; the condensation will facilitate its deterioration.

✔ Keep the coffee maker and pot clean. If you don't, oils from the coffee will build up and turn rancid, affecting the taste of the coffee.

Scallion Butter

Here's as good a place as any to start buttering up friends and relatives. This herbed butter goes well with any savory meal and is great spread on freshly baked bread.

Preparation time: *10 minutes*

Yield: *1 cup*

2 sticks unsalted butter, at room temperature	*3 tablespoons finely chopped scallions (or snipped chives)*

1 Combine the butter and scallions in a small bowl. Blend well.

2 Spoon the mixture onto a piece of wax paper about 12 inches square. Shape the butter into an even log about 6 to 7 inches long. (The ease of doing this depends on the consistency of your butter.) Gently roll the wax paper around the log, shaping and smoothing as you go. (See Figure 8-1.) When completely rolled, gently twist the ends simultaneously in opposite directions. You should end up with a fairly symmetrical log. Refrigerate. Cut in slices to serve.

Vary It! *In addition to the scallions, add 2 teaspoons lemon juice and ¼ teaspoon ground white pepper to the butter.*

Vary It! *Soften 2 sticks of unsalted butter. Add one of the following ingredients: 4 teaspoons chili powder; 2 tablespoons finely chopped basil; 2 teaspoons finely chopped tarragon; ¼ cup finely chopped black olives (or green or mixed); ½ cup ground, toasted hazelnuts; ¼ cup strawberry jam; 2 tablespoons finely chopped capers; 2 teaspoons grated orange zest; 2 tablespoons Dijon mustard; 5 tablespoons honey; 4 teaspoons curry powder; or 2 tablespoons snipped dill.*

Tip: *Zip strip the leaves of most fresh herbs by holding the tip in one hand and running your fingers down the stalk toward the root end.*

Per serving: *Calories 101 (From Fat 100); Fat 11g (Saturated 7g); Cholesterol 31mg; Sodium 2mg; Carbohydrate 0g (Dietary Fiber 0g); Protein 0g.*

STEPS FOR MAKING COMPOUND BUTTERS

Figure 8-1:
Rolling a
butter log in
wax paper.

PUT THE BUTTER IN A BOWL AND LET IT GET SOFT... BUT DON'T MELT IT!

USE A FORK TO BLEND IN YOUR SEASONINGS!

TURN BUTTER OUT, ONTO A PIECE OF WAXED PAPER AND ROLL INTO A UNIFORM CYLINDER.

TWIST ENDS OF PAPER WRAP IN OPPOSITE DIRECTIONS.

Butter comes in two basic models: unsalted (also known as sweet) and salted. Unsalted butter doesn't contain sugar — it just doesn't have any salt. It has a delicate, clean flavor (although if you're used to salted butter, you may find it bland at first). Unsalted butter is preferred by cooks, bakers, and other control freaks, because the amount of salt in a dish can be regulated. Salted butter, obviously, contains salt, which is added as a preservative. The amount of salt can vary from brand to brand and from region to region.

If you need to find a way to soften butter, here are some tips:

- ✔ Let it sit at room temperature.

- ✔ Microwave the butter on medium-low (30 percent power on a 600- to 700-watt microwave) for about 20 seconds. Repeat in 5-second increments, if necessary.

- ✔ To help the butter soften a little faster, slice the butter with a vegetable peeler or shred it on the side of a box grater with the largest holes.

Pat as much moisture as possible out of ingredients such as olives, capers, and washed herbs that you use in your flavored butters.

Ancient lore holds that butter was invented when, one very hot day, an Asian horseman carried a goatskin sack of sour milk. The galloping motion of his horse churned the milk into a wondrous, thick substance.

Spoon flavored butter into a decorative crock and include a butter spreader as part of the gift. Or shape into 1½-inch-thick logs. Wrap in plastic wrap and tie ribbons at the ends to look like party "poppers." Try colored plastic wrap for a more festive look. (For more information on wrapping ideas, see Chapter 14.)

Of course, butter, in any way, shape, or form tastes great on bread, but you can enjoy the rich flavor in other ways, too. The French have traditionally served an herbed butter pat over meat and fish. But how about flavored butter melting into a freshly baked potato? Or swirl it in a pan before scrambling eggs. You can also try flavored butter on steak, fish, chicken, vegetables, sauces, or grilled cheese sandwiches. The possibilities are endless!

Chapter 9

Preserving the Seasons: Gems under Glass

Glittering jars full of gem-colored fruits and vegetables are as tempting, I think, as all the gems in Tiffany's window. No wonder Audrey Hepburn wanted to have breakfast there!

Years ago, the jelly cupboard in the kitchen was the Tiffany's window of the home. Preserving and canning were a way of life before refrigeration and freezing. Today, convenience rules. Most food is available fresh or frozen all year round, and canning or preserving is a matter of preference rather than survival.

So choosing to make someone a gift of jam, conserve, relish, or salad dressing is a gem indeed. But the gems in this chapter, unlike the ones in Tiffany's window, are a feast for the taste buds as well as the eyes.

All Dressed Up and Ready to Go: Flavored Oil and Vinegar

Some oils are good for us. Some oils are not so good for us. (Don't we love them!) All of them serve a culinary purpose: They bring life to food. Sometimes the simplest way to enjoy oils is to flavor them with herbs or spices so you can dunk bread into them or drizzle them over vegetables. You can also pair them up with a flavored vinegar. Pour the oils and vinegars into pretty bottles, and you have simple but elegant gifts.

Pressing details about olive oil

Olive oil is the queen of the kitchen. It is the most written-about type of oil and certainly can be the most expensive. Gourmet stores and supermarkets present a dizzying array of olive oils. So instead of just closing your eyes and pointing at one, this section is a primer to help you pick the right one for your cooking needs.

Olive oil is a monounsaturated oil that hails from countries like Italy, France, Greece, and Spain as well as from California. The flavor, color, and aroma can vary greatly from one country to the next. The best olive oils are made from ripe olives picked from the tree (not the ones that have fallen off). After the harvest is collected, the olives are ground into a paste and then pressed. The finest oils are cold pressed, with no heat or chemicals applied.

Here are the types of olive oil:

- **Extra-virgin olive oil:** This variety is the product of the first cold pressing and has the lowest acidity of all. It's the fruitiest of all and most expensive. The best time to use it is when you can show off its flavor — such as drizzling it over fish or dipping bread into it. It's also perfect for a simple vinaigrette dressing.

- **Virgin olive oil:** This oil is also from the first pressing but has a slightly higher acidity. Use it for salad dressing, dipping, marinades, and cooking.

- **Fino (fine) olive oil:** This oil is a blend of extra-virgin and virgin oils. Use it for salad dressings, dipping, marinades, and cooking. It's also good for sautéing.

- **Pure olive oil:** This oil is a combination of extra-virgin or virgin olive oil and refined olive oil. (In refined olive oils, heat is applied — not a good thing — to an oil from a second or third pressing.) Use it for marinating, cooking, and sautéing.

- **Light olive oil:** This oil is highly filtered and loses much of its olive oil taste. Don't be fooled into believing it's lower in calories; it's just lighter in color and flavor. It's recommended for baking.

Remember, the more important the flavor of the olive oil, the better the quality should be. Keep that in mind when you stock up for gift oils in glass.

Chive-Flavored Oil

The light oniony flavor of this oil enhances salad dressings. But don't stop there. Try dipping bread in it. Brush it on fish or poultry before grilling. Pour some in a pan before you scramble eggs. Even drizzle some over a baked potato. Include some of these suggestions on the gift tag so the recipient will know how versatile this present is. (See the picture of it in the color section of this book.) You'll have to plan ahead with this gift as the flavors need 2 weeks to develop.

Special equipment: *2-cup glass jar with screw top, funnel, paraffin (if desired)*

Preparation time: *5 minutes*

Yield: *1 cup*

1 cup good-quality olive oil	½ cup dried chives

1 Combine the oil and chives in a glass jar.

2 Put the top on the jar and let it sit for 2 weeks in a cool place (not the refrigerator). After that time, taste the oil. If you want it stronger, let it sit for another week.

3 Before giving, strain the oil and pour into a gift bottle, using a funnel if necessary. (For more on food containers, see Chapters 14 and 18.) Close the top and seal with paraffin, if desired. (See Chapter 14 for more on using paraffin.)

Remember: *Although many recipes call for fresh herbs in oil, fresh herbs can cause bacterial problems. Dried herbs are recommended here for safety reasons. You can sprinkle fresh chopped chives over a salad, potato, or into the serving portion of oil to enhance the flavor.*

Vary It! *You can blend any combination of your favorite dried herbs in place of the chives. Use the basic proportions of ½ cup dried herbs to 1 cup olive oil. You can also add dried red pepper flakes for a little zing.*

Per serving: *Calories 120 (From Fat 120); Fat 14g (Saturated 2g); Cholesterol 0mg; Sodium 0mg; Carbohydrate 0g (Dietary Fiber 0g); Protein 0g.*

Distilling facts about vinegar

In the fifth century B.C., Hippocrates recommended the medicinal power of vinegar. A bit later, the Romans reportedly dipped their bread into vinegar. But it took a long time for vinegar to be recognized as an indispensable pantry item — and the soul mate of olive oil.

Dressing a salad

Salad bowls are a prime destination for deliciously flavored oils and vinegars, which are often best accented on simple green salads. Here are some tips to make your salads memorable:

✔ Salad dressings are classically mixed in a proportion of 3 parts oil to 1 part vinegar. You also can substitute lemon juice for all or part of the vinegar.

✔ Salad greens should be absolutely dry. Water will dilute the dressing and keep it from coating the leaves. A salad spinner for drying greens is a great, inexpensive investment.

✔ Don't dress a salad until just before serving. Add only enough dressing to coat the leaves. It's a salad bowl, not a swimming pool!

✔ Sea salt or kosher salt sprinkled on a salad just before serving brings out the flavor.

Their large grains cling to the leaves and don't dissolve as quickly as regular table salt does.

✔ Make a party out of your salad. The best salads are explosions of color, texture, and flavors. Give your salad more than pale pink tomatoes and sliced cucumbers. Try adding a selection of the following ingredients to your bowl of greens: roasted peppers, pepperoncini, chickpeas or other beans, marinated artichokes, chunks of cheese (for example, feta, fontina, mozzarella, or blue), sliced apples, sliced cooked potatoes, nuts, chopped chives, peas, cauliflower florets, broccoli florets, jicama, mandarin oranges, beets, scallion, asparagus, Oriental crispy noodles, pomegranate seeds, grapes, or corn off the cob. Honestly, my favorite salad has no lettuce but is loaded with these ingredients.

As you prepare to make the flavored vinegar in this section, refresh your understanding about the wide, wide range of vinegars available at the grocery:

✔ **Red and white wine vinegar:** Made from red or white wine, this vinegar is the all-around hero of the kitchen. It has an assertive but not harsh flavor. Use it for just about everything, including salads, marinades, and sweet-and-sour dishes. Color is the only determining factor. Red wine vinegar makes potato salad look pretty yucky, so try white instead.

✔ **Cider vinegar:** Made from fermented apple juice, this vinegar is mild and slightly sweet, making it suitable for salads but best used in pickling. Some believe that apple cider vinegar has health benefits.

✔ **Malt vinegar:** This robust vinegar, made from beer, is popular in England for pickling and chutneys. It's an absolute requirement on fish and chips. Try it on your French fries.

✔ **Distilled white vinegar:** Made from grain alcohol, this vinegar is harsh. The job it does best is pickling.

✔ **Rice wine vinegar:** As you may have guessed, this vinegar is made from rice. It's delicate and slightly sweet. A must for sushi and other Japanese and Chinese dishes, it can also make a light vinaigrette for salads. Flavored rice wine vinegar is also available.

✔ **Sherry vinegar:** As the name implies, this vinegar is made from sherry. It has a slightly nutty flavor that adds a nice touch to a dressing for chicken salads. It's also good as a dressing for other types of salad.

Berry-Berry Vinegar

Capture the essence of summer in this colorful vinegar. Use it in salad dressings — it's particularly delightful on a spinach salad. Or add a little oil and try marinating poultry in it before grilling or broiling. The color section of this book includes a picture of Berry-Berry Vinegar in the bottle and ready to go.

Special equipment: 1-quart wide-mouth jar, funnel, paraffin (if desired)

Preparation time: 15 minutes

Cooking time: 2 minutes

Yield: 2 cups

1½ cups raspberries	**Garnish:** *(needed 10 to 14 days later)*
1 cup blackberries	6 to 8 raspberries
2 cups white wine vinegar	6 to 8 blackberries
1 tablespoon sugar	

1 Rinse the raspberries and blackberries and drain on paper towels. Pat as dry as possible. Crush the berries slightly in a small bowl. Transfer to a wide-mouth jar.

2 Bring the vinegar to a boil in a small saucepan. Remove from the heat. Dissolve the sugar in it and pour over the berries.

3 Allow the berries to cool to room temperature. Screw on the cover and store in a cool spot (not the refrigerator) for 10 to 14 days.

4 Taste after 10 days for flavor. If it's not strong enough, let it sit longer. If the flavor is strong enough, strain out the old berries. Pour into a gift bottle. (Use a funnel if needed.) Add fresh raspberries and blackberries as a garnish. Seal with top and dip in paraffin, if desired. (See Chapter 14 for more on using paraffin.)

Remember: Discard any old or moldy berries before giving this vinegar as a gift.

Vary It! Add 2½ cups of your favorite fruit to 2 cups of white wine or cider vinegar. Red wine vinegar can also be used for additional color. Or try strawberries and champagne vinegar for an elegant taste treat.

Per serving: Calories 7 (From Fat 0); Fat 0g (Saturated 0g); Cholesterol 0mg; Sodium 2mg; Carbohydrate 2g (Dietary Fiber 0g); Protein 0g.

A more pleasant way to taste vinegar is to dip a sugar cube in it and then suck the vinegar from the cube.

Relishing the Thought of Scrumptious Spreads

Candied yak rind, asparagus and pistachio conserve, violet and watermelon jam. Okay, maybe I'm exaggerating the varieties of condiments available today, but a walk down the supermarket jelly aisle does seem like a voyage of culinary experimentation.

You can do some experimenting of your own by making the special gifts of jam, jelly, conserve, or relish that you can find in this section.

With the proliferation of jarred, sweet spreads available in markets these days, it's no wonder that the definitions of these products can be confusing. Here are some explanations to help you sort it out:

- ✔ **Jelly** is clear and has no pieces of fruit. It is juice or essence of fruit and sugar thickened with natural or commercial pectin.
- ✔ **Jam** is made with crushed berries and sugar cooked down until thickened.
- ✔ **Conserve** is chunky, made with more than one fruit plus nuts and cooked down with sugar until thickened.
- ✔ **Marmalade** is a clear type of jelly usually made with slices of citrus fruit and sugar that are cooked down until thickened and the peels are tender.
- ✔ **Preserves** are translucent, with large pieces of fruit cooked in sugar syrup.
- ✔ **Chutney** is a condiment that contains fruit, vinegar, sugar, and spices that are cooked down until thickened. It can be smooth or chunky and can range from mildly spiced to hot.
- ✔ **Relish** is a condiment that is made up of chopped, pickled vegetables or fruits, or small ingredients, such as corn.

Always use unblemished fruits or vegetables when making jams, jellies, and other similar products.

Grainy Apricot Mustard

In this recipe, the sweet tang of dried apricots is teamed up with mustard seeds to create a mustard that wakes up everything from sandwiches to salads.

Preparation time: *20 minutes, plus 30 minutes for the apricots to soften and 48 hours sitting*

Cooking time: *5 minutes*

Yield: *4 cups*

1⅔ cups chopped dried apricots	*2 tablespoons packed brown sugar*
2¼ cups water	*½ teaspoon nutmeg (preferably freshly grated)*
⅔ cup mustard seeds	
¾ cup cider vinegar	*¼ teaspoon salt*

1 Simmer the apricots and water in a medium saucepan over low heat for 5 minutes. Remove from the heat and let soften for 30 minutes.

2 Blend the mustard seeds in a blender until coarsely chopped. Add the apricots, vinegar, brown sugar, nutmeg, and salt. Puree until the apricots are smooth. The mustard seeds will remain coarse. Add a little water if the puree is too thick, although the mustard should be a thick consistency.

3 Spoon the mustard into jars that have been thoroughly washed with hot, soapy water. Cover with clean lids.

4 Store in the refrigerator. Allow the flavors to develop for 2 days before using. The mustard keeps for 1 month or longer.

Tip: *You can divide the recipe into half-pint or pint jars depending on how many gifts you need.*

Remember: *Tell the recipient of the mustard gift that it must be kept refrigerated.*

Vary It! *Thin the mustard with a healthy splash of a vinaigrette salad dressing and use it as a basting sauce for grilling or as a tangier dressing for the salad.*

Per serving: Calories 20 (From Fat 5); Fat 1g (Saturated 0g); Cholesterol 0mg; Sodium 1mg; Carbohydrate 4g (Dietary Fiber 1g); Protein 1g.

Hot Diggity Dog Relish

Once upon a time, someone grew tired of just mustard on his hot dog. At that same magical moment, someone else was inspired to combine all the odds and ends from the garden into one concoction suitable as a hot dog topping. This may be a fairy-tale explanation of how relish was created, but it is fun to speculate about the beginnings of this classic combination. Peppers, onions, and zucchini are cooked together in this recipe to make a relish that hot dogs and hamburger will cry out for. And it has a taste that will stand up to the mustard.

Preparation time: *40 minutes*

Cooking time: *15 minutes*

Yield: *8 cups*

1½ pounds (about 3 large) red bell peppers	*2 teaspoons salt*
1½ pounds (about 3 large) green bell peppers	*1 teaspoon coriander seed*
1 pound (about 2 medium) zucchini	*¾ teaspoon celery seed*
1 pound (about 2 large) sweet onions	*¾ teaspoon powdered mustard*
2 cups cider vinegar	*¾ teaspoon turmeric*
2 tablespoons sugar	

1 Wash and dry the red and green bell peppers. Remove the stems, seeds, and veins from the peppers. Coarsely dice them. Pulse on and off in a food processor fitted with a metal blade until finely chopped. Scrape the peppers into a large pot.

2 Wash, dry, and trim the ends off the zucchini. Coarsely dice them. Pulse on and off in a food processor fitted with a metal blade until finely chopped. Add to the peppers in the pot.

3 Peel the onions. Coarsely dice them. Pulse on and off in a food processor fitted with a metal blade until finely chopped. Add to the peppers and zucchini in the pot.

4 Add the vinegar, sugar, salt, coriander seed, celery seed, mustard, and turmeric to the vegetables in the pot. Bring to a boil. Partially cover and simmer for 15 minutes, stirring occasionally.

5 Cool the relish slightly. Ladle into jars that have been thoroughly washed with hot, soapy water. Cover with clean lids. The relish keeps for 2 weeks in the refrigerator.

Tip: *You can divide the recipe into half-pint or pint jars depending on how many gifts you need. Quantities can vary each time you make this recipe due to variations in the produce, so have an extra jar or two on hand.*

Remember: *Tell the recipient of the relish gift that it must be kept refrigerated.*

Tip: Make a confetti salad dressing with this relish. Start by mixing ⅓ cup relish (including some liquid) with ½ cup olive oil or other oil. Taste and add more oil or relish to suit your palate. It makes a scant cup.

Per serving: Calories 6 (From Fat 0); Fat 0g (Saturated 0g); Cholesterol 0mg; Sodium 37mg; Carbohydrate 1g (Dietary Fiber 0g); Protein 0g.

If you have a "tube steak at the Umbrella Room in New York City," you're eating a hot dog from a pushcart vendor.

Down to earth: Organic produce

You can find certified organic produce in most supermarkets — and you may want to select organic for some of the recipes in this chapter. A little background on organic produce may help you decide.

Getting certified is a very stringent procedure with strict guidelines from the United States Department of Agriculture. An independent, third party certifies a farm organic only if, among other things, the following conditions are met:

- Soil on a standard farm has gone through a three-year transition period to become organic.

- No chemical herbicides, fumigants, synthetic fertilizers, or unapproved pesticides are used.

- Labeling requirements are met.

- Strict records of materials and operations are kept.

- Farms are inspected annually.

Consumers are accustomed to getting bigger, faster, better. But sometimes you pay a price. It is reported that, daily, the average person comes into contact with well over a few hundred chemicals. Think about that mousse you just put on you hair, the dry-cleaned sweater you wore today, or the deodorant you put on this morning. Organic produce is one step toward eliminating some of the chemicals in our lives. The downside of organic produce is that it's very labor intensive. Although it tends to be higher priced, there is greater value to these healthful crops:

- Some studies show that organic produce contains more vitamins and nutrients than standard produce.

- Organic produce is never irradiated.

- Organic farming helps protect the environment.

- Organic produce is never genetically modified.

Banana-Mango Chutney

Chutneys have always been a great accompaniment to curry. Here the sweet bananas and mango lend themselves to the exotic spices and are a good contrast to the heat of some curries. Try this thick mahogany-colored condiment on a ham sandwich or in place of applesauce with bratwurst or potato pancakes.

Special equipment: *Medium-sized wide-bottomed pot*

Preparation time: *30 minutes*

Cooking time: *1 hour and 15 minutes to 1 hour and 30 minutes*

Yield: *3½ cups*

2 pounds ripe, but not mushy, bananas (about 6 medium)

1 cup cider vinegar

1 cup chopped onions

2 cloves garlic

1½ cups diced mango (from 2 medium mangoes)

½ cup diced roasted red pepper

⅓ cup brown sugar

3 tablespoons tomato paste

1½ teaspoons allspice

1 teaspoon cinnamon

½ teaspoon nutmeg (preferably freshly grated)

½ teaspoon salt

⅛ to ¼ teaspoon cayenne

1 Peel the bananas and break into chunks. Drop them into a blender jar. Add about half the vinegar and puree until smooth. Pour into a medium-sized wide-bottomed pot.

2 Place the remaining vinegar, onions, and garlic in the blender jar. Puree until smooth. Add to the banana puree.

3 Add the mango, red pepper, brown sugar, tomato paste, allspice, cinnamon, nutmeg, salt, and cayenne to the banana puree mixture.

4 Partially cover and simmer over medium-low heat for 1 hour and 15 minutes, until thick, stirring often. The thicker it gets, the more carefully you should watch it.

5 Cool the chutney slightly. Spoon into jars that have been thoroughly washed with hot, soapy water. Cover with clean lids. The chutney keeps in the refrigerator for 2 weeks.

Tip: You can use frozen or canned mango instead of fresh. If you can't find mango, use fresh or frozen peaches. Feel free to add a cup of raisins if you want additional texture and sweetness.

Tip: You can divide the recipe into half-pint or pint jars depending on how many gifts you need. Quantities can vary each time you make this recipe due to variations in produce, so have an extra jar or two on hand.

Remember: Tell the recipient of the chutney gift that it must be kept refrigerated.

Per serving: Calories 26 (From Fat 0); Fat 0g (Saturated 0g); Cholesterol 0mg; Sodium 33mg; Carbohydrate 7g (Dietary Fiber 1g); Protein 0g.

Testing jam for doneness

To test jam or conserve for doneness, place a small plate in the freezer for a few minutes. Remove the jam from the heat. Spoon ½ teaspoon or so of jam on the plate and return it to the freezer for a minute. It will cool down, and you can see how thick the jam is. Tilt it and determine how quickly it runs, or if it runs at all. Keep checking until it reaches the desired thickness. Figure 9-1 gives you a quick visual reminder of this process.

TESTING JAM FOR DONENESS

Figure 9-1: The jam test, step by step.

1. PLACE A SMALL PLATE IN THE FREEZER FOR A FEW MINUTES.

2. REMOVE THE JAM FROM HEAT SPOON ½ TEASPOON OF JAM ON TO THE PLATE. RETURN TO THE FREEZER FOR A FEW MINUTES.

3. IT WILL COOL DOWN. YOU CAN SEE HOW THICK IT IS. TILT IT AND DETERMINE HOW QUICKLY IT RUNS. KEEP CHECKING UNTIL IT REACHES THE DESIRED THICKNESS.

YOU CAN ALSO TAKE ITS TEMPERATURE! IT SHOULD READ 219°. READY!

You can also take the temperature of the jam. (See Chapter 6 for information about thermometers.) When done, the jam should read 219 degrees.

Start testing for doneness 10 minutes or so before the estimated finish time. You can always return jam that's too thin when it's cooled to the pot to be further reduced. If you've run out of time, leave it thin and call it a topping.

Strawberry-Pineapple Jam

The sunny sweetness of strawberries joins up with the tropical piquant pineapple to make an easy jam. Many supermarkets have already-trimmed pineapples available, which makes it even easier. Try it with the Pineapple-Ginger Scones or the Cornmeal Toasting Bread, both in Chapter 11.

Preparation time: *35 minutes (50 minutes if pineapple is not already trimmed)*

Cooking time: *30 to 40 minutes*

Yield: *3 cups*

2 cups finely chopped or shredded fresh pineapple (about 14 ounces)

2 cups sugar

4 cups fresh strawberries, stems and hull (hard core) removed

1 Combine the pineapple and sugar in a medium-sized, heavy-bottomed saucepan. Simmer for 10 minutes over medium-low heat.

2 Add the strawberries to the pineapple. Crush the strawberries slightly. Continue cooking until the jam tests done (see the section "Testing jam for doneness," earlier in this chapter), about 20 to 30 minutes.

3 Cool the jam slightly. Ladle into jars that have been thoroughly washed with hot, soapy water. Cover with clean lids. The jam keeps in the refrigerator for 3 weeks.

Tip: *You can divide the recipe into half-pint or pint jars depending on how many gifts you need. Quantities can vary each time you make this recipe due to variations in produce, so have an extra jar or two on hand.*

Remember: *Tell the recipient of the jam gift that it must be kept refrigerated.*

Per serving: Calories 40 (From Fat 1); Fat 0g (Saturated 0g); Cholesterol 0mg; Sodium 0mg; Carbohydrate 10g (Dietary Fiber 0g); Protein 0g.

For centuries, sea captains returning from long voyages would impale a pineapple on their gatepost to show they were receiving visitors. The pineapple is now known as a universal sign of welcome.

Rhubarb-Fig Conserve

Rhubarb forsakes its lifetime partner, strawberries, and takes up with dried figs to make a delicious conserve. The walnuts add a contrasting texture.

Here's a word of caution about rhubarb: Rhubarb leaves are poisonous, so be sure to completely remove them before cutting up the rhubarb.

Preparation time: *30 minutes, plus 30 minutes sitting*

Cooking time: *45 minutes*

Yield: *4¼ cups*

6 cups rhubarb (about 1½ pounds after trimming)

3 cups sugar

½ cup chopped dried figs

¼ cup orange juice

1 cup chopped walnuts

2 teaspoons grated orange zest

1 Wash and dry the rhubarb. Trim and cut the stalks into ½-inch dice.

2 Combine the rhubarb, sugar, figs, and orange juice in a large, heavy saucepan. Let sit for 30 minutes.

3 Heat the rhubarb mixture on low, stirring until the sugar dissolves and the rhubarb starts to give up its juices. Increase to medium-high heat and bring to a boil. Skim off any foam on top . Reduce to a simmer over medium-low heat. Cook for 45 minutes, stirring more frequently the thicker it gets.

4 Add the nuts and orange zest to the rhubarb jam during the last 10 minutes of cooking.

5 Test for doneness. (See the section "Testing jam for doneness," earlier in this chapter.)

6 Cool the conserve slightly. Spoon into jars that have been thoroughly washed with hot, soapy water. Cover with clean lids. This jam keeps in the refrigerator for 3 weeks.

Tip: *You can divide the recipe into half-pint or pint jars depending on how many gifts you need. Quantities can vary each time you make this recipe due to variations in produce, so have an extra jar or two on hand.*

Remember: *Tell the recipient of the conserve that it must be kept refrigerated.*

Per serving: *Calories 49 (From Fat 10); Fat 1g (Saturated 0g); Cholesterol 0mg; Sodium 1mg; Carbohydrate 10g (Dietary Fiber 0g); Protein 0g.*

Shedding tears of joy for the onion

Onions have always been a foundation of cooking — one of the essential flavors. No stock or soup starts without them. For a period in time, no army would fight without them — they were thought to make men valiant. The French have long dedicated a soup and a tart to them. And now, with the advent of the super sweet onions, like Vidalia, more opportunities are available to make the onion a star rather than an understudy. Before you stick your hand in the onion bin, here are a few things to know about the different onions:

- **Yellow onions** are the strongest of all the onions. The mainstay of the kitchen, they're best used in cooked dishes. They are round, in varying sizes, with a golden skin. They're world travelers, adapting well to any cuisine.

- **White onions** are milder and have a sleek white skin. The smaller sizes are often seen lounging in a cream sauce. The tiny variety is often spotted at the bottom of a cocktail glass.

- **Red onions** are mild and sweet. They're vain about their purplish color and like to be eaten raw in order to show it off.

- **Bermuda onions** are large and slightly flat and are often confused with the Spanish onion. Mild and delicate, it is good raw in salads or on sandwiches.

- **Spanish onions** are very large, often ½ pound each. They're round and golden but can also be white. They're stronger than Bermuda onions but still mild.

You often can't help crying when cutting onions. They give off fumes (propanethiol S-oxide, if you must know) that combine with the liquid in your eyes to form sulfuric acid. Because a dull knife drags and tears, creating more fumes, a sharp knife and good ventilation are your best friends.

Oh-so-sweet onions

Super-sweet onions are in a class by themselves. Onion lovers agree that they're so sweet they can be eaten raw like an apple. The big three are Vidalia, Maui, and Walla Walla, grown in Georgia, Hawaii, and Washington, respectively. Location is everything. If the same onion is planted in another location, it will taste completely different. Sweet onions have a shorter season than regular onions. Growers have produced copycats of the big three, like the Texas 1015 and the South American Oso Sweet. Vidalias were the first to be mass marketed. They have very light golden skin, are usually a bit flat on both ends, and wear a sticker with the PLU (Price Look Up) number 4159.

Sweet Onion Marmalade

Thick strips, not too sweet, deep amber color. This sounds like the description of a good English marmalade. Well, not quite in this case. This actually also describes a delicious sweet and savory onion condiment that's slowly cooked to release all the natural sweetness. Its flavor also gets some help from raisins and brown sugar and a little tang from balsamic vinegar. It goes particularly well with ham and pork, but a naked hamburger or hot dog would also savor its cover. Don't overlook it as an appetizer on crostini (kroh-STEE-nee) — toasted Italian breads — or Melba toast. And, yeah, you could just plain slather it on French bread.

Preparation time: *35 minutes*

Cooking time: *2 hours*

Yield: *6 cups*

6 pounds (about 9 large) Vidalia or other sweet onions	¼ cup brown sugar
1½ cups water	4 teaspoons paprika (not hot)
1 cup golden raisins	2½ teaspoons salt
½ cup balsamic vinegar	2 teaspoons caraway seed
	½ teaspoon pepper

1 Peel and trim the onions. Cut them in half lengthwise and then cut crosswise into ½-inch-thick slices. Separate the slices into individual pieces.

2 Combine the onions and the water, raisins, vinegar, brown sugar, paprika, salt, caraway seed, and pepper in a large saucepot. Bring the liquid to a boil and then reduce the heat to medium-low. Cover the pot and simmer for 1½ to 1¾ hours, until the onions are very tender. Stir often in the beginning and then less frequently when the onions start to reduce in volume.

3 When the onions are very tender, increase the heat to medium-high and reduce the liquid to about ½ cup, stirring if necessary.

4 Cool the marmalade slightly. Ladle into jars that have been thoroughly washed with hot, soapy water. Cover with clean lids. The marmalade keeps in the refrigerator for 2 weeks.

Tip: *You can divide the recipe into half-pint or pint jars depending on how many gifts you need. Quantities can vary each time you make this recipe due to variations in produce, so have an extra jar or two on hand.*

Remember: *Tell the recipient of the marmalade that it must be kept refrigerated.*

Per serving: *Calories 19 (From Fat 1); Fat 0g (Saturated 0g); Cholesterol 0mg; Sodium 62mg; Carbohydrate 5g (Dietary Fiber 1g); Protein 0g.*

Scarborough Fair Herb Jelly

Country fairs and hot summer days and homegrown produce are all captured in this jar of jelly. Fresh parsley, sage, rosemary, and thyme make a delicate jelly that can accompany lamb or poultry.

Preparation time: *40 minutes, plus cooling time*

Cooking time: *5 minutes*

Yield: *4½ cups*

¼ cup chopped parsley, tightly packed

¼ cup chopped sage, tightly packed

¼ cup chopped rosemary

¼ cup chopped thyme

4 cups white wine vinegar

1 teaspoon grated lemon zest

1.75-ounce no-sugar-needed pectin (I used Ball)

1¼ cups sugar

Green food coloring (optional)

1 Simmer the parsley, sage, rosemary, thyme, and vinegar in a medium saucepan over medium-low heat for 3 minutes. Remove from the heat. Allow to cool to room temperature.

2 Strain out the herbs and discard them. Return the vinegar to the saucepan. Add the lemon zest. Sprinkle the pectin gradually over the surface, stirring the whole time. Bring the mixture to a boil over medium-high heat, stirring constantly. If you get some lumps, try using a wire whisk to break them up.

3 Add the sugar and return the mixture to a boil for 1 minute. Remove from the heat. Skim off the foam. Add a few drops of food coloring, if desired.

4 Pour the jelly into jars that have been thoroughly washed with hot, soapy water. Cover with clean lids. The jelly keeps in the refrigerator for 3 weeks.

Tip: You can divide the recipe into half-pint or pint jars depending on how many gifts you need.

Remember: Tell the recipient of the jelly that it must be kept refrigerated.

Per serving: Calories 16 (From Fat 0); Fat 0g (Saturated 0g); Cholesterol 0mg; Sodium 3mg; Carbohydrate 4g (Dietary Fiber 0g); Protein 0g.

Sometimes a jelly needs a little help. It just doesn't have the strength to thicken on its own. Pectin can come to the rescue. While some fruits (including apples, blueberries, grapes, and lemons) are naturally high in pectin, others (such as bananas, peaches, and raspberries) are not. Most often, teaming a high-pectin fruit with a low-pectin fruit does the thickening trick. A process of cooking down apples will yield pectin that you can add to any jam. A few forms of commercial pectin are also available that do the job quickly (although sometimes the quality of the flavor suffers).

Part IV
Into the Mixing Bowl

In this part . . .

Choices abound in this part. Whether you feel like baking a pie or making quick bread, yeast bread, or a cake to give, it's all here — including a recipe for fruitcake that restores a good measure of respect to the word. If you need a change of pace from sweets, check out the dips, spreads, and spiced nuts in Chapter 12. And see how you can give the gift of time with homemade mixes in Chapter 13.

Chapter 10

Let Them Eat Cake . . . and Pies

In This Chapter

▶ Whipping up cakes

▶ Baking pies

Recipes in This Chapter

▶ Pecan-Cream Cheese Pound Cake

▶ Bountiful Fruitcake with Almond Paste "Wrapping Paper"

▶ Buttermilk-Streusel Coffee Cake

▶ Orange Cannoli Pie

▶ Lemon-Lime Icebox Pie

▶ Plum-Almond Tart

Cakes are the exclamation points of many special events — birthdays, anniversaries, weddings. This chapter isn't about exclamation point cakes, however, but simple gift cakes that underscore the little, day-to-day celebrations in life. These cakes end in a question mark, as in, "May I have some more?"

The pies in this chapter are a whole other story. I think that pies evoke a very different response than cakes do. Some people who routinely turn down an offering of cake practically inhale a pie. My politically incorrect and statistically unverifiable conclusion is that most of these individuals are men. And it's usually a fruit pie. So I include a delicious plum tart recipe in this chapter just for them. You also find two tantalizing icebox pies for everyone's enjoyment.

No matter where your preferences lie, cakes and pies are welcome gifts practically anytime. I've never been one to let nutrition stand in the way of a good thing, so I strongly advocate putting into practice the saying "Life is uncertain. Eat dessert first." I'm sure that everyone under the age of 10 will be right behind me on this one. So if you know anyone under 10 — or anyone over 10 — you'll find a gift here for them.

Bake Me a Cake as Fast as You Can

Some cakes live on as Hall of Famers. They're passed down like family jewels through the decades. Simple cakes like angel food, sponge, devil's food, and, of course, pound cake are delicious in their own right, but then each new cooking generation tweaks them a little to showcase their favorite ingredients.

Pound cake is one of the classic beauties, dating from the early 18th century. It has a very dense texture and a buttery flavor. Like a little black dress, it needs no adornment, but it also makes a great backdrop for anything you want to put in it.

A pound cake has very little chemical leavening (sometimes none), so the height it reaches in the oven depends on the amount of air beaten into the batter. Always take the extra few minutes to thoroughly beat the butter, sugar, and egg mixture.

Pecan-Cream Cheese Pound Cake

The cream cheese in the recipe gives the cake an incredibly dense, almost velvetlike texture. The rich nuttiness adds to the very lightly sweetened flavor. This cake is a good gift for many different taste buds. Slice it on the thin side to serve with coffee or afternoon tea. Slice it thicker to raft a scoop or two of your favorite ice cream.

Preparation time: *40 minutes*

Cooking time: *55 to 60 minutes*

Yield: *Two 9-inch loaves (sixteen ½-inch slices)*

3½ cups all-purpose flour	16-ounce box light brown sugar (sifted if lumpy)
1 teaspoon salt	2 teaspoons vanilla extract
¼ teaspoon baking soda	10 eggs, at room temperature
1 cup (2 sticks) butter, at room temperature	1½ cups pecans, toasted (see Chapter 6) and finely chopped
2 packages (3 ounces each) cream cheese, at room temperature	

1 Preheat the oven to 350 degrees. Line two 9-x-5-inch loaf pans with wax paper or parchment paper. Grease and dust with flour and set aside.

2 Sift together the flour, salt, and baking soda. Set aside.

3 With an electric mixer on medium, cream the butter and cream cheese together in a large bowl. Increase to high and beat until light and fluffy, about 2 minutes. Add the sugar. Continue beating on high until very light and fluffy. Add the vanilla. Scrape down the mixture occasionally.

4 Begin adding the eggs one at a time. Start the mixer on low. Gradually increase to medium-high. Beat for about 20 seconds. Scrape down the bowl. Repeat these steps with each egg.

5 Add the flour mixture. Beat on medium until just blended. Fold in the pecans.

6 Divide the batter evenly between the pans. Give each pan a shake back and forth on the counter a couple of times to smooth the top. Bake for 55 to 60 minutes (rotating once during baking) or until a toothpick inserted in the cake comes out clean. (See the sidebar "Is it done yet?")

7 Remove from the oven and allow to cool for 15 minutes in the pan on a cooling rack. Remove from the pan, peel off the paper, and cool completely on a wire rack. Wrap tightly. This cake stays good for 4 days.

Tip: Toasting nuts brings out more of their flavor.

Per serving: Calories 231 (From Fat 115); Fat 13g (Saturated 6g); Cholesterol 88mg; Sodium 311mg; Carbohydrate 26g (Dietary Fiber 1g); Protein 4g.

 Pound cake doesn't weigh a pound, but just about everything in it does; that's where the name came from. Although we often vary the recipe today, how much easier could it have been for housewives of yesteryear to remember the ingredients in this recipe? Take 1 pound of butter, 1 pound of sugar, 1 pound of flour, and 1 pound of eggs. What was not easy was beating all those ingredients before the invention of the electric mixer.

Fruitcake?! Absolutely, and without apologies

Pity the plight of the poor fruitcake. Few foods are the object of so much ridicule. But fruitcake endures. And the real joke is on those who don't know that fruitcake can be delightful, as a gift at Christmas or any other time of the year. If you're still in doubt, check out the heart-tugging short story by Truman Capote called "A Christmas Memory." An elderly woman stands at the window one morning and announces, "Oh my, it's fruitcake weather." Thus begins the story of a young boy, Buddy, and his elder female cousin and their all-consuming adventure to gather the ingredients for their annual fruitcake ritual. Read it, and you may find that fruitcake is more about the making and giving than it is about the eating. And if you do read it, just so you know, a satsuma (sat-SOO-muh) is a mandarin orange.

Bountiful Fruitcake with Almond Paste "Wrapping Paper"

Fruitcake ingredients have come a long way since the origin of the cake. More dried fruits (including dried melon) and nuts are available than ever before. Dates, dried cranberries, apricots, and three kinds of nuts make this recipe incredibly flavorful and sumptuous. No more picking the funny red things out of your slice of cake. And no need to look for tape and ribbon — you can decorate this fruitcake with its own edible wrapping paper made from rolled almond paste. You can sample a slice of Bountiful Fruitcake in the color section of this book.

Preparation time: *35 minutes*

Cooking time: *l hour and 35 minutes*

Yield: *Two 8½-x-4½-inch loaves (total of fifteen ½-inch slices)*

2 cups dried cranberries

8-ounce box chopped dates (about 1½ cups)

1½ cups walnuts, left in large pieces

1½ cups Brazil nuts, whole

1 cup shelled, unsalted pistachios

1 cup dried apricots, quartered

¼ cup candied orange peel

¼ cup candied lemon peel

1¾ cup all-purpose flour

¾ teaspoon salt

¾ teaspoon cinnamon

½ teaspoon nutmeg (preferably freshly grated)

½ teaspoon ginger

½ teaspoon baking soda

¾ cup (1½ sticks) butter

⅔ cup light brown sugar, firmly packed

8 eggs, at room temperature

1 tablespoon vanilla extract

⅔ cup brandy, plus additional as needed (optional)

Almond Paste "Wrapping Paper" (optional)

1 Preheat the oven to 300 degrees. Line the bottom of two 8½-x-4½-inch loaf pans with wax paper or parchment paper. Grease and flour them. Set aside.

2 Combine the cranberries, dates, walnuts, Brazil nuts, pistachios, apricots, orange peel, and lemon peel in a large bowl. Toss well. (If you don't care for candied peels, leave them out. The cake contains plenty of other good stuff, so it won't suffer if you omit the peels.)

3 Sift together the flour, salt, cinnamon, nutmeg, ginger, and baking soda. Set aside.

4 Cream the butter and sugar in a medium bowl on medium-high until light and fluffy. Add the eggs, beating after each one to incorporate. The mixture will be thin and look curdled. Add the vanilla.

5 Add the flour mixture and beat just until incorporated. Pour over the fruit mixture. Toss well until the nuts and fruits are coated. The batter will just cover them. Divide the mixture evenly between the 2 pans. Smooth the top as much as possible, pressing down any ingredients sticking up.

6 Bake for l hour and 35 minutes, rotating once during baking. Remove from the oven to a cooling rack. If you aren't using brandy, let them cool for 15 minutes. Remove from the pans and peel off the paper if necessary. Let cool completely and then wrap in an airtight bag or container. The cakes will keep in the refrigerator for 2 weeks.

If you're using brandy, let the cakes cool for 15 minutes. Remove from the pans and peel off the paper if necessary. Turn the cakes over and, using ⅓ cup of brandy for each cake, generously brush the bottom and the sides with brandy, and then brush the remaining brandy on the top of each cake. Cool completely. Wrap in cheesecloth that has been soaked with brandy. Wrap tightly and store in the refrigerator. Brush with additional brandy every few weeks. The fruitcake keeps for 2 months.

Tip: *Fruitcake cuts best when cold and sliced with a serrated knife. Most people think thin slices are the way to go.*

Almond Paste "Wrapping Paper"

When people say that this gift is too pretty to unwrap, it really is true. You make the edible gift wrap from rolled almond paste, which you can tint to suit different occasions. Its other purpose is to help keep the cake fresh, but nobody has to know that.

4 tubes (7 ounces each) pure almond paste (not marzipan)

1½ cups confectioners' sugar

4 tablespoons light corn syrup, plus additional syrup for brushing the appliqués

3 teaspoons lemon zest

1 teaspoon vegetable oil

Food coloring (optional)

1 Knead the almond paste, confectioners' sugar, 4 tablespoons corn syrup, and lemon zest together until smooth. Gather into a ball. (The almond paste should be soft when you purchase it. If it's not fresh, work a little extra corn syrup into it.)

2 Remove one-fourth of the ball. Set aside. Divide the rest of the ball in half. At this point, tint the dough, if desired. You can use the same color for both balls or use different colors.

3 Roll one of the two larger balls of dough into a 10½-x-13-inch rectangle. Roll out on a surface that's been dusted with a little confectioners' sugar. Wrap around one of the fruitcakes. Press to seal. Repeat with the other large almond-paste ball.

4 Tint the remaining smaller ball of dough if desired. (Or divide it further and tint it a few colors). Roll out to ⅛ inch. Cut ribbon and shapes freehand or use small cookie cutters to cut out shapes. Brush one side of the shape lightly with corn syrup. Apply to the wrapped fruitcake. Allow the cake with appliqués to set for about 45 minutes and then carefully wrap the cakes in a plastic bag to keep them from drying out.

Tip: *Using paste food coloring gives you more intense colors than liquid. Just remember that a little goes a long way.*

Per serving without "wrapping paper": *Calories 287 (From Fat 150); Fat 17g (Saturated 6g); Cholesterol 69mg; Sodium 102mg; Carbohydrate 32g (Dietary Fiber 5g); Protein 6g.*

Per serving with "wrapping paper": *Calories 437 (From Fat 217); Fat 24g (Saturated 7g); Cholesterol 70mg; Sodium 108mg; Carbohydrate 52g (Dietary Fiber 6g); Protein 8g.*

Buttermilk: It brings culture to cakes

They say that Southern cooks know all the secrets of buttermilk. They drink it and cook with it, and I'm told that they even bathe in it. Well, I can assure you that at least two of those options are true.

Buttermilk has a wonderful moisturizing talent when added to baked goods. As you find in the streusel coffee cake in this section, buttermilk gives cake a rich, soft texture with melt-in-your-mouth flavor. Who knows? Maybe it works on skin, too.

If you have no buttermilk on hand, here's a quick fix. Add 1 tablespoon lemon juice or distilled white vinegar plus enough milk to make 1 cup. Let it sit for 5 to 10 minutes at room temperature. You can also find powdered buttermilk on grocery shelves and at gourmet shops.

Buttermilk-Streusel Coffee Cake

This dessert is the stuff that Welcome Wagons are made of. What could be a better way to say "hello" to a new neighbor than a down-home, simple, tasty coffee cake? And members of that committee you're on are sure to see the sensibility of your suggestions after eating some of this dessert. Grandparents will enjoy reminiscing about the good old days over this cake and coffee. Coming from the German word for sprinkle or scatter, the *streusel* (not to be confused with *streudel,* the flaky pastry) topping adds texture and sweetness to the cake.

Preparation time: *35 minutes*

Cooking time: *40 minutes*

Yield: *24 squares, approximately 2 inches each*

Streusel:

1 cup all-purpose flour
½ cup light brown sugar, firmly packed

7 tablespoons butter, at room temperature

Cake:

1¾ cups flour
1 teaspoon baking powder
½ teaspoon baking soda
½ teaspoon salt
½ teaspoon cinnamon
¼ teaspoon nutmeg (preferably freshly grated)

1 cup sugar
½ cup (1 stick) butter, at room temperature
2 eggs, at room temperature
1 teaspoon vanilla extract
1 cup buttermilk, at room temperature

1 To make the streusel, thoroughly combine the 1 cup flour, brown sugar, and 7 tablespoons butter in a small bowl with a fork or your fingers. The topping will be crumbly. Refrigerate until ready to use.

2 Preheat the oven to 350 degrees. Line a 13-x-9-inch baking pan with wax paper or parchment paper and lightly grease. Set aside.

3 For the cake, sift together the flour, baking powder, baking soda, salt, cinnamon, and nutmeg. Set aside.

4 With an electric mixer on medium-high, cream the sugar and butter together in a medium bowl until light and fluffy. Add 1 egg at a time, beating on low and increasing to medium-high. Add the vanilla. Scrape down the sides occasionally.

5 Beat in about one-third of the flour mixture until just smooth. Add ½ cup buttermilk and beat until just smooth. Repeat, ending with the last one-third of the flour. Scrape down the sides of the bowl occasionally.

6 Spread the cake batter evenly into the prepared pan. Sprinkle the streusel topping over the batter and pat very gently. Be sure to sprinkle the topping all the way out to the edges and into the corners of the pan. If you don't, when the cake rises and the topping is pushed inward, the edges of the cake may wind up without any topping.

7 Bake for 40 minutes or until a toothpick inserted in the cake comes out clean. Cool on a wire rack for 15 minutes. Remove from the pan and peel off the paper. Wrap well. The cake will keep for 4 days.

Per serving: Calories 175 (From Fat 70); Fat 8g (Saturated 5g); Cholesterol 37mg; Sodium 110mg; Carbohydrate 24g (Dietary Fiber 0g); Protein 2g.

Is it done yet?

You have three ways to test if a cake is done — but you only have to use one:

- ✔ Insert a toothpick or wooden skewer near the center of the cake. It should be clean or have just a few dry crumbs on it when removed.

- ✔ Push lightly on top of the cake with a finger. The cake should spring back up.

- ✔ The edge of the cake will be just starting to pull away from the side of the cake pan.

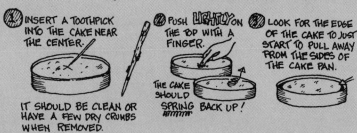

3 WAYS TO TEST CAKE DONENESS

① INSERT A TOOTHPICK INTO THE CAKE NEAR THE CENTER.
IT SHOULD BE CLEAN OR HAVE A FEW DRY CRUMBS WHEN REMOVED.

② PUSH LIGHTLY ON THE TOP WITH A FINGER.
THE CAKE SHOULD SPRING BACK UP!

③ LOOK FOR THE EDGE OF THE CAKE TO JUST START TO PULL AWAY FROM THE SIDES OF THE CAKE PAN.

Filling the Seasons with Pie

Pie in the sky is no longer a dream. You can give pie any time, for any reason. With the recipes here, the seasons blur into one. Citrus fruit is available all year-round so the two icebox pies taste as refreshing after a hot bowl of chili by the fire as they do at a cookout by the grill. The rich plum tart has a raspberry variation that allows you to keep on giving it through the year.

Orange Cannoli Pie

Say Sicily to someone, and cannoli probably won't be the first thing to come to mind. More often it is an image of volcanoes, guns, and men of few words. But this Mediterranean isle holds cannoli dear, especially at Carnevale time. The traditional tubular, fried pastry shells are filled with delicate sweetened ricotta cheese, candied orange rind, and grated chocolate. Unlike cannoli, this pie shell is made with pignoli nuts and then baked, and the pie can be filled ahead of time. Give it in February before Lent or in the summer for a refreshing end to a barbecue.

Special equipment: *10-inch tart pan with removable bottom*

Preparation time: *1 hour*

Cooking time: *20 to 25 minutes*

Yield: *8 servings*

Crust:

½ cup confectioners' sugar

½ cup pine nuts (pignoli), toasted (see Chapter 6 for advice on toasting nuts and Chapter 12 for more about pine nuts)

1 cup all-purpose flour

½ teaspoon baking powder

¼ teaspoon salt

½ cup (1 stick) butter, chilled

1 egg yolk

Filling:

1 package unflavored gelatin, softened in ¼ cup water (see the sidebar "Unflavored gelatin: The inside story")

15-ounce container ricotta cheese, at room temperature

1 cup confectioners' sugar

⅓ cup chopped, good-quality semisweet chocolate

2 tablespoons grated orange zest (see Chapter 8)

1 teaspoon vanilla extract

½ cup heavy cream

Garnishes:

Curls from a 7-ounce milk chocolate candy bar, such as Hershey's (see the tip at the end of the recipe)

2 teaspoons confectioners' sugar mixed with ¼ teaspoon cinnamon

1 Preheat the oven to 350 degrees.

2 Make the crust: Combine the confectioners' sugar and pine nuts (pignoli) in the bowl of a food processor fitted with a metal blade. Pulse until the nuts are ground.

3 Add the flour, baking powder, and salt. Pulse a few times to blend. Cut the butter into pieces and add to the flour mixture. Pulse a few times until a coarse meal forms. Add the egg yolk. Pulse a few times until the mixture just starts to come together. Don't over-process.

4 Turn the dough out on a lightly floured surface and pat into a ball. Place the dough between two pieces of wax paper and gently roll into a 10-inch circle. If the dough is too soft, chill for 20 minutes. Remove one sheet of wax paper. Carefully flip the dough into the tart pan. Peel off the wax paper. Push the dough evenly up the sides. If there are any tears, just pat them closed. The dough is very giving. Prick the bottom with a fork.

5 Bake for 15 to 20 minutes, until light golden in color. Cool. Set aside.

6 Melt the gelatin (see the sidebar "Unflavored gelatin: The inside story" in this chapter) in a small saucepan. Set aside to cool slightly.

7 Combine the ricotta cheese, confectioners' sugar, semisweet chocolate, orange zest, and vanilla.

8 Whip the cream in a small bowl with an electric mixer until soft peaks form. (See the section "Whipping cream — it won't hurt," later in this chapter.)

9 Stir the gelatin into the ricotta cheese mixture. Fold the whipped cream into the mixture. Refrigerate for 10 to 15 minutes, until the mixture just starts to set. Watch that it doesn't get too firm.

10 Mound the filling into the crust. Refrigerate for 2 hours, until set. Right before serving or giving, garnish with the chocolate curls. Using a small strainer, dust the pie with the confectioners' sugar. This pie keeps in the refrigerator for 3 days.

Tip: *Here's an easy way to make chocolate curls. Using a vegetable peeler, scrape the long, narrow edge of the chocolate bar to make big corkscrew curls. Scrape along the short edge to make smaller, tighter curls. Refrigerate until ready to use. This technique works well with milk chocolate and white chocolate bars, but with dark chocolate, you may get shavings, not curls.*

Per serving (without garnish): *Calories 419 (From Fat 231); Fat 26g (Saturated 14g); Cholesterol 84mg; Sodium 146mg; Carbohydrate 38g (Dietary Fiber 2g); Protein 11g.*

Controlling how the cookie crumbles: Making crumb crusts

Crumb crusts are a great invention (probably concocted by a frugal house-wife) for those who are short on time or patience. They're extremely easy to make, and the only drawback is that you can't bake a filling in this crust. Here are two tips to make preparing crumb crusts even easier:

- Here's a technique you may want to try if you have time. Line the pie plate with a double thickness of plastic wrap, allowing some overhang. Proceed with the recipe for the crumb crust. Freeze the crust for 2 hours. Gently lift the crust up by the plastic wrap. Carefully tilt into one hand and gently remove the plastic wrap. Replace the crust in the pie plate. Proceed with the rest of the recipe. This technique makes the pie easier to serve.

- Use the bottom of a ¼ or ⅓ cup metal measuring cup to smooth and press the crumbs into the bottom of the pie crust. Push the crumbs all the way up the side of the pie plate, extending up about ¼ inch past the rim, with the side of the measuring cup. Press the crumbs between the edge of the measuring cup and your thumb to form an edge. Using a measuring cup makes it easier to form an even pie crust.

Lemon-Lime Icebox Pie

Wow. This recipe is a wake-up call for your taste buds. This tangy duo of lemon and lime just dances around your mouth. It's a great refresher in the warmer months. *Note:* To ensure the success of this recipe, it's important to use only fresh lemon and lime juice; the pie may disappoint if you use juice from a bottle.

Preparation time: *40 minutes*

Yield: *8 servings*

Crust:

One-half 9-ounce box chocolate wafers (21 cookies), broken up

½ cup unsalted macadamia nuts

2 tablespoons light brown sugar

4 tablespoons (½ stick) softened butter

Filling:

2 cans (14 ounces each) sweetened condensed milk (not evaporated milk)

½ cup fresh (not bottled) lemon juice, seeds removed (2 to 3 lemons)

½ cup fresh (not bottled) lime juice (3 to 4 limes)

1 teaspoon grated lemon zest (see Chapter 8)

1 teaspoon grated lime zest (see Chapter 8)

Garnishes:

¼ *cup chopped unsalted macadamia nuts*   *Whipped cream*

1 Process the wafers and nuts in a food processor fitted with a metal blade until finely ground. Add the brown sugar and butter. Pulse on and off until just combined.

2 Place the crumb mixture in a 9-inch pie plate. Pat the crumbs evenly across the bottom and all the way up the side, extending up about ¼ inch. Smooth and press into place. (See Figure 10-1.) If you use a tablespoon or ¼ cup metal measuring cup to smooth and press the sides of the crust, you'll have less sticking to your fingers. Chill while making the filling.

3 Combine the sweetened condensed milk, lemon juice, lime juice, and zests in a medium bowl. Whisk until combined. The mixture will start to thicken. Pour into the chilled crust. Refrigerate for at least 6 hours. Garnish, if desired, with the macadamia nuts and whipped cream. This pie keeps for 2 days in the refrigerator.

Tip: *To get more mileage from lemons and limes, roll room-temperature fruit back and forth while pressing down firmly on them. Then proceed with the juicing.*

Tip: *If you don't have a juicer, here's how to extract the juice from a citrus fruit. Cut the lemon or lime in half. Insert the tines of a fork and twist the fruit around the fork while squeezing. This job can be a little messy, so do it over a small bowl.*

Vary It! *Use 1¼ cups graham cracker crumbs (about 16 cracker squares or 8 whole crackers) instead of the chocolate wafers and increase the butter to 5 tablespoons.*

Per serving (without garnish): Calories 518 (From Fat 206); Fat 23g (Saturated 11g); Cholesterol 49mg; Sodium 220mg; Carbohydrate 73g (Dietary Fiber 1g); Protein 10g.

Figure 10-1:
Crumb-crust
technique
for an
icebox pie.

PRESSING CRUMB CRUST INTO A PIE PLATE

1. PLACE CRUMB MIXTURE IN A PIE PLATE.

2. PAT CRUMBS EVENLY ACROSS THE BOTTOM AND ALL THE WAY UP THE SIDE. SMOOTH AND PRESS INTO PLACE.

Sweetened condensed milk dates back to 1856, when Gail Borden introduced it. Civil War soldiers used it because it didn't spoil.

Unflavored gelatin: The inside story

Unflavored gelatin is the unseen fortifier in the food world. It is a light-colored powder that comes in ¼-ounce packets. It has no discernible flavor and should not be confused with the box of colored, highly sugared powders that become wiggly desserts. Here are some things you should know about working with gelatin:

✔ Gelatin should almost always be softened before you use it. To soften, place 1 envelope (a scant tablespoon) in at least ¼ cup cold water (the recipe usually tells you exactly how much liquid) for about 5 minutes. During this time, the powder will absorb the liquid and soften into a slushy-looking glob. The only exception to this advice occurs when the recipe calls for mixing sugar and gelatin together and then pouring boiling liquid over it.

✔ After softening, melt the gelatin (if the recipe says to melt) in a small saucepan over low heat. Gelatin doesn't need a lot of heating to melt. Stir for less than a minute, bringing it to just a simmer. The liquid will turn clear. You won't feel any more granules when stirring.

✔ Test the gelatin by taking some liquid off the spatula and rubbing it between your fingers. It will feel sticky, but no granules of powder will be left.

✔ Gelatin doesn't freeze well, so you can't freeze any desserts containing gelatin.

Whipping cream: It won't hurt

Having too much fat isn't a problem in the world of whipped cream. Lucky cream. In fact, in order to be whipped, cream needs to contain at least 30 percent fat. Whipping cream has the minimum amount needed; heavy cream (or heavy whipping cream) has even more. Cream is now being pasteurized, which adds an extra dimension to the whipping equation. The heating process destroys some of the cream's capability to be whipped, so whipping it to the desired stage may take longer. If you have a choice, use heavy cream because the additional fat will work in your favor. Here are some additional tips on working with cream:

✔ Store cream in the coldest part of the refrigerator — toward the bottom and back away from the door.

✔ Chill the beaters (detachable) and bowl for at least 20 minutes in the freezer before whipping.

✔ If you're sweetening the cream, add the sugar, as well as the vanilla, when the cream starts to thicken.

✔ Use confectioners' sugar for sweetening (unless a recipe calls for something else). It dissolves easier and stabilizes the cream.

✔ Vary the sweetness level of whipped cream to complement the dessert it is to accompany. Use more sugar for a tangy dessert and less sugar for a sweeter dessert.

✔ Be careful not to overwhip the cream. If you're folding it into another mixture, beat only to soft peaks. If you want it stiffer for serving alone, start to decrease the speed of the mixer as it gets thicker or you'll have butter.

✔ Cream that's whipped ahead of time and stored in the refrigerator will start to deflate and "leak." A gentle beating will fluff it back up.

✔ Cream can be frozen, but once defrosted, it will not whip. However, you can use it straight in beverages or in baking.

Demystifying the pie crust

A dear friend once proudly served a pie and announced that the crust was a never-fail recipe. As I ate it, I remember thinking that the crust was misnamed — it was so awful that in this case it definitely had failed. No, I'm not trying to be a total food snob, but I don't think that a commercial pie crust should start tasting better to me than a homemade one. Making pie crusts is tricky, but I can offer some techniques to help you navigate.

Unfortunately, several variables can affect a pie crust. Fortunately, most of them are in your control. A pie crust is a delicate balance of dry, wet, and fat elements. Things like humidity, which affects the moisture in flour, may give you varying results — even from season to season. But after you get accustomed to the feel of the dough, this is in your control, too. Follow these tips:

✔ Pay attention to how the flour is measured (see Chapter 4); don't pack it into the cup.

✔ Make sure that the butter and shortening are very cold.

✔ Use only very cold water.

✔ Make sure that your kitchen isn't too warm.

✔ Don't use excessive amounts of flour to roll out the dough or to dust the rolling pin.

✔ Try using a pastry cloth and rolling pin cover or roll the dough out between two pieces of parchment paper.

✔ Don't overwork the dough.

✔ Allow the dough to rest as long as possible. (See the section "Letting the dough take a nap," later in this chapter.)

May I cut in?

Flakiness may not be a desirable trait in hair or blind dates, but in pie crusts, it's tops on the list. Keeping the butter and shortening as chilled as possible is a key to success. Hot hands do not a flaky crust make, either, so it's best to use an implement other than your fingers to break the butter into small pieces. The simplest tools in your drawer for cutting in the butter and shortening are two dinner knives, as shown in Figure 10-2. Here's what you do:

1. **Hold one knife in each hand.**

2. **Criss-cross your wrists and hold them inside the bowl at the 9 o'clock and 3 o'clock positions.**

3. **Simultaneously draw the knives in opposite directions, bringing the 9 o'clock knife to the 3 o'clock position and the 3 o'clock knife to the 9 o'clock position.**

4. **Keep repeating this crossing motion.**

   You'll go faster and faster as you become more experienced in this technique.

   Turn the bowl occasionally as you cut in the butter. It's a little like patting your head and rubbing your stomach at the same time, but the technique will get easier the more you practice it.

Instead of using knives, you can use a pastry blender, a gadget consisting of several loops of stiff wire held together with a handle. It essentially functions like several knives cutting through at once.

Although cooks often use a food processor for making pie crusts, I'm not a big fan of using that machine for pastry crust. It's too easy to go past the point of no return. You can use it to cut the butter and vegetable shortening into the flour by carefully pulsing off and on. But when adding liquids, I suggest removing the mixture from the bowl and adding them by hand.

CUTTING BUTTER INTO FLOUR

Figure 10-2:
Using dinner knives to cut butter into flour.

HOLD A KNIFE IN EACH HAND. CRISS-CROSS WRISTS AND HOLD INSIDE BOWL AT 9 AND 3 O'CLOCK.

PULL IN OPPOSITE DIRECTIONS. KEEP REPEATING! IT GETS FASTER AND FASTER!

TURN BOWL OCCASIONALLY

OR TRY A PASTRY BLENDER

OR

FOOD PROCESSOR

Choosing the right ingredients

Butter really is better than margarine when making pie crusts. Butter tastes better than margarine, which is bloated with water, thus affecting the overall chemistry of your crust. So unless you have dietary restrictions, stick with butter.

I have to say it: Lard really does make a better crust than vegetable shortening. If your diet allows, substitute lard for the vegetable shortening. Lard gives the crust flakiness, and butter gives it flavor. Make sure that the lard is fresh and has no odor.

Splish splash: Adding the right amount of water

Here's where the sailing gets a little choppy. Adding liquid into the flour and shortening takes a little bit of stopping and testing. If your flour is old or it's a humid day, the amount of liquid you need may vary. Add the smallest amount called for in the recipe. Pick up a wad in your fingers and press it together. If it's crumbly, it still needs a little more liquid. Sprinkle a small amount of liquid over the crust mixture and gently work it in. Test again. Usually that's all it takes.

Letting the dough take a nap

After you get the crust to the right consistency, it needs beauty sleep. Gather the dough up into a ball and then flatten it into a disk about 6 inches in diameter. Wrap it in plastic wrap and tuck it into the fridge for a nap. After about an hour, when it is totally cold, roll it into the desired size. (Some doughs may be very hard and have to sit for 10 to 15 minutes before rolling, or they will crack.) If you have a lot of time, shape it into the tart pan or pie plate, cover it, and let it snuggle in for the night in the fridge. If you don't have that much time, do let it rest for at least 2 hours. Otherwise, it will be cranky and get twisted out of shape when it bakes.

Consider these three ways to transfer the dough into the pan:

- Roll it totally around the rolling pin. Hold it just at one edge of the pie plate or tart pan, gently unroll it over the plate or pan, and then shape.

- Gently fold the pie crust in quarters. Lift and place the point in the center of the pie plate or tart pan. Gently unfold and then shape.

- If you have rolled the dough between wax paper, peel off one piece of paper. Invert the dough onto the pie plate or tart pan, gently peel off the second piece of wax paper, and then shape.

Plum-Almond Tart

What a good pie am I! The filling in this pie is called frangipane (FRAN-juh-payn), a classic ground almond filling. The pie takes advantage of seasonal fruits and complements it with the flavor of almond. Although this tart is good anytime, it's best when plums are in season — from summer to early fall. The pie crust recipe makes 2 crusts for 9-inch tarts.

Special equipment: 9-inch tart pan with removable bottom

Preparation time: 55 minutes, plus at least 2 hours chilling time

Cooking time: 50 to 55 minutes

Yield: 8 servings

Pie crust:

2 cups all-purpose flour

2 teaspoons sugar

¾ teaspoon salt

7 tablespoons butter, chilled

6 tablespoons solid vegetable shortening, chilled

1 egg yolk

1 teaspoon lemon juice

3 to 4 tablespoons ice water

Filling:

3 medium plums (about 9 ounces total)

1 cup whole blanched almonds

⅔ cup confectioners' sugar

6 tablespoons butter, softened

2 eggs, at room temperature

½ teaspoon almond extract

Pinch of salt

Confectioners' sugar

1 For the pie crust, combine the flour, sugar, and salt in a medium bowl. Set aside.

2 Cut the butter and vegetable shortening into small pieces — about ¼ inch. Cut the butter and shortening pieces into the flour mixture until it resembles coarse meal.

3 Make a well in the center of the flour mixture. Add the yolk, lemon juice, and 3 tablespoons of water. Start whisking the liquids together with a fork and gradually spiral outward, incorporating the flour and the liquid. Do not overcombine. (See the section "Demystifying the pie crust," earlier in this chapter.) Add more water, if necessary.

4 Gather up the dough in a ball. Divide into 2 equal parts. Pat into 6-inch disks. Wrap in plastic wrap and refrigerate for 1 hour or longer. You need only one disk for this recipe, so you can wrap the second disk and freeze it for up to 2 months for another purpose. (Or make 2 pies and keep one for yourself!)

5 Roll the pie crust out to an 11-inch circle. Place in the tart pan. Fold the excess edge over toward the center of the pie and gently press it, making the crust even with the top of the tart pan. Cover and chill for at least 2 hours.

6 Preheat the oven to 375 degrees. Prick all over the bottom of the pie crust with a fork. Line the crust with a piece of aluminum foil. Fill the foil with a pound of dried beans (or enough rice to cover the bottom and up the sides or a pie weight bought for that purpose). This is called *blind baking*. You can use the dried beans or rice used as pie weights again for pie duty but not for use in recipes calling for cooking dried beans or rice.

7 Bake for 10 minutes. Carefully lift out the foil and bake for 5 more minutes. Prick the bottom again, if necessary. Remove the crust to a cooling rack. Cool while continuing with the recipe. Lower the oven temperature to 350 degrees.

8 For the filling, wash and dry the plums. Cut in half along the "seam" and remove the pit. Cut each half into 6 wedges. Repeat with the remaining plums. Set aside.

9 Pulse the almonds in the bowl of a food processor fitted with a metal blade. Add the sugar and process until very finely ground, about 20 to 30 seconds. Remove the mixture to a small bowl.

10 With an electric mixer on medium-high, beat the almond mixture and butter until light and fluffy. Beat in the eggs, one at a time, on low, until incorporated. Stir in the almond extract and salt. Spread the mixture into the cooled pie crust. Fan about two-thirds of the plums around the top at the edge, ½ inch away from the crust. Fan the remaining plums in the opposite direction in a circle around the center. The plums will sink somewhat during baking.

11 Bake for 35 to 40 minutes, until the crust is golden brown and the center springs back when you touch it. Remove from the oven and place on a cooling rack until completely cool. Cover the pie with foil. It will keep for 3 days in the refrigerator. Bring to room temperature before serving. Dust with confectioners' sugar before presenting.

Tip: *Chilling the crust or actually resting it in a cold place allows the gluten in the crust to relax. This prevents the crust from becoming a contortion artist when it is baked. If you can shape the crust the day before baking, so much the better.*

Vary It! *Replace the plums with 1 cup raspberries. As a garnish, sprinkle the top with 2 tablespoons sliced almonds.*

Per serving: *Calories 550 (From Fat 360); Fat 40g (Saturated 15g); Cholesterol 130mg; Sodium 257mg; Carbohydrate 41g (Dietary Fiber 2g); Protein 9g.*

Chapter 11

A Loaf of Bread and Thou

Magic happens. Mix one packet of little yeast granules into a big bowl of flour. Add some water and a pinch of salt and sugar. Put it in the oven and out emerges the staff of life. Cultures 5,000 years ago were doing the same thing.

However, back then, man was baking bread because he needed to stay alive. Bread was one of his more reliable food resources. The staff of life was not just a saying in those days, so when someone gave you bread, the gesture was sincere. Today, that custom is carried on when people bring bread to a new neighbor. But don't stop with a neighbor and don't stop with just white bread. Bring a Prosciutto-Fig Quick Bread to a walkathon (it's practically a meal in itself), make Pineapple-Ginger Scones for the book club (particularly if you're reading *Jane Eyre*), or bring Banana-Blueberry Bread to soccer practice (for the moms and dads who schlepp there every week).

This chapter shows you the basic techniques of making bread with yeast and with leavening agents such as baking soda and baking powder. I include a range of sweet and savory recipes from which to choose as well as easy, I-have-no-time recipes and more involved recipes for those rainy Sundays when you find yourself wondering what you'll do today.

Making Quick Breads — Time Is on Your Side

Your kids forgot to tell you that the school bake sale is tomorrow. Your new mother-in-law is coming to visit on short notice. For moments like these, when you're short on time but you really don't want to serve store-bought products again, you don't need to panic. Quick breads can come to the rescue. They're one of the most satisfying culinary treats. Certainly the time factor is an advantage, and the fuss factor is low. And when you're done, a glorious loaf of bread is waiting to be sliced and devoured.

Pan handling

Sometimes smaller is better when making quick breads. Sometimes more is more. By dividing bread into smaller loaves, you can create a sampler basket of different breads to give to a few friends. With a little experimenting, you'll find that the pan sizes listed in recipes aren't carved in stone. You can use mini loaf pans for the quick breads or divide free-form loaves into smaller breads. Just follow these guidelines:

- ✔ Fill mini loaf pans or even muffin tins at least half full but not more than two-thirds full.

- ✔ Even if you divide a recipe in half, the baking time is still longer than half of the baking time called for in the basic recipe. Start watching a little after halfway through the original baking time. Halving a recipe probably takes two-thirds to three-fourths of the stated time.

- ✔ Use these tips for testing doneness of quick breads:

  - • Insert a toothpick in the center of the bread. If the bread is done, the toothpick will have no crumbs or only a few dry crumbs clinging to it when removed.

  - • Bread starts to pull away from edges of the pan when it's done.

  - • If you push the top of the loaf lightly with your finger, it will spring back when it's done.

  - • Use other senses besides touch. The bread will acquire a golden brown hue. You'll start to smell the bread shortly before it's done.

- ✔ The more often you open the oven door, the harder it is for the heat to return to preset temperature. Keep your checking of doneness to a minimum.

- ✔ If you use a glass baking dish, lower the oven temperature 25 degrees. You may also need to do the same with dark pans or pans with a dark nonstick coating. Always check the manufacturer's instructions.

Top: Easy Alabaster Mints (Chapter 6); bottom: Tea Party Sugar Cubes (Chapter 6)

Pear-Cranberry Compote (Chapter 8);
Rise-and-Shine Waffle Mix (Chapter 13)

Top: Lemon-Cardamom Shortbread (Chapter 7);
bottom: Freckled Chocolate, Cinnamon, and Hazelnut Biscotti (Chapter 5)

Top: 1-2-3 Milk Chocolate Chunky Clusters (Chapter 5);
bottom: No-Bake Black Forest Bites (Chapter 5)

Cranberry-Walnut Monkey Bread (Chapter 11)

Bountiful Fruitcake (Chapter 10)

Left: Chive-Lemon Flavored Oil (Chapter 9);
right: Berry-Berry Vinegar (Chapter 9)

Left: Marinated Olives (Chapter 12);
right: Shrimp in Green Sauce Dip (Chapter 12)

Life after the oven: Cooling and storing

Nothing is more tempting than hot bread coming out of the oven, but do try and resist sampling it until after it cools. Bread is easier to slice and has better flavor if it's allowed to cool completely. Also keep in mind that bread slices easiest if cut with a serrated bread knife.

When the bread is totally cool, wrap it in a plastic bag or plastic wrap. Store it at room temperature (unless the recipe specifies otherwise) for 1 to 3 days, depending on the bread. Bread stored in the refrigerator actually goes stale faster than bread stored at room temperature. But breads freeze very well. Make sure that the loaf is very well wrapped, with no air pockets, to help prevent freezer burn. Frozen bread keeps about 3 months. Defrost unsliced bread for 2 to 3 hours at room temperature. Reheat, wrapped in foil, in a 350-degree oven for about 20 to 25 minutes. For a crispier crust, wrap foil loosely around the loaf and do not completely seal it.

Always give a loaf of bread that is freshly baked. Not only it will be at peak flavor and freshness, but the recipient can also enjoy it longer.

Baking soda versus baking powder

Baking soda and baking powder may seem the same to you, but they're not. Baking soda was the first chemical leavener and has a very specific job description. It is a leavener, yes, and a strong one. You have to use only a small amount (compared to baking powder). But its additional asset is that it neutralizes acids. And some of these acids are very well concealed. The obvious ones are buttermilk, lemon juice, yogurt, sour cream, and vinegar. Acids also lurk in molasses, honey, brown sugar, and chocolate. So you should always see baking soda called for when these ingredients are present.

Baking powder, on the other hand, prefers using a one-two punch. Double-acting baking powder is the easiest type to find and the one that's most often called for in recipes. It contains two sets of leavening agents. One set starts working immediately when you mix it (you'll see bubbles forming right away), and the other agents start working in the oven.

Baking soda and baking powder may be quick, but they demand respect. They suffer as a result of delays. Once the liquid is added, especially in recipes with baking soda, turn the dough into the pan as soon as possible so the leavening doesn't lose its potency.

You also do not want to overmix quick breads, especially when you're making muffinlike breads or scones in which the shortening is cut into the flour. The resulting bread will be tough. So always mix the ingredients (usually by hand) until just blended. If kneading is called for in a quick bread recipe, use a light touch and just a few pushes to bring the dough together.

Banana-Blueberry Bread

If this wonderful combination of ripe, sweet bananas, tangy blueberries, and toasted almonds sounds like breakfast in a bread, you're right. Banana-Blueberry Bread is a great gift for dashboard diners on the go — so save some for yourself. It's a fine way to mellow a commuter's day. But don't be tempted to sample the bread when it's still warm. At that point, the bread will be a little gummy, and the blueberries will still be oozing.

Preparation time: *30 minutes*

Cooking time: *55 to 60 minutes*

Yield: *One 9-x-5-inch loaf (sixteen ½-inch slices)*

2 cups all-purpose flour	*2 teaspoons lemon juice*
1 teaspoon baking soda	*¾ cup sugar*
½ teaspoon salt	*½ cup (1 stick) butter, at room temperature*
¾ cup small blueberries, washed, picked over, and dried	*1 teaspoon vanilla extract*
	2 eggs, at room temperature
1½ cups mashed ripe banana (3 medium to large bananas)	*1 cup sliced almonds, lightly toasted (see Chapter 6 for information on toasting nuts)*
¼ cup plain yogurt, at room temperature	

1 Preheat the oven to 350 degrees. Grease a 9-x-5-inch loaf pan and dust with flour. Line it with parchment paper, if you want. Set aside.

2 Sift together the flour, baking soda, and salt. Remove 1 teaspoon of the mixture and toss with the blueberries. This helps prevent the blueberries from sinking to the bottom of the bread. Set aside.

3 Combine the banana, yogurt (measured in a dry measuring cup), and lemon juice in a small bowl. (The lemon juice helps keep the banana from darkening.) Set aside.

4 With an electric mixer on medium speed, cream the sugar, butter, and vanilla in a medium bowl until the mixture lightens in color. (The mixture will remain granular.) Beat in 1 egg at time until smooth, about 1 minute. Stir in the banana mixture. The batter will look curdled, but it's not. Add the flour mixture and beat until combined. Fold in the blueberries and ¾ cup of the almonds.

5 Spoon into the prepared pan. Smooth the top. Sprinkle with the remaining ¼ cup almonds. Bake for 55 to 60 minutes, until the bread tests done. (See the section "Pan handling," earlier in this chapter.) Cool in the pan for 15 minutes on a cooling rack. Remove from the pan. Peel off the paper and cool completely on the rack. Wrap tightly. The bread keeps for 3 days.

Tip: *Speckly, soft bananas that nobody loves are the best for banana bread. The speckles mean the bananas are at their sweetest — they just may be too soft to eat.*

Tip: If you're unsure of the freshness of your baking soda, put 1 teaspoon of baking soda in 2 teaspoons of vinegar or lemon juice. If it fizzes, it's still good.

Tip: You thought you had time to make banana bread, but now you're just watching the bananas get riper and riper? Peel and mash them. Measure out 1½ cups and mix it with 2 teaspoons of lemon juice. Place it in a plastic bag and squeeze out the air. Freeze until your schedule frees up again.

Per serving: Calories 214 (From Fat 88); Fat 10g (Saturated 4g); Cholesterol 42mg; Sodium 164mg; Carbohydrate 29g (Dietary Fiber 2g); Protein 4g.

 Ellis Island guides tell the story that as immigrants came through the gateway to America, some of them were held in the infirmary, where they were given bananas. But this strange yellow fruit was virtually unknown in many of their homelands. They had no idea how to eat it and often tried to chew the whole thing, peel and all.

Mock Devon Cream

Devon Cream, as well as cream from other English counties, is a clotted cream, meaning that it's made from unhomogenized milk that thickens when it is heated. Clotted cream and jams are traditionally served with scones. This version is thinner than the English version but just as tasty.

Preparation time: 10 minutes

Yield: 2 cups

1 cup whipping cream, chilled

2 teaspoons confectioners' sugar

⅓ cup sour cream (measured in a metal measuring cup), chilled

1 Beat the whipping cream in a chilled bowl with the chilled beaters of an electric mixer on high speed until it starts to thicken.

2 Add the sugar. Continue beating until soft peaks form. Fold in the sour cream.

3 Serve immediately or keep refrigerated for 2 to 3 hours.

Tip: The Devon cream should be made just before giving. If this isn't possible, attach the recipe for the cream along with the scones.

Per serving: Calories 38 (From Fat 35); Fat 4g (Saturated 2g); Cholesterol 13mg; Sodium 6mg; Carbohydrate 1g (Dietary Fiber 0g); Protein 0g. (per tbsp.)

Chili-Cheese Muffin Loaf

This cheesy, moist bread is a great accompaniment to a Tex-Mex dinner, or use it to spice up a turkey or roast beef sandwich. Come to think of it, homegrown tomatoes all by themselves would be tasty on this bread.

Preparation time: *25 minutes*

Cooking time: *50 to 55 minutes*

Yield: *One 8-inch loaf (sixteen ½-inch slices)*

2¼ cups flour

2 teaspoons baking powder

1 teaspoon chili powder

¾ teaspoon salt

¼ teaspoon baking soda

⅓ cup solid vegetable shortening

1½ cups grated cheddar cheese

1 cup buttermilk, at room temperature

1 egg, at room temperature

1 Preheat the oven to 350 degrees. Lightly grease a 8½-x-4½-inch loaf pan with nonstick cooking spray. Set aside.

2 Sift together the flour, baking powder, chili powder, salt, and baking soda into a medium bowl.

3 Add the shortening and cut in the flour mixture with a pastry blender. Stir in the cheddar cheese.

4 Make a well in the center of the flour mixture. Add the buttermilk and egg. Combine the ingredients, starting in the center and spiraling outward. Stir only until just blended. Do not overmix.

5 Turn the batter into the prepared pan. Smooth the top with a spatula or spoon.

6 Bake for 50 to 55 minutes, until a toothpick inserted in the bread tests clean. (See the section "Pan handling," earlier in this chapter.) Cool on a wire rack. Store wrapped in foil or a plastic bag for up to 3 days.

Tip: *You can combine the sifting and the blending of the shortening in a food processor.*

Vary It! *Omit the chili powder and add ¾ cup chopped dried apples.*

Per serving: *Calories 155 (From Fat 76); Fat 8g (Saturated 4g); Cholesterol 25mg; Sodium 264mg; Carbohydrate 14g (Dietary Fiber 1g); Protein 5g.*

Prosciutto-Fig Quick Bread

Like Bogie and Bacall, prosciutto and figs are one of the enduring classic combinations. And when you join those ingredients in a moist ricotta-based quick bread, the result is a great brunch addition or a teatime pick-me-up.

Preparation time: *25 minutes*

Cooking time: *45 to 50 minutes*

Yield: *One 12-inch loaf (twenty-four ½-inch slices)*

3 cups all-purpose flour

4 teaspoons sugar

2½ teaspoons baking powder

1 teaspoon salt

15-ounce container ricotta cheese, at room temperature

3 eggs, at room temperature

1 cup chopped prosciutto

½ cup chopped dried figs

1 Preheat the oven to 375 degrees. Line a baking sheet with parchment paper or grease lightly.

2 Sift together the flour, sugar, baking powder, and salt. Set aside.

3 Thoroughly combine the ricotta cheese and eggs in a large bowl. Stir in the prosciutto and figs.

4 Stir as much as possible of the flour mixture into the ricotta mixture. Turn out onto a lightly floured surface and knead the remaining flour mixture into the dough.

5 Shape the dough into a 12-inch-long loaf and place on the baking sheet. Cut a ¼-inch-deep slit on the top of the loaf, starting and ending about 2 inches from the ends.

6 Bake for 45 to 50 minutes, until the bread is a deep golden brown. Test for doneness. (See the section "Pan handling," earlier in this chapter.) Remove to a cooling rack. Do not slice until completely cool. Wrap in foil and store in the refrigerator for up to 3 days.

Tip: *Some delis sell prosciutto ends or the pieces that are too small to slice for a lesser price. If you can't locate prosciutto at your deli or supermarket, use a good-quality smoked ham.*

Per serving: *Calories 125 (From Fat 35); Fat 4g (Saturated 2g); Cholesterol 41mg; Sodium 278mg; Carbohydrate 16g (Dietary Fiber 1g); Protein 6g.*

Pineapple-Ginger Scones

Parliamentary procedure, the Beatles, and scones — three of the best things the United States has received from the British. Forget that we once tossed English tea overboard. We've remedied that tax problem and can enjoy a comforting afternoon nibble of warm scones and tea. Take along a gift basket of Pineapple-Ginger Scones the next time you're invited out.

Preparation time: *35 minutes*

Cooking time: *18 to 20 minutes*

Yield: *8 scones*

2 cups all-purpose flour	½ cup (1 stick) cold butter
¼ cup plus 1 tablespoon sugar	1 cup chopped dried pineapple
1½ teaspoons baking powder	2 tablespoons finely chopped crystallized ginger
½ teaspoon baking soda	¾ cup buttermilk, at room temperature
½ teaspoon salt	1 egg, at room temperature
¼ teaspoon nutmeg	

1 Preheat the oven to 400 degrees. Line a baking sheet with parchment paper or grease lightly.

2 Thoroughly combine the flour, ¼ cup sugar, baking powder, baking soda, salt, and nutmeg in a medium bowl.

3 Cut the butter into ½-inch chunks. Cut into the flour mixture with a pastry blender. (For more on cutting in ingredients, see Chapter 10.) Mix in the pineapple and ginger.

4 Make a well in the flour mixture. Add the buttermilk and egg. Stir together with a fork until just about mixed. Turn out onto a lightly floured surface and gather together loose clumps, kneading 7 to 8 times. If the dough is still sticky, add a very small amount of flour at a time. Try to work in as little flour as possible because more flour will dry the texture.

5 Pat into an 8-inch disk. Cut into 8 wedges. Space evenly on the baking sheet. Sprinkle the remaining 1 tablespoon sugar over the wedges.

6 Bake for 18 to 20 minutes, until golden brown and the top springs back when touched.

7 Remove from the oven. Remove from the baking sheet and cool on a wire rack. These scones are best eaten on the same day they're baked.

Vary It! *To make Emerald Isle Scones, reduce the sugar to 1 tablespoon and substitute ¾ cup currants and 1 tablespoon caraway seeds for the pineapple and ginger. Do **not** sprinkle the top with sugar.*

Per serving: *Calories 316(From Fat 116); Fat 13g (Saturated 8g); Cholesterol 58mg; Sodium 332mg; Carbohydrate 46g (Dietary Fiber 2g); Protein 5g.*

Let's Have a Tea Party

Well, why *not* have a tea party? This chapter shows you how to make one of the important elements of an English tea, scones, so it's entirely proper to rediscover the fun you had at tea parties when you were a kid. Review how to brew a great cup of tea, and then combine a few of the recipes in this book to make a three-course tea.

I suggest that you start with an assortment of finger sandwiches spread with Shrimp in Green-Sauce Dip, Downtown Lox Spread, Uptown Smoked Salmon Spread, and Pâté 101 (all in Chapter 12). The second course is scones with Mock Devon Cream (a recipe that I provide earlier in this chapter). Rhubarb-Fig Conserve or Strawberry-Pineapple Jam (see Chapter 9) also would taste good. Serve a nice slice of Plum-Almond Tart (see Chapter 10) as the third course.

I admit this is a lot of work, so trust me when I say no one will complain if you instead decide to simply serve a nice cup of tea and a warm fresh scone.

Tea is an age-old repast that can be as simple as you want or filled with pomp and circumstance. It's a very satisfying menu as well as a social event.

"High tea" is often thought of as the more elegant of the teas, but in fact it has its origins in the British working class. It's the meal they ate after a long day of labor. Afternoon tea is the formal, often three-course interlude around 4 in the afternoon. It originated with the upper-class people who dined fashionably late and needed an afternoon pick-me-up.

Picking a tea

Teas fall into three categories:

- **Black:** Leaves that have been fermented and dried. Known for its hearty flavors, it has more caffeine than other teas. Black teas are the most popular category of teas. Darjeeling, Ceylon, and Lapsang Souchong are all black teas.

- **Green:** Leaves that are unfermented and dried. They have a more delicate flavor and almost no caffeine. Gunpowder and Bancha are green teas.

- **Oolong:** Leaves that have been fermented for only a short time. The flavor is somewhere between black and green teas. Black Dragon and Jasmine are oolongs.

Herbal teas are in a class by themselves. They're not actually made from tea leaves but from infusions of herbs, flowers, and berries in boiling water. They're commonly known as tisane (tih-ZAHN).

Brewing tea

Always use a glass, pottery, or china teapot — never metal — when brewing tea. Here are the steps for brewing the perfect pot of loose tea for your tea party:

1. **Bring a kettle of cold water to a boil, but don't boil it for long.**

2. **Meanwhile, run very hot tap water into the empty teapot.**

   Swirl it around and let it sit a few minutes. Pour out the water.

3. **Place in the teapot a generous 1 teaspoon of loose tea for each cup of tea.**

4. **Pour the boiling water over the tea leaves. Cover the pot and allow the tea to steep between 3 and 5 minutes.**

Don't overbrew, or the tea will become bitter.

Iced tea was invented on a scorching hot day at the 1904 World's Fair in St. Louis.

Yeast Breads: Rising to the Next Level

Entire books are devoted to the topic of yeast breads, so you may be intimidated by that culinary task if you've never baked bread before. After you make one loaf of yeast bread, however, you'll find that it's not so hard after all — just time-consuming. This chapter contains all sorts of bread recipes for varying tastes and skill levels. You can plunge right in with the ooey-gooey Cranberry-Walnut Monkey Bread (a recipe where neatness definitely doesn't count!).

Choosing a yeast

Three kinds of yeast are available:

- **Active dry (regular) yeast** is in granular form and needs to be added to warm water to rehydrate and activate before using.

- **Fast-rise (quick) yeast** is also in granular form, but it can be added directly to the flour before baking. A higher water temperature than active dry yeast is required, usually 130 degrees.

- **Cake yeast,** also known as compressed yeast, comes as a cube that is crumbled and to which a barely warm liquid is added. It is highly perishable and has a very short shelf life.

The three types of yeast are all basically interchangeable, but keep in mind that they all require slightly different usage techniques.

To me, just like Goldilocks, only one yeast is just right. That's the active dry yeast. All the recipes in this book use active dry yeast. Although the fast-rise type may save a few minutes — and this may sound old-fashioned — I like to know that the yeast is alive and kicking. When I see it bubble, I know that I'm off to a good start. I'm investing time in making the bread, so a few minutes doesn't matter. I also think the taste is better in the end with regular active yeast.

In the 13th century, bakers were harshly fined for short-weighting loaves of bread. So, for every 12 loaves of bread they sold to a customer, a 13th loaf was added free. That's where the expression *baker's dozen* comes from.

Proofing the yeast

Proof is the term that means testing to make sure that the yeast is actually alive (as shown in Figure 11-1). Reliability was more of an issue in years past when live yeast was not always a sure thing. The active dry yeast is now pretty foolproof (no pun intended). The yeast only has two basic requirements:

- ✔ The water it is placed in should be warm, not hot, between 105 and 115 degrees.
- ✔ Add a little sugar to the water. Yeast needs a little snack food before it decides to grow.

Use a thermometer to determine the liquid temperature. If the temperature is too hot, it will kill the yeast. If it's too cold, it will greatly retard the growth of the yeast.

If your thermometer happens to drop and break just as you're about to use it, here's a guide. Your body temperature is 98.6 degrees, so a range of 105 to 115 degrees would just feel quite warm to your touch. This step is not unlike testing the liquid in a baby bottle.

Figure 11-1:
Proof positive in the yeast department.

Mixing the dough

You can mix bread dough by hand, by a combination of stand mixer and hand, or with a heavy-duty mixer. (You can also use a food processor, but the method is slightly different so it's best to consult the manufacturer's directions or cookbooks dedicated to processor recipes.) With all three methods, start mixing by combining the yeast, liquid, and enough flour to make a batterlike consistency. Doing so helps develop the gluten (which is the substance that gives bread dough its elasticity). Then gradually add the remaining flour. If you use a stand mixer, at some point it will start to complain, and you'll have to switch to hand mixing. A heavy-duty mixer can complete the whole process, but you may want to do the initial very wet stages with a paddle attachment, switching later to the dough hook. Consult the manufacturer's directions for speeds appropriate to your machine.

It's best to add salt at a later stage in the mixing because it fights with the flour to absorb the most liquid. Put salt in later, and the flour wins.

A bread recipe doesn't always use the same amount of flour, due to variables such as the age of the flour and weather conditions. Always add flour in the smallest increments, using the minimal amount possible.

A little plastic implement called a bowl scraper can make your bread-making life a little easier. It is a 5-inch-wide hand-held spatula made of hard plastic with no handle. One side is curved to easily scrape the bottom of the bowl.

Kneading the dough

The Surgeon General has yet to announce that kneading dough increases endorphins and makes you happier. But he should. You've probably heard that you can take your aggressions out on the dough, and you can. Bread dough can take a fair amount of abuse. But it is the rhythmical repetition of kneading that produces a trancelike peace. Repetition is also what stretches the gluten in the flour and builds a structure for the air bubbles to hang out in which makes the bread rise. Here are the steps in kneading:

- ✓ Turn the ball of dough out onto a lightly floured surface. Work the final amount of flour into the dough.

- ✓ Press the heel of your preferred hand into the dough and simultaneously push it away from you a few inches.

- ✓ Without even taking the heel of your hand out of the dough, close your fingers around the edge and bring the dough back toward you, folding it over on itself.

- ✓ Give the dough a quarter turn and repeat the motion. Keep repeating the process for however long the recipe requires, usually about 10 minutes.

Making it to the first rise

After the kneading is done, place the dough in a lightly greased bowl. Roll the dough over in the bowl to coat it with grease. Doing so helps prevent a skin from forming while it rises. Cover the bowl with a clean tea towel or dish towel or plastic wrap. Place the dough in a warm place (80 to 85 degrees) away from any drafts. Allow the dough to rise until double in size, usually 1 to 1½ hours. To test whether the dough has risen enough, gently poke a finger about ½ inch into dough (see Figure 11-2). If the indentation stays, start punching, as I explain in the next section.

Figure 11-2:
How to test whether the dough has risen enough.

TO TEST IF THE DOUGH HAS RISEN, GENTLY POKE A FINGER INTO THE DOUGH A ½".

IF THE INDENTATION STAYS THERE, THE DOUGH IS READY FOR PUNCHING.

PROOFING RISING DOUGH

Cozy places such as tops of refrigerators are nice, warm spots to let dough rise. Just ask your cat about other such places.

Punching down and shaping

Literally, make a fist and sink it into the middle of the dough, deflating it. Bring the edges inward toward the spot where you punched. Begin to shape the dough according to the recipe. For example, the Oat and Ale Bread is round. To make this shape, remove the dough from the bowl and turn it upside down, making the side that was just on the bottom of the bowl the top. Massage the sides downward and under, pinching them in place under the ball of dough. You want to form a smooth, taut surface on the ball.

Reaching the second rise, baking the bread

Place the dough on a baking sheet and cover with a clean tea or dish towel. (Don't use plastic wrap because it may stick to the loaf.) Let rise in a warm, draft-free place until double in size, usually about 45 minutes. Slash the top with a sharp knife or single-edge razor, if the recipe instructs you to do so. "Wash" the dough, if the recipe requires it. Traditionally, washes can be egg (only the white, only the yolk, or both), milk, or cornstarch mixed with water.

They enhance the appearance of the loaf and help things like nuts or oats stick on top, which also improves the appearance. Bake in a preheated oven. Wait for the magic to happen.

Testing for doneness

When the shortest baking time is up, turn the bread over (if it's a free-form loaf) or slip the bread out of the pan and knock on the bottom. You should hear a hollow thumping sound. If you don't get the right answer, put the loaf back in the oven. You can remove a loaf from its pan about 5 minutes before finish time and place it on the oven rack. Doing so adds to the crispiness and color of the crust.

When bread is done, always remove the loaf from the pan to a wire rack to cool, unless the recipe directs otherwise.

Cranberry-Walnut Monkey Bread

Nobody really knows where the name of this whimsical bread comes from. There are a few theories — the pieces are squished in like a barrel of monkeys, or so many hands reach for the bread that it looks like a tribe of monkeys. Regardless of the origins, it's guaranteed to be finger-lickin' good. (For proof, see the color section of this book.)

Preparation time: 45 minutes, plus 2½ hours rising time

Cooking time: 50 minutes

Yield: 9-inch bread (about 15 servings)

¼-ounce package active dry yeast

¼ cup warm water (105 to 115 degrees)

½ cup sugar

4 tablespoons (½ stick) butter

½ cup milk

1 egg, at room temperature

2 egg yolks, at room temperature

1 teaspoon vanilla extract

3¼ to 3¾ cups all-purpose flour

2 teaspoons salt

Coating:

1½ cups walnuts

¾ cup dried cranberries

6 tablespoons (¾ stick) butter

½ cup light brown sugar

Confectioners' sugar (optional)

1 Proof the yeast in the warm water with a pinch of sugar from the ½ cup sugar.

2 Meanwhile, melt the 4 tablespoons butter in a small saucepan. Remove from the heat and add the milk. Put into a large mixing bowl.

3 Add the remaining sugar, egg, yolks, vanilla, and proofed yeast. Stir well. Add 1 cup of the flour. Mix by hand or start beating with an electric mixer or a heavy-duty mixer fitted with a dough hook. Incorporate 1 more cup of flour. Add the salt and 1 more cup of the flour. If you mix by hand or with a stand or hand electric mixer, you'll have to turn the dough out onto a surface somewhere at this point. A heavy-duty (KitchenAid-type) mixer with a dough hook will keep going.

4 The dough will still be sticky. Start kneading in the last ½ cup to ¾ cup of flour a little at a time. (See the section "Mixing the dough," earlier in this chapter.) Continue kneading for 10 minutes.

5 Grease a large bowl with butter or nonstick cooking spray. Place the dough in the bowl and turn over a few times to coat the surface of the dough. Cover with a clean dish towel and place in a warm (80 to 85 degrees), draft-free place until double in size, about 1½ hours. (See the section "Making it to the first rise," earlier in this chapter.)

6 Meanwhile, grind the nuts in a food processor fitted with a metal blade until chopped. Add the dried cranberries and pulse on and off 4 or 5 times until the cranberries are partially chopped. Place in a pie plate or shallow bowl.

7 Just before the time the dough is finished rising, melt the 6 tablespoons butter and the brown sugar in a small saucepan. Remove from the heat. Set aside to cool slightly.

8 Grease a 9-inch tube pan or spray with nonstick cooking spray. Wrap the outside bottom and sides of the pan with a piece of heavy-duty foil (just in case your pan leaks!). Set aside.

9 Punch down the dough. Tear off small pieces and roll in balls about 1½ inches in diameter. You should have about 30. Neatness and total accuracy don't count at all here. Dip a ball in the melted butter-sugar mixture and then coat with the nut-cranberry mixture. Place in the tube pan. Repeat with the remaining balls of dough. Place the balls randomly in the pan — close to each other but not snug. It's okay if you have small gaps between the balls of dough. You will have two, not necessarily even, layers. If you have any nut mixture left, sprinkle it on top.

10 Cover loosely with the clean dish towel and let rise in a warm, draft-free place until double in bulk, about 1 hour.

11 Preheat the oven to 375 degrees 15 minutes before the rising is done.

12 Bake for 50 minutes. Cover the bread with a piece of aluminum foil after 30 minutes to prevent overbrowning. Remove from the oven after the bread tests done. You'll know it's done when the dough springs back when pushed and a skewer inserted in the dough comes out clean. (You can't do the thumping-on-the-bottom test with this bread.) Cool in the pan for 30 minutes on a cooling rack. (If you remove the bread from the pan sooner, the bread could break apart.) Run a knife around the edge of the pan to loosen.

13 Remove the cake in the tube portion of the pan from the side portion. Run a knife between the cake and the bottom of the pan and invert immediately onto a plate. Cool completely. Sprinkle with confectioners' sugar, if desired. This bread keeps for 3 days, but it's best the first day it's made.

14 To serve, forget the knife and just pull it apart with your hands.

Per serving: Calories 330 (From Fat 145); Fat 16g (Saturated 6g); Cholesterol 64mg; Sodium 325mg; Carbohydrate 43g (Dietary Fiber 3g); Protein 6g.

Jumbo Pretzels

Dense and oversized may not be attributes everyone wants, but they look good on these pretzels. The water bath gives them a crusty outside with an inside that's not all air. You can vary the toppings according to your preference. This recipe requires a little patience, but you'll be rewarded when you tote them off to Little League practice.

Preparation time: 60 minutes

Cooking time: 15 to 18 minutes

Yield: 10 pretzels

¼-ounce package active dry yeast

1¼ cups warm water (105 to 115 degrees)

Pinch of sugar

3¼ to 3½ cups all-purpose flour

1 tablespoon salt

Kosher salt

1 Proof the yeast in a large bowl with the warm water and the sugar. (See the section, "Proofing the yeast," earlier in this chapter.)

2 Mix 2½ cups of the flour into the yeast by hand or with a mixer or a heavy-duty mixer. Beat until incorporated. Add the 1 tablespoon salt. Add ½ cup flour. Turn out onto a lightly floured surface and knead as much remaining flour as needed, a little at a time. Smooth into a ball and cover with a clean tea towel for 10 minutes.

3 Lightly grease a baking sheet and the bottom of a roasting pan that's at least 12 x 17 inches. Put a large kettle or pot of water on to simmer.

4 Divide the dough into 10 equal pieces. Roll out the pieces, one at a time, to 20-inch strands. (See the tip at the end of the recipe.) Keep the pieces and strands that you're not working with covered with a clean tea towel.

5 Preheat the oven to 450 degrees.

6 Shape the pretzels by taking one end in each hand. Twist one end over the other, twice, about 5 inches from the ends. Fold them back over the looped part of the dough, letting the ends hang over the loop slightly. Moisten with water under each overhanging end and press down. Place in the roasting pan.

7 Carefully pour the simmering water over the pretzel dough. Let stand about 45 seconds. The pretzels will want to float, so briefly submerge each pretzel during that time with a slotted spatula. Remove from the water with a slotted spatula, allowing as much water to drain off as possible. Place on the baking sheet.

8 Sprinkle the desired amount of kosher salt evenly over the pretzels. Bake for 15 to 18 minutes, rotating once halfway through, if necessary, until light golden. Remove to a cooling rack. These pretzels are best if eaten the day they're made.

Tip: *If the strands have a mind of their own while you're dividing and rolling them out, try these hints: Instead of lightly flouring your hands to form the strands, moisten your hand very slightly before rolling. Doing so gives you some "traction." Roll the strand as far as it wants to go. Push the ends down onto the surface so that the strand doesn't recoil, and let it rest while you start another one. Keep all the strands covered while you're working with them.*

Vary It! *If you want to make The Everything Pretzel, try this recipe. Combine 2 teaspoons poppy seeds, 2 teaspoons sesame seeds, 2 teaspoons dried minced onion, 2 teaspoons dried minced garlic, and 2 teaspoons kosher salt. Dried onion and garlic burn easily if spilled on a baking sheet, so wipe up any excess toppings.*

Vary It! *If you're a believer in the less-is-more school of thought, then just sprinkle on the topping that appeals to you.*

Per serving: *Calories 150 (From Fat 4); Fat 0g (Saturated 0g); Cholesterol 0mg; Sodium 1,034mg; Carbohydrate 31g (Dietary Fiber 1g); Protein 5g.*

Philadelphia, where the first commercial pretzel was produced in 1861, is nicknamed the "Big Pretzel." The city is known for selling big yeast pretzels served with a squirt of yellow mustard. Take a lead from the City of Brotherly Love and give your pretzels with a jar of Grainy Apricot Mustard (a recipe you can find in Chapter 9).

A pretzel-shaped sign hanging over a storefront in Scandinavia indicates there's a bakery inside.

Oat and Ale Bread

Give your sandwiches a more exciting life. This robust bread is full of flavor that adds a new dimension to the lunchbox. It is chock-full of oatmeal and nuts, with just a smidge of onion. The ale? It just adds character to the loaf.

Preparation time: *45 minutes, plus 1 hour and 45 minutes rising*

Cooking time: *25 minutes*

Yield: *Two 7-inch round loaves (fourteen ½-inch slices per loaf)*

½ cup coarsely chopped sweet onion	*¾ cup ale or beer, room temperature*
½ cup water	*¼ cup light molasses*
¼-ounce package active dry yeast	*1 tablespoon vegetable oil*
¼ cup warm water (105 to 115 degrees)	*3¾ to 4 cups all-purpose flour*
Pinch of sugar	*2 teaspoons salt*
1 cup old-fashioned rolled oats	*1 cup chopped walnuts*

Glaze:

1 egg beaten with 1 teaspoon water	*2 tablespoons oatmeal*

1 Combine the onion and water in a blender; puree about 20 seconds, until almost liquid. Set aside.

2 Proof the yeast in the warm water with the pinch of sugar. Meanwhile, combine the oats and ale in a large bowl. Let sit while yeast is proofing. Add the proofed yeast, the pureed onion, molasses, and oil. Mix thoroughly.

3 Add 2 cups of the flour to the oat mixture. Mix until smooth. Add 1 more cup flour. Mix until smooth. Add the salt. Add ½ cup of flour. Turn out on a lightly floured surface and begin kneading in the remaining ¼ cup flour. Knead in additional flour until no longer sticky. Use the smallest amount flour at a time. Knead the dough for 10 minutes.

4 Lightly grease a large bowl with nonstick cooking spray. Put the dough in the bowl and turn to coat the surface. Cover with a clean tea towel. Place in a warm, draft-free place to rise until double in bulk, about 1 hour. Line a baking sheet with parchment paper or lightly grease it.

5 Punch down the dough. Turn out onto a lightly floured surface and knead in the walnuts. Divide the dough into 2 equal parts. Shape each part into a 5-inch disk. (See the section "Punching down and shaping," earlier in this chapter.) Place on the baking sheet. Cover with a clean tea towel. Set in a warm, draft-free place to rise until double in bulk, about 45 minutes.

6 Preheat the oven to 375 degrees 15 minutes before the dough rising time is done.

7 Brush the top of the dough with the beaten egg. Sprinkle with 1 tablespoon of the oatmeal. Repeat with the other dough.

8 Bake for 25 minutes, until it tests done. Cool on a wire rack. Wrap in a plastic bag or foil.

Per serving: *Calories 117 (From Fat 35); Fat 4g (Saturated 0g); Cholesterol 8mg; Sodium 170mg; Carbohydrate 18g (Dietary Fiber 1g); Protein 3g.*

Chapter 12

Hearty Party Fare: Dips, Spreads, and Cheesy Things

In This Chapter

▶ Adding flavor to nuts

▶ Dipping into foreign flavors

▶ Touring the town with smoked salmon spreads

▶ Branching out with olive recipes

Alice in Wonderland knew the feeling well. She wasn't paying attention, fell down a hole, and wound up at a tea party without bringing a thing. Of course, everyone was mad.

You won't have that problem. Parties are a bit more casual than they used to be. The emphasis is on friends, not fussing. So if your host or hostess jumps at your offer to bring a dish, use this chapter as your guide.

Going Nuts

Nuts. Now there's a misnomer if ever I heard one. To think that one of nature's perfect foods, wrapped in one of nature's perfect packages, has come to mean loony is — well, nuts. Everyone knows how welcome nuts are as party fare. The bonus is how good they are for you to *eat*. Nuts are high in good (mono-unsaturated) oil, with pecans the highest. They contain fiber, something the ancients apparently knew, because they believed that nuts aided digestion. It may well be that the Aborigines of Australia experienced long ago the original "Mac Attack" and went straight for a handful of macadamias. So get cracking on these nut recipes with the satisfaction of fixing something that's doubly good.

Curried Cashews

Aromatic, spicy, and sweet, these nuts cook up in a jiffy while the flavor transports you to another land. Try a stronger curry, if you're bold. The giving possibilities are endless — take them to poker night or serve them around a campfire while telling ghost stories.

Preparation time: *10 minutes*

Cooking time: *About 6 minutes*

Yield: *About 6 cups*

4 teaspoons mild curry powder	*1 cup dark raisins*
3 tablespoons butter	*1 cup shredded sweetened coconut*
2 cans (10 ounces each) lightly salted whole cashews	*1 teaspoon kosher salt*

1 Heat the curry powder in a large skillet over low heat until fragrant, about 30 seconds. Stir continually and do not allow to burn.

2 Add the butter and increase the heat to medium. Add the cashews and coat with the curry. Cook for 5 minutes, stirring occasionally. Remove from the heat. Toss in the raisins, coconut, and salt. Allow to cool. Store in an airtight container for up to 5 days.

Per serving: Calories 190 (From Fat 128); Fat 14g (Saturated 4g); Cholesterol 4mg; Sodium 206mg; Carbohydrate 14g (Dietary Fiber 2g); Protein 4g.

Barbecue Almonds

Enjoy the flavor of your barbecue without all the smoke. These nuts would feel at home at a friend's cookout, but don't overlook wintertime events like an after-tobogganing party. Their smoky flavor transcends the seasons.

Special equipment: *Parchment paper*

Preparation time: *20 minutes*

Cooking time: *30 minutes*

Yield: *About 3½ cups*

2 tablespoons light brown sugar

1 tablespoon cornstarch

3 to 4 teaspoons chili powder

1 teaspoon kosher salt

¾ teaspoon cumin

½ teaspoon onion powder

3 tablespoons tomato paste

1 teaspoon liquid smoke

Few drops hot pepper sauce (optional)

1 egg white, at room temperature

16-ounce bag whole almonds with skins

1 Preheat the oven to 300 degrees.

2 Line a jelly roll pan with parchment paper. Coat with nonstick cooking spray.

3 Combine the brown sugar, cornstarch, chili powder, salt, cumin, and onion powder in a small bowl. Blend well.

4 Combine the tomato paste, liquid smoke, and hot pepper sauce, if desired, in a medium bowl. Add the brown sugar mixture and blend well. Set aside.

5 Beat the egg white in a medium bowl with an electric mixer until it just holds a peak. Fold one-fourth of the beaten egg white into the tomato mixture. The mixture will be thick. Fold in the remaining egg white. The mixture will deflate somewhat. Add the almonds and thoroughly coat.

6 Spread the almonds on the prepared jelly roll pan, separating the almonds. Bake for 30 minutes. Loosen and stir the nuts halfway through baking.

7 Remove from the oven and cool. Store in an airtight container for up to 1 week.

Per serving: Calories 211 (From Fat 148); Fat 16g (Saturated 1g); Cholesterol 0mg; Sodium 93mg; Carbohydrate 10g (Dietary Fiber 4g); Protein 7g.

Dipping into a World of Flavor

Travel the globe, and you'll experience the spices and aromas of the foods each country claims to be its own. In this chapter you can sample the Middle Eastern love of sesame paste and chickpeas in the Red Pepper Hummus recipe. You can sample the Spanish penchant for seafood and herbs in the Shrimp in Green-Sauce Dip recipe. Or follow the Rio Grande with South-of-Somewhere Salsa and enjoy the Tex-Mex sensation of corn, cilantro, and jalapeño peppers.

When it comes to chili peppers, usually the smaller it is, the hotter it is. This is because the big-time heat conductors in the chili peppers are the white veins and the seeds. Removing these incendiaries is necessary before using a pepper in a dish. See Figure 12-1 for a step-by-step.

Shrimp in Green-Sauce Dip

Here's a dip that will make the party circuit year-round. It's a vibrant summer dip full of fresh tasty green leaves. Or dress it for the winter holidays by adding chopped red or orange peppers. Serve with sturdy crackers or party breads. For a view of the finished product, see the color section of this book.

Preparation time: *25 minutes*

Yield: *About 3 cups*

½ cup mayonnaise

1 cup watercress leaves

½ cup Italian parsley, packed

8 ounces cream cheese, at room temperature

¼ cup chopped chives

2 teaspoons drained, prepared horseradish

1 teaspoon lemon juice

⅛ teaspoon salt

1½ cups minced cooked shrimp

1 Process the mayonnaise, watercress, and parsley in the bowl of a food processor fitted with a metal blade for about 30 seconds, until green and speckled. Stop once to scrap down the sides of the bowl. Add the cream cheese. Pulse on and off until just smooth. Remove to a medium bowl.

2 Add in the chives, horseradish, lemon juice, and salt. Stir until blended. Add the shrimp. Store in an airtight container for up to 2 days.

Tip: If watercress isn't available, use fresh spinach leaves instead, and add a healthy twist of freshly ground pepper.

Vary It! *Use 8 ounces of crabmeat instead of shrimp. Pick over the crabmeat carefully to remove tiny (and sometimes not so tiny) pieces of cartilage. Take small amounts at a time and rub between your fingers, feeling for anything sharp.*

Vary It! *If you are landlocked and can't find real crabmeat, you may find yourself standing in the supermarket staring at something called "imitation crabmeat" or "sea legs." Faced with what looks like white tubes painted with iodine, you're thinking, "Should I or shouldn't I?" What you're looking at is not fake crab; it's usually real pollock. It's actually called surimi (soo-REE-mee) and is formed fish. And, yes, you can use it in the dip, but I make it my last choice.*

Per tablespoon: Calories 38 (From Fat 32); Fat 4g (Saturated 1g); Cholesterol 15mg; Sodium 44mg; Carbohydrate 0g (Dietary Fiber 0g); Protein 1g.

South-of-Somewhere Salsa

This salsa combines Southwest ingredients with a few from south of the border. Corn, beans, and tomato make for a hearty salsa. Pepitas add a crunchy texture. You can find pepitas (or green pumpkin seeds) at health food stores; they usually come raw or toasted. Add more fresh jalapeño if you're feeling bold. Take a look at the picture of this salsa in the color section of this book.

Preparation time: *30 minutes*

Cooking time: *5 minutes*

Yield: *4¼ cups*

⅔ cup pepitas (shelled green pumpkin seeds)

1½ cups chopped tomatoes

15½-ounces can black beans, drained

1 cup cooked fresh corn kernels (grilled if possible)

⅓ cup finely chopped red onion

2 tablespoons chopped fresh cilantro

3 tablespoons vegetable oil

1 tablespoon lime juice

½ fresh jalapeño pepper, deveined, seeded, and minced

½ teaspoon salt

1 Preheat the oven to 350 degrees. Spread the pepitas on a jelly roll pan. Toast for about 5 minutes. They'll puff up and pop, so watch them as they're baking. A few may fly around your oven. (If you can find already toasted pepitas, skip this step.)

2 Combine the tomatoes, black beans, corn, onion, cilantro, oil, lime juice, jalapeño, and salt in a medium bowl. Chill for 2 hours. Bring to room temperature before serving. Toss the pepitas with the other ingredients just before serving. Serve with sturdy dipping chips. Store in an airtight container for up to 3 days.

Per serving: *Calories 78 (From Fat 47); Fat 5g (Saturated 1g); Cholesterol 0mg; Sodium 84mg; Carbohydrate 6g (Dietary Fiber 2g); Protein 3g.*

SEEDING A JALAPEÑO

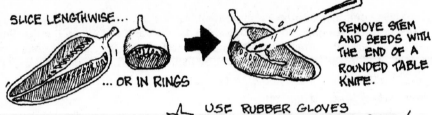

Figure 12-1: How to seed a jalapeño pepper without getting burned.

SLICE LENGTHWISE...

... OR IN RINGS

REMOVE STEM AND SEEDS WITH THE END OF A ROUNDED TABLE KNIFE.

USE RUBBER GLOVES AND NEVER TOUCH YOUR EYES!

Red Pepper Hummus

Tahini — no, it's not the tropical island where Gauguin painted. It's a paste made from ground sesame seeds and one of the major ingredients in hummus, a chickpea dip. It adds a rich nutty flavor to this and other traditional Middle Eastern dishes. In this recipe, orange juice replaces the expected lemon juice for a refreshing twist. You can find tahini in supermarkets, health food stores, and Middle Eastern markets.

Preparation time: *10 minutes*

Yield: *2 cups*

15.5-ounce can chickpeas (also known as garbanzo beans), drained, juice reserved

2 cloves garlic, chopped

½ cup tahini, stirred well

2 tablespoons orange juice

2 tablespoons olive oil

1 teaspoon orange zest

¾ teaspoon salt

½ teaspoon cumin

Pinch of cayenne

7-ounce jar roasted red peppers, drained

Pita bread, crackers, or crudités

Combine the chickpeas, garlic, tahini, orange juice, olive oil, orange zest, salt, cumin, and cayenne in the bowl of a food processor fitted with a metal blade. Pulse on and off until smooth. Add the red peppers. Pulse on and off until incorporated, leaving some pepper pieces. If necessary, add chickpea juice if the mixture is too thick. Serve with pita bread, crackers, or crudités. The hummus keeps for 3 days.

Tip: *If the tahini doesn't stir easily, put it in a saucepan and heat it gently just until warm. Remove from the heat. Mash the lumps until it smoothes out.*

Per tablespoon, not including bread: *Calories 40 (From Fat 27); Fat 3g (Saturated 0g); Cholesterol 0mg; Sodium 76mg; Carbohydrate 3g (Dietary Fiber 1g); Protein 1g.*

Two Tales of a City

From New York City's melting pot of ethnic foods you can ladle out such popular opposites as traditional French cuisine and soul-satisfying Jewish dairy fare — one uptown and one downtown; one for dinner Saturday night and one for brunch Sunday morning.

The two recipes in this section both use the same smoked salmon and cream cheese base, but that's where the similarity ends. Downtown Lox Spread is gutsy and bold; the Uptown Smoked Salmon Spread is subtle and delicate. You decide which direction to go.

Downtown Lox Spread

Even though many of the dairy restaurants (which serve no meat products) of the Lower East Side of New York have succumbed to gentrification, a lexicon of culinary slang lives on. Order lox on a bialy (bee-AH-lee) with a schmear. And don't forget the onion. That loosely translates to smoked salmon on a flat onion roll with a thin layer of cream cheese. Enjoy all these flavors in one generous schmear on the bread you most enjoy.

Preparation time: *25 minutes*

Yield: *1½ cups*

8 ounces Neufchâtel cream cheese, at room temperature

2 tablespoons sour cream

2 tablespoons chopped scallion with some green parts

2 tablespoons drained, chopped sun-dried tomatoes (packed in oil)

¼ pound smoked salmon, chopped

Crackers, crudités, or bagels

Blend the cream cheese, sour cream, scallion, and tomatoes in a small bowl. Stir in the smoked salmon. Serve with crackers, crudités, or, the obvious, a bagel. Store in an airtight container for up to 2 days.

Vary It! *Add 2 teaspoons prepared, drained horseradish.*

Per tablespoon: *Calories 33 (From Fat 23); Fat 3g (Saturated 2g); Cholesterol 8mg; Sodium 137mg; Carbohydrate 1g (Dietary Fiber 0g); Protein 2g.*

Uptown Smoked Salmon Spread

The fancy French restaurants in New York are offering appetizers of thinly sliced smoked salmon served with capers, lemon, and toast points. Enjoy this taste at home without having to pay for the expensive wine.

Preparation time: *20 minutes*

Yield: *1½ cups*

8 ounces Neufchâtel cream cheese, at room temperature

2 tablespoons sour cream

2 tablespoons finely chopped red onion

1 tablespoon small capers, rinsed

1 teaspoon lemon juice

⅛ teaspoon white pepper

¼ pound smoked salmon, chopped

Melba toast, pumpernickel bread, or crudités

Blend the cream cheese, sour cream, onion, capers, lemon juice, and pepper in a small bowl. Stir in the smoked salmon. Serve with Melba toast, pumpernickel bread, or crudités. Store in an airtight container for up to 2 days.

Vary It! *Add 2 teaspoons snipped dill instead of the capers.*

Per tablespoon: *Calories 32 (From Fat 22); Fat 3g (Saturated 2g); Cholesterol 8mg; Sodium 202mg; Carbohydrate 1g (Dietary Fiber 0g); Protein 2g.*

Pâté 101

An unwritten list is floating around the universe that tells kids of each new generation which foods they should categorically refuse to eat. Liver is at the top. But now that you're an adult (ahem), perhaps it's time to revisit that list. By adding a few camouflaging ingredients, you can turn that infamous ingredient into a timeless spread.

Preparation time: *45 minutes*

Cooking time: *12 to 15 minutes*

Yield: *2 cups*

⅔ cup walnuts, toasted (see Chapter 6)

1 pound chicken livers

½ cup chopped sweet onion (such as Vidalia)

½ cup (1 stick) butter

2 tablespoons Calvados (or unsweetened apple juice)

1 teaspoon salt

½ teaspoon pepper

⅛ teaspoon allspice

¼ cup chopped walnuts (optional)

2 tablespoons chopped parsley (optional)

French bread

Crackers

1 Place the walnuts in the bowl of a food processor fitted with a metal blade. Process until finely ground. Leave in the bowl.

2 Wash and pat dry the chicken livers. Trim off the connecting membrane. Cut into 1-inch pieces. Set aside.

3 Cook the onions and 5 tablespoons of the butter in a medium sauté pan over medium-low heat. (This may seem like a lot of butter, but it will be incorporated into the recipe.) Stir frequently until translucent, about 5 to 7 minutes. Scrape the onions and all the butter into the bowl of the food processor.

4 Add the remaining 3 tablespoons of butter to the sauté pan. Heat slightly over medium-high heat. Add the chicken livers. Sauté until they start to firm up but are still pink inside, about 2 to 3 minutes. Add the Calvados and cook for 30 seconds longer. Scrape the livers into the food processor bowl.

5 Add the salt, pepper and allspice to the food processor bowl. Scrape down the sides. Process until smooth, about l minute. Scrape into a serving crock. Refrigerate. Cover after it has cooled for 30 minutes. Bring to room temperature before serving. Sprinkle with the chopped nuts and parsley, if desired. Serve with sliced crusty French bread or crackers. The pâté will keep for 2 days.

Tip: *Pâté is traditionally served with cornichon (KOR-nih-shohn) pickles. These darling little bites pack a wallop of tanginess. If you can't find any, use the smallest dill pickles you can find and cut them in slices.*

Per tablespoon, bread not included: Calories 59 (From Fat 43); Fat 5g (Saturated 2g); Cholesterol 75mg; Sodium 79mg; Carbohydrate 1g (Dietary Fiber 0g); Protein 3g.

Extending the Olive Branch

If you love olives, you may imagine that heaven is where you pluck them off the branch. But give pause, for here on earth, olives on the branch are incredibly bitter fruit. Olives must be cured first, a messy business involving baths in lye and other industrial-sounding processes. But all that is taken care of before you buy them at the store and get to work on the recipes in this section.

Some of the better-known olives include the following:

- ✔ **Picholine:** This medium-size, green, brine-cured olive is from France.
- ✔ **Nicoise:** Also from France, this olive is small, brownish-purple to purple-black, and brine cured.
- ✔ **Manzanilla:** This Spanish olive is medium size, green, and brine cured.
- ✔ **Gaeta:** This medium-size, black, dry-cured olive is from Italy.
- ✔ **Kalamata:** This native of Greece is brownish purple and brine cured.
- ✔ **Moroccan:** This medium-size, black, oil-cured olive is from, yep, Morocco.

Marinated Olives

Olive dishes have adorned cocktail and buffet tables for generations without losing their appeal. It's like expecting an old friend will always be there. Well, your old friend is showing up with a new "do." The addition of garlic, fennel, and rosemary remakes an old standby. For the presentation, see the color section of this book.

Preparation time: 30 minutes

Yield: About 3½ cups, including oil

3 cup olives, green or black or mixed

3 cloves garlic

1 tablespoon fennel seed

2 sprigs (4 inches each) rosemary

4 strips of lemon zest, about 3 inches each

1¾ to 2 cups olive oil

1 If any olives are brine-cured, rinse and pat dry. Pit the olives if you want.

2 Peel the garlic and cut the cloves in half lengthwise. Add to the olives.

3 Bruise the fennel seed slightly by rolling over them once or twice with a rolling pin. They should release an aroma without being crushed. Toss with the olive mixture.

4 Transfer the olive mixture to a container. Add the rosemary and lemon zest. Add enough olive oil to cover the olives. Cover the container and let it marinate in the refrigerator for 1 week. Stir or agitate occasionally. The olives keep for 1 month in the refrigerator.

Per tablespoon: Calories 79 (From Fat 76); Fat 9g (Saturated 1g); Cholesterol 0mg; Sodium 105mg; Carbohydrate 1g (Dietary Fiber 0g); Protein 0g.

Smokin' salmon

The velvety, rosy-hued slices of smoked salmon that you take home from the seafood counter have gone through quite a regime to look so beautiful. Fillets from places like Norway, Denmark, Scotland, Nova Scotia, and the Pacific Northwest all vie for the title of "Best Salmon."

Salmon fillets take a cure either in a brine or dry salt, sometimes with sugar and spices added. Traditionally, it is cold-smoked (below 90 degrees). It remains raw but firms up and acquires a delectable woody perfume and flavor.

Whenever possible, taste before you buy. Smoked salmon should not be dry, nor should it be overly smoky or overly salty. These levels vary greatly from one piece to another.

Many people call smoked salmon *Nova*, a name that derives from Nova Scotia salmon. Nova encompasses all the smoked salmons, like Norwegian, Scottish, Irish, and so on. Smoked salmon is also generically called *lox* (from the Yiddish *laks* and Scandinavian *lax*, meaning salmon). It actually is belly lox, which is fattier and saltier than other smoked salmon. A cousin in this family is *gravlax*. It hails from Scandinavia, where fillets are not smoked but rubbed with salt and sugar and layered with lots of dill.

You can give olives, such as the Marinated Olives in this chapter, in a 1-quart jar. For the Marinated Olives, arrange the rosemary and lemon zest against the sides of the glass jar before adding the olives for an attractive presentation. If you're dividing the olives into 2 jars, divide the rosemary, zest, and garlic equally.

Provençal Cheese and Olive Bites

This recipe is like a mini-excursion to the South of France. Enjoy cheese, herbs, and olives all rolled into one bite-size taste treat. Close your eyes and go.

Special equipment: *Parchment paper*

Preparation time: *30 minutes*

Cooking time: *15 minutes*

Yield: *24 bites*

24 medium pitted ripe olives (about ¾-inch long, from a 3.8-ounce can)	*Pinch of salt*
	Pinch of pepper
1 cup grated Gruyère cheese (about 4 ounces)	*4 tablespoons Neufchâtel cheese also called ⅓ fat-reduced cream cheese, at room temperature*
½ cup flour	
¼ teaspoon dried thyme, crushed	*Paprika*

1 Drain and pat the olives dry.

2 Preheat the oven to 400 degrees. Line a baking sheet with parchment paper.

3 Thoroughly toss the Gruyère cheese, flour, thyme, salt, and pepper in a small bowl. Blend in the Neufchâtel cheese. Knead a few times until the dough becomes smooth.

4 Divide the dough into 24 equal pieces. Working with 1 piece at a time, flatten each into a disk about 1½ inches. Enclose an olive in it. Repeat with the remaining pieces of dough and olives. Dust with the paprika. Place on the baking sheet.

5 Bake for 14 to 15 minutes, until golden. Remove to a cooling rack. Serve warm or store in the refrigerator in an airtight container for up to 4 days. Bring to room temperature before serving.

Vary It! *A wealth of stuffed olives is starting to appear on the market — with flavors ranging from almond to garlic to tuna. Look for them in your market or check Chapter 17.*

Vary It! *You can also try different herbs, such as rosemary or basil. You can even leave out the herbs and put in a good pinch of cayenne to spice it up.*

Per serving: *Calories 40 (From Fat 23); Fat 3g (Saturated 1g); Cholesterol 7mg; Sodium 69mg; Carbohydrate 2g (Dietary Fiber 0g); Protein 2g.*

Layered Goat Cheese Mold

Yes, goat cheese is tangy. So here's a recipe that takes baby steps toward helping you learn to love this flavorful cheese. The goat cheese is combined with Neufchâtel cream cheese and layered with three different flavor combinations. Try and find a good source for your goat cheese, especially if you're trying it for the first time. Too often a sour supermarket cheese ruins the experience. Perhaps you'll just want to think of this recipe as assertive cream cheese.

Special equipment: One 5-x-3-x-2½-inch mini loaf pan or a 2-cup mold

Preparation time: 30 minutes (longer for additional molds), plus 2½ hours chilling time

Yield: 1 loaf

2 tablespoons pine nuts (pignoli)	1 tablespoon heavy cream
10½-ounce goat cheese log (fresh with no rind or ash), at room temperature	2 tablespoons drained, chopped sun-dried tomatoes (packed in oil)
6 ounces Neufchâtel cream cheese (also called ⅓ reduced-fat cream cheese), at room temperature	1½ teaspoons chopped fresh basil or ½ teaspoon dried basil, crumbled

1 Line a mini loaf pan across the long sides with aluminum foil. Leave an overhang for lifting the mold out of the pan. Grease lightly. Evenly sprinkle the pine nuts on bottom of the pan. Set aside.

2 Thoroughly blend the goat cheese, Neufchâtel, and cream in a small bowl. Divide the mixture in half. Place one half in another small bowl. Mix the sun-dried tomatoes into the first half. Place small spoonfuls of the mixture into the loaf pan, trying not to disturb the nuts. Gently spread the mixture evenly in the pan. Make the edges as smooth as possible. Chill for 30 minutes.

3 Meanwhile mix the basil into the second half of the mixture. After the loaf has chilled, spread the basil mixture on top of the tomato mixture. Smooth the top. Cover with plastic wrap. Gently press down to fill in any gaps in the mixture. Chill for 2 hours. Store well wrapped in the refrigerator for up to 5 days.

Vary It! Try using 2 tablespoons chopped walnuts instead of the pine nuts, 2 tablespoons chopped olives (patted dry) instead of the tomatoes, and ½ teaspoon dried thyme, crumbled, instead of the basil.

Per 1-ounce serving: Calories 95 (From Fat 72); Fat 8g (Saturated 5g); Cholesterol 21; Sodium 125mg; Carbohydrate 1g (Dietary Fiber 0g); Protein 5g.

Chapter 13

Mixes — the Gift of Time

Mr. Fiorella, my high school Latin professor, used to say "Tempus fugie, non come backie." He was right. You can't get time back, but you can delight the harried and the hassled people in your life with a food gift that saves time, like the mixes in this chapter.

A premeasured packet for cookie dough or a soup mix, for example, is like drawing a "free spin" card — good for one homemade treat with almost no work.

Making Mixes for Everyone

Mixes are so easy to prepare and such popular gifts that I suggest making them assembly-line style — buying a sufficient quantity of ingredients to produce, say, half a dozen units of a recipe rather than just one. So buy ingredients in quantity and mix up packets for all your busy friends. You're blending good taste and efficiency in handy little packages.

You can personalize a gift with your own label, and I include some ready-to-copy labels later in this chapter.

Check out some of the catalogs and Web sites in Chapter 18 for ideas about packaging your mixes. You can find all sorts of things, like small spice bottles, metal containers, and cellophane envelopes, for example. Use your imagination — as long as the container is food safe.

Mixing ingredients to ensure equal distribution is crucial to the success of the recipes in this chapter, particularly when you double, triple, or apply a larger factor.

Bloody Mary Mix

Some like it hot; some like it alcohol free. It doesn't matter how your gift is enjoyed. The combination of spices in this mix adds a zesty flavor to Bloody Marys or Virgin Marys.

Preparation time: *20 minutes*

Yield: *¾ cup*

4 tablespoons dried lemon peel	*2 tablespoons salt*
4 tablespoons pepper	*2 tablespoons onion powder*
2 tablespoons celery seed	*2 to 4 teaspoons wasabi powder*

Combine all the ingredients in a spice grinder, although you can use a blender in a pinch. Process until finer in texture but specks of ingredients are still visible. Place in an airtight jar or tin. Prepare a label with instructions for use and attach to the jar or tin.

Vary It! *For a Bloody Bullshot, add sixteen 0.19-gram packets of dried beef bouillon.*

Remember: *Depending on where you buy wasabi, which is dried ground Japanese horse-radish, the strength will vary. Supermarket brands tend to be weaker because they have ingredients such as cornstarch in them.*

Per tablespoon: *Calories 23 (From Fat 4); Fat 0g (Saturated 0g); Cholesterol 0mg; Sodium 1184mg; Carbohydrate 6g (Dietary Fiber 2g); Protein 1g.*

The tomato-and-vodka drink Americans enjoy most at brunch originated in the 1920s in Paris at Harry's New York Bar, where it was christened "Bucket of Blood." Some time later it was renamed "Bloody Mary," after the English queen Mary Tudor, who had a murderous reputation.

Clarifying the juice issue

Not as lip-smackin' good as apple cider, apple juice is readily available in supermarkets. Usually clarified, it is pasteurized and vacuum sealed in bottles. Apple cider, by comparison, is most often available at apple orchards and farm stands in the fall, although more and more supermarkets carry it. Cider is sold unclarified and, until recently, unpasteurized. Refrigeration is necessary to retard fermentation. Pasteurized cider is now also available at most orchards. Hard cider has some degree of alcohol fermentation.

Mulled Cider Mix

Nothing says welcome more than the aroma of spices and oranges wafting through the air. The perfect ending to a day of apple picking is a warm mug of fragrant cider. It makes those doughnuts you got at the orchard taste even better.

Special equipment: *Cheesecloth, butcher's twine*

Preparation time: *30 minutes*

Cooking time: *1½ minutes*

Yield: *6 bundles*

2 large oranges

6 cinnamon sticks (3½ inches each), each broken into about 3 equal-size pieces

6 teaspoons chopped crystallized ginger

24 whole cloves

36 whole allspice berries

1 Cut six 7-x-7-inch double-thick squares of cheesecloth. Lay out all six.

2 Peel the zest off the oranges in fairly even strips. (Eat the oranges or save them for another purpose.) Microwave on high for about 1½ minutes, until dried. Check often to turn or to remove smaller pieces when dried. Break into pieces about ½ inch long. Divide evenly among the cheesecloth squares, a scant tablespoon in each one.

3 Place 3 pieces of cinnamon stick on each cheesecloth square. Put 1 teaspoon ginger, 4 cloves, and 6 allspice berries on each square.

4 Gather up the cheesecloth squares into a bundle and tie tightly with string so that no ingredients fall out. Trim off the excess cheesecloth above the string.

Per tablespoon: *Calories 7 (From Fat 0); Fat 0g (Saturated 0g); Cholesterol 0mg; Sodium 2mg; Carbohydrate 2g (Dietary Fiber 0g); Protein 0g.*

 Package gifts such as the bundles of Mulled Cider Mix in a decorative airtight tin or canning jar. Attach the appropriate preparation label.

Hot Chocolate Mix

Americans think of hot chocolate as a winter beverage. The French have other ideas. To them, hot chocolate is a delicious beverage that's on the menu all year-round. This mix is so rich and chocolaty that you may not want to give it up when spring arrives.

Preparation time: *20 minutes*

Yield: *Eight ½-cup servings*

3 cups powdered milk

½ cup Dutch-processed cocoa

4 ounces milk chocolate, grated

¼ cup sugar

1 Thoroughly combine all the ingredients.

2 Divide the ingredients equally into 8 packets. Copy the appropriate preparation label and attach to the packet or gift container.

Tip: *A mouli grater makes grating the chocolate go quickly.*

Per serving: *Calories 347 (From Fat 161); Fat 18g (Saturated 11g); Cholesterol 50mg; Sodium 191mg; Carbohydrate 36g (Dietary Fiber 2g); Protein 15g.*

Tie a long cinnamon stick, for use as a stirrer, to gifts such as the Hot Chocolate Mix packets. Include a pouch of mini marshmallows for an added touch.

Do you have any idea what a marshmallow actually is? It's named for an ingredient it no longer contains — the marsh mallow, a root extract that gave the sugary puffball its name. Now cornstarch and gum arabic hold the airy confection together.

Thai Bean Soup Mix

When snow and ice surround your world, follow the aroma of this flavorful soup to more temperate climes. The spices of Thai cooking will warm recipients of this mix down to their fingertips on a frigid winter day.

Preparation time: *20 minutes*

Yield: *2 packets, about 1¾ cups each*

1 pound dried small red beans	*1½ teaspoons coriander*
1 cup dried unsweetened shredded coconut	*1 teaspoon turmeric*
½ cup dried minced onions	*1 teaspoon ginger*
1 tablespoon salt	*½ teaspoon garlic powder*
3 packets (4 grams each) dried chicken broth	*½ teaspoon cayenne*
3 teaspoons dried lemon zest	*½ teaspoon pepper*

1 Carefully pick over the dried beans to remove pebbles or other un-beanlike things.

2 Combine the beans, coconut, and onions in a medium bowl or on wax paper. Toss thoroughly to distribute the ingredients. Divide evenly in half. Put into 2 plastic bags or directly into gift containers.

3 Thoroughly combine the salt, chicken broth, lemon zest, coriander, turmeric, ginger, garlic powder, cayenne, and pepper. Divide in half. Mix one portion in each bag.

4 Copy the appropriate preparation labels and attach to the gift container.

Tip: *Dried (also known as desiccated), unsweetened coconut is available at health food and gourmet stores.*

Per serving: *Calories 329 (From Fat 108); Fat 12g (Saturated 10g); Cholesterol 0mg; Sodium 1,305mg; Carbohydrate 43g (Dietary Fiber 18g); Protein 16g.*

U.S. Senate Bean Soup Mix

This recipe is derived from a recipe that has been on the U.S. Senate dining room menu for well over half a century. Instant mashed potato buds set it apart from other bean soup recipes.

Preparation time: *15 minutes*

Yield: *Two 2½-cup packets*

1 pound dried white beans (preferably navy beans)

1½ cups dried instant potato buds

¾ cup dried minced onion

6 tablespoons dried celery

3 tablespoons dried chives

1 tablespoon dried parsley

4 packets (4 grams each) jambon seasoning (I used Goya brand)

2 teaspoons salt

¾ teaspoon pepper

¼ teaspoon garlic powder

1 Pick over the beans to remove any pebbles or other un-beanlike objects.

2 Thoroughly combine the beans and potato buds in a medium bowl or on wax paper. Divide equally in half. Put in two plastic bags or directly into a gift container.

3 Thoroughly combine the onion, celery, chives, and parsley in a small bowl or on wax paper, tossing well to distribute the ingredients. Divide in half and place one-half in each packet of the bean mix.

4 Thoroughly combine the jambon seasoning, salt, pepper, and garlic powder in a small bowl or on wax paper. Divide in half. Add one-half to each half of the bean mixture.

5 Copy the appropriate preparation label and attach to the bag or gift container.

Tip: *Jambon seasoning is ham flavor seasoning. Check the Spanish section of your super-market.*

Per serving: *Calories 225 (From Fat 6); Fat 1g (Saturated 0g); Cholesterol 0mg; Sodium 779mg; Carbohydrate 45g (Dietary Fiber 13g); Protein 12g.*

Basic Cookie Mix

This mix is really handy to have around. It makes it so easy to have warm, tasty cookies quickly when the kids come home from school or when neighbors — like you — drop in.

Preparation time: *30 minutes plus packaging*

Yield: *4 packets, about 3⅔ cups each*

2½ cups granulated sugar

½ vanilla bean

2 cups packed light brown sugar, free of lumps

7 cups flour

3 teaspoons baking soda

2½ teaspoons salt

20-ounce package butter-flavored vegetable shortening (3 cups)

1 Place the sugar in a very large bowl. Split the vanilla bean lengthwise and scrape out the seeds. Add to the sugar and work into the sugar to distribute evenly. Fingers are great for this task. Add the brown sugar and combine thoroughly.

2 Add the flour, baking soda, and salt and combine thoroughly. A wire whisk is great for this task, but no matter what tool you use, make sure that the ingredients are evenly distributed.

3 Add the shortening and beat on low until very evenly incorporated, about 3 to 4 minutes. The mixture will be crumbly, but all the bits of mixture should be the same size.

4 Divide the mixture evenly into packages. Copy the appropriate preparation label and attach to the package or gift container.

Remember: *The success of the mix depends on the even distribution on the ingredients. Each package has to have the same quantity in it to work properly. So don't rush the combining steps.*

Per serving: *Calories 107 (From Fat 46); Fat 5g (Saturated 1g); Cholesterol 0mg; Sodium 87mg; Carbohydrate 14g (Dietary Fiber 0g); Protein 1g.*

Hot off the griddle

If you're not a bright-eyed, bushy-tailed morning person, then let these hints help make your waffle making easier:

- Not sure the waffle iron is hot enough? If a few drops of water jump off it, you're good to go.

- When the waffle iron stops steaming, the waffle should be done. If the waffle sticks to the top, it may need a little more time.

- The first waffle is often downright ugly. Save it for yourself. If you're not awake anyway, you won't notice.

- Put cooling racks on a jelly roll pan or baking sheet. Place in a 200-degree oven to keep waffles crisp without steaming for up to 20 minutes.

- If you really can't face breakfast, waffles at night are okay, too!

Rise-and-Shine Waffle Mix

Who doesn't want to wake up to the aroma of tantalizing spices in the morning? Give these packages of easy waffle mix (there's a picture in the color section of this book), and ordinary mornings will become special in a jiffy for the recipients of this breakfast favorite. Send along another eye-opener — the Blissful Blueberry Citrus Syrup in Chapter 8.

Preparation time: *15 minutes*

Yield: *6 packets (2⅓ cups each)*

10 cups flour	3 tablespoons baking soda
2 cups dried buttermilk powder	3 tablespoons salt
¾ cup sugar	2 tablespoons cinnamon
3 tablespoons baking powder	1 teaspoon nutmeg (preferably freshly grated)

1 Thoroughly mix together all the ingredients in a large bowl.

2 Divide the mixture into 6 equal portions — about 2⅓ cups each.

3 Wrap each portion in individual packages. Copy the appropriate preparation label and attach to the packages or gift containers.

Tip: *Dried buttermilk powder is available in most supermarkets. If you can't locate it, see the list of resources in Chapter 18.*

Tip: *A wire whisk isn't good only for liquid ingredients; it efficiently combines dry ingredients, too.*

Per serving: *Calories 170 (From Fat 7); Fat 1g (Saturated 0g); Cholesterol 5mg; Sodium 1,026mg; Carbohydrate 34g (Dietary Fiber 1g); Protein 6g.*

Duncan Hines — the name you see on all those boxes of cake mix — was indeed a real person. Traveling the United States in the1930s and 1940s, he was probably the first food critic. Hines was known for scrutinizing restaurants for cleanliness as well as good food before awarding recommendations. Though often asked for the use of his name on a product, he declined. He finally sold it for a mix, but only on the condition that the mixing directions were guaranteed to include a fresh egg.

Label Me Easy

Give your gift mixes a touch of class with a label. This section contains a label for each of the recipes in the chapter. Use a photocopier to reproduce as many labels as you need. Then glue it to the container or attach it with a length of ribbon, jute, or yarn.

You don't have to use the labels full size. Try setting the copier at 65 percent, for example, to make labels for smaller jars or bottles.

From the Kitchen of: _____

Bloody Mary

The proportions of this drink are entirely personal. Start with these proportions and go from there.

Yield: *1 Bloody Mary*

1 ounce vodka

3 ounces tomato juice

½ to 1 teaspoon Bloody Mary Mix

Combine all the ingredients and pour into a tall glass filled with ice.

Vary It! *Add a dash or two of Tabasco if you like it hotter!*

From the Kitchen of: _____

Mulled Cider

Cooking time: *5 minutes*

Yield: *Two 8-ounce cups*

1 packet Mulled Cider Mix *16 ounces apple cider*

Combine the cider mix and apple cider in a small saucepan. Simmer on low for 5 minutes.

From the Kitchen of: _____

Hot Chocolate

Yield: *1 cup*

1 packet Hot Chocolate Mix *Cinnamon stick*
¾ cup boiling water *Marshmallows*

Place 1 packet of mix in a cup or mug. Add the boiling water. Stir with the cinnamon stick. Top with marshmallows.

Tip: *Substitute milk for water for an even richer drink.*

Tip: *Add whipped cream instead of marshmallows for total indulgence.*

From the Kitchen of: _____

Thai Bean Soup

Cooking time: *1 hour and 30 minutes to 1 hour and 45 minutes*

Yield: *Four 1-cup servings*

1 packet Thai Bean Soup Mix
5 cups water (or chicken broth) or more if needed

Combine the mix and water in a large saucepan. Boil for 2 minutes. Cover and turn off heat for 1 hour. Bring back to a boil. Reduce the heat to medium-low. Partially cover and cook 1 hour and 30 minutes to 1 hour and 45 minutes, until the beans are tender. Stir occasionally. Adjust the seasoning, if desired.

From the Kitchen of: _____

U.S. Senate Bean Soup

Cooking time: *1 hour and 15 minutes to 1 hour and 30 minutes*

Yield: *Five 1-cup servings*

1 packet U.S. Senate Bean Soup Mix

6 cups water (or chicken broth)
or more if needed

1 cup chopped baked ham (optional)

Combine the mix and water in a large saucepan. Boil for 2 minutes. Cover and turn off the heat for 1 hour. Bring back to a boil. Reduce the heat to medium-low. Add the ham, if desired. Partially cover and cook until the beans are tender, about 1 hour and 15 minutes to 1 hour and 30 minutes. Stir occasionally. Adjust the seasoning, if desired.

From the Kitchen of: _____

Basic Cookies

Preparation time: *15 minutes*

Cooking time: *10 to 11 minutes*

Yield: *About twenty-eight 2½-inch cookies*

1 packet Basic Cookie Mix

1 large egg

5 tablespoons water

Sugar or colored sugar (optional)

1 Preheat the oven to 375 degrees.

2 Combine the mix, egg, and water in a medium bowl. Beat on medium with an electric mixer until thoroughly combined.

3 Drop by tablespoonfuls on ungreased baking sheets. Sprinkle with sugar, if desired. Bake for 10 to 11 minutes, until the edges are golden. Cool on a wire rack. Store in an airtight container.

Vary It! *Add 1 cup chocolate chips and 1 cup chopped nuts. Drop by tablespoonfuls on ungreased baking sheets. Bake for 11 to 12 minutes. This variation makes about 3 dozen 2½-inch cookies.*

From the Kitchen of: _____

Rise-and-Shine Waffles

Preparation time: *5 minutes*

Cooking time: *Follow manufacturer's instructions*

Yield: *l packet makes six 8-inch round waffles*

1 packet Rise-and-Shine Waffle Mix	*2 tablespoons vegetable oil*
1 large egg	*10 ounces club soda, seltzer, or water*

1 Preheat a waffle iron according to the manufacturer's instructions.

2 Empty the packet of waffle mix into a medium bowl. Make a well in the center.

3 Pour the egg, oil, and club soda into the well. Stir until almost smooth. Do not overmix.

4 Pour about ½ cup batter onto the griddle. Cook until golden.

Part V

Tying Up Loose Ends: Wrapping, Packaging, and Mailing

The 5th Wave   By Rich Tennant

"Oh look, Stan. Miss Muffet brought us a gift basket. There's homemade curried curds and whey, curds and whey chutney, a curds and whey Mandelbrot — my, what a surprise."

In this part . . .

The cooking's done, and it's time to deliver your gift. This part includes creative ideas for wrapping your delicious presents and nestling them in secure packaging. I also suggest unusual places to find interesting and offbeat containers to delight Granny or whoever is the recipient of your kitchen creation.

Chapter 14

Wrap Rap

• •

In This Chapter

▶ Looking to nature for inspiration

▶ Creating your own edible containers

▶ Finding containers in all kinds of stores

▶ Using paraffin to seal bottles

• •

Recipes in This Chapter

▶ Pepparkakor Bowl

▶ Pastillage Containers

▶ Chocolate Nest

"**W**rap rap."

"Who's there?"

"Can."

"Can who?

"Can you find a better way to open this chapter?"

Sure I can, and that's the point of this chapter. The presentation of your homemade food gift can often be a gift in itself. If you're creative with the containers or packaging for your gift, the recipient is likely to appreciate that as much as the contents themselves. Attractive packing may require you to think outside the box, but often you don't have to look far for ideas. The first person to consult about packaging for your food gifts is Mother Nature herself. She supplies a multitude of garden-grown containers waiting to be filled with your handmade goodies.

You can also fashion your own edible containers or discover still other container treasures in the least likely places. This chapter shows you how to cook up gift wrapping and tease out wrappers from the closet, attic, and hardware store. So start thinking: If an object has sides, what can it hold?

Edible Containers Courtesy of Nature

As clever as the packaging industry is with container design, nature has been there first and done it better. Consider an egg, a walnut, or a head of garlic. Each is perfectly suited to its purpose and incredibly imaginative. But you can be imaginative, too. Consider vegetables such as squash, pumpkins, or cabbage as containers for your gifts. (I warned you that you have to think outside the box.) Nature has already done most of the design work; all you have to do is a bit of remodeling.

Broccoli

Broccoli makes a lovely contrasting container for the Shrimp in Green-Sauce Dip in Chapter 12. Choose a nice, full head and cut the stem near the base to keep it from tilting. Carve a hollow in the top of the head to insert a small, clear, glass bowl. This will keep the dip from oozing through the stems.

Cauliflower

Cauliflower is a great, dense vegetable that you can hollow out and fill with a dip like Red Pepper Hummus in Chapter 12. Cut the stem so that the cauliflower sits level on the platter. Then carve a crater in the top with a knife. If the cauliflower is dense enough and there are no spaces between florets, spoon the dip directly into the hollow. If the head is not absolutely solid, insert a small clear glass bowl to hold the dip. Place the whole head on a platter and surround with crudités, such as carrots, peppers, zucchini, and broccoli. Don't forget to use the florets you remove from the cauliflower as additional crudités.

Pumpkin

Think of this type of squash as more than a Halloween decoration. A smaller pumpkin makes a great container for all sorts of foods, including the South-of-Somewhere Salsa in Chapter 12. You can also use a bigger pumpkin for a more dramatic presentation. Just carve off the lid with a knife like a Halloween jack-o-lantern. You don't have to remove all the strings and seeds, however. You can use the pumpkin to hold a small amount of food by simply inserting a small bowl in the opening. You can also use the bowl to keep gifts like the Curried Cashews in Chapter 12 dry and away from the moisture of the pumpkin's insides. The diminutive cousin of the pumpkin is Jack Be Little. You can hollow out a few of these cute little squashes to hold a variety of foods. Remove the strings and seed so that you can spoon the salsa directly into the Jack Be Little.

Red cabbage

If you can find a red cabbage with the outer leaves still attached, it can make a pretty display. As with some other vegetables, you may have to carve out a hollow with a knife. Then insert a clear glass bowl to hold the dip and to prevent any leakage. If you can find a Savoy cabbage, which is a crinkly version of the regular green cabbage, that's also a pretty alternative.

Talk to the produce department people in your supermarket and ask them to save you a cabbage that hasn't had the outer leaves removed.

Squash

One of the most fascinating squash around is the gooseneck. It fully lives up to its name, with a long curving neck and a bulbous base. Lay it on its side and cut out a cavity with a knife in the thick bulbous base. Pile it with a tasty treat, like the Marinated Olives in Chapter 12. Depending on the size of the base, it may not hold a lot, but the overall presence is decorative and impressive. Squash are available during the late summer and fall. And, of course, some old standbys are more readily available year-round, including acorn and butternut.

Slice a section of the roundest part of the bottom of the squash to keep it from rolling.

Edible Containers Courtesy of You

If you're bold enough to challenge Mother Nature, this section contains a few recipes that should put you squarely in the running.

Two of the recipe names have non-English origins, so a bit of history is in order. "Pepparkakor Bowl" comes from the Scandinavian *pepparkakor*, or spice cookie, a staple at holiday time. It is the first cookie my *Farmor* (father's mother in Swedish) taught me to make. In the creative spirit of this chapter, there's a variation to make gingerbread men; they'll be real comfy hanging out in the bowl.

The other imported title is "Pastillage Containers," a borrowing from the French. The containers look like porcelain from Limoges — what a surprise to discover they're good to eat!

Pepparkakor Bowl

Pepparkakor Bowl is a sturdy transport but should be made during the cooler months to keep its shape. See Figure 14-1 for a quick overview and step-by-step instructions. And don't let the gingerbread men (variation at end of recipe) hog the bowl. Freckled Chocolate, Cinnamon and Hazelnut Biscotti (Chapter 5) or 1-2-3 Milk Chocolate Chunky Clusters (Chapter 5) will love being delivered in this container.

Special equipment: *One (two if making multiple gingerbread bowls) 1½-quart metal bowl, about 8 inches in diameter and 3 inches deep; miniature aspic cutters or any other ¾-inch cookie cutter*

Preparation time: *40 minutes, plus overnight refrigeration and additional 1-hour refrigeration*

Cooking time: *25 minutes*

Yield: *Four 8-inch bowls*

6½ cups flour	*1 cup (2 sticks) butter, at room temperature*
2 teaspoons ginger	*¾ cup granulated sugar*
2 teaspoons cinnamon	*¾ cup dark brown sugar*
1 teaspoon baking soda	*¾ cup light molasses*
¾ teaspoon salt	*2 eggs*
½ teaspoon cloves	*2 teaspoons orange extract*
½ teaspoon allspice	

1 Sift together the flour, ginger, cinnamon, baking soda, salt, cloves, and allspice. Set aside.

2 With an electric mixer on medium speed, beat the butter, granulated sugar, brown sugar, and molasses in a large bowl until light in color, about 1 minute. Scrape down the sides of the bowl with a rubber spatula. Add the eggs and orange extract and beat until just incorporated.

3 Add one-third of the flour mixture to the butter mixture and beat until incorporated. Scrape down the sides of the bowl with a rubber spatula. Repeat with the remaining flour. Depending on the strength of your mixer, you may have to mix in the last addition by hand. This dough is fairly stiff.

4 Divide the dough into four pieces and wrap in plastic wrap. Refrigerate overnight to allow the flavors to develop.

5 Invert a bowl and line the outside with aluminum foil. Use the back of a spoon to smooth out as many crinkles in the foil as possible. (The dough likes to stick to them.) Grease lightly with nonstick cooking spray.

6 Roll out one portion of dough between two pieces of wax paper to a 10½-inch circle. Peel off one piece of wax paper. Gently invert the dough onto the bowl and center it. Carefully peel off the second piece of wax paper. Ease the dough flat onto the bowl. Refrigerate the dough for 1 hour.

7 Preheat the oven to 350 degrees. Cut the edge of the bowl with a sharp knife to make it straight. Cut gently so that you don't cut through the foil. If desired, cut out a decoration with miniature cookie cutters around the circumference of the bowl. Make each cutout about ¾ inch to 1 inch from the edge and space the cutouts about 1 to 2 inches apart. (Make evenly spaced marks with a toothpick before using the cookie cutter. Doing so helps ensure that the designs are level and evenly spaced.) Place on a baking sheet.

8 Bake for 25 minutes, until the dough springs back when touched. Remove the bowl from the baking sheet and cool on a wire rack until almost cool, about 30 minutes.

9 Carefully separate the metal bowl from the gingerbread bowl. Carefully peel the foil away from the gingerbread bowl. Place the gingerbread bowl on a wire rack to finish cooling. Repeat the process with the remaining three pieces of dough.

10 Store the bowls in an airtight container for up to 2 weeks.

Vary It! *You don't have to make all the bowls. Make one instead of four and use the remaining three portions of dough to make gingerbread cookies (Or make two bowls and use the remaining two portions for cookies or whatnot.) Roll one section (one-fourth of the whole batch) at a time out to a thickness of ⅛ inch. (See the cookie tips in Chapter 7.) Cut out cookies with 3-inch cookie cutters. Place on a lightly greased baking sheet. Bake at 350 degrees for 6 to 8 minutes, until lightly browned on the bottom and the cookies spring back when touched. Cool on a wire rack. Repeat with the remaining portions of dough. Keep in an airtight container for 1 week. One-fourth of the dough makes about 2 dozen 3-inch cookies.*

 Weave a ribbon in and out though the cutouts before filling the bowl. If you want to show off the decorating techniques you picked up in Chapter 6 (or if you have any flowers left over from the Tea Party Sugar Cubes, Chapter 6), pipe a border on the edge of the gingerbread bowl.

 If you don't want to pipe the edge of the Pepparkakor Bowl, you can also decorate the edge of the bowl with pastillage (recipe follows in this chapter). Make the pastillage. Working with small portions (keep the rest covered) roll the portion out to ⅛ inch or a little thinner and cut out a shape with a small (1-inch) cookie cutter. Lay the cutouts side by side around the edge of the bowl. Press any overhanging edges of the pastillage downward over the edge of the gingerbread bowl. Allow to dry for 3 to 4 hours. Mix a small batch of Royal Icing (Tea Party Sugar Cubes, Chapter 6). Pick up the cutouts, apply icing as "glue," and reposition the cutouts. Allow to dry at least 1 hour.

 Custom in Sweden dictates that an odd number of cookies (at least 7!) be served to a guest.

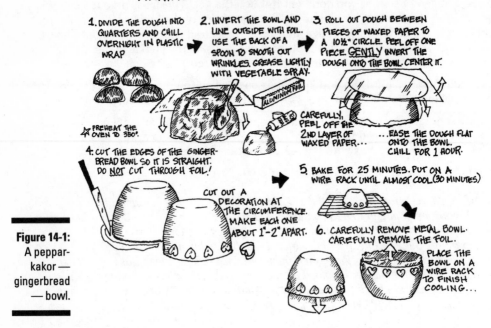

MAKING A GINGERBREAD BOWL

1. DIVIDE THE DOUGH INTO QUARTERS AND CHILL OVERNIGHT IN PLASTIC WRAP

2. INVERT THE BOWL AND LINE OUTSIDE WITH FOIL. USE THE BACK OF A SPOON TO SMOOTH OUT WRINKLES. GREASE LIGHTLY WITH VEGETABLE SPRAY.

3. ROLL OUT DOUGH BETWEEN PIECES OF WAXED PAPER TO A 10½" CIRCLE. PEEL OFF ONE PIECE. GENTLY INVERT THE DOUGH ONTO THE BOWL. CENTER IT.

PREHEAT THE OVEN TO 350°.

CAREFULLY, PEEL OFF THE 2ND LAYER OF WAXED PAPER...

...EASE THE DOUGH FLAT ONTO THE BOWL. CHILL FOR 1 HOUR.

4. CUT THE EDGES OF THE GINGERBREAD BOWL SO IT IS STRAIGHT. DO NOT CUT THROUGH FOIL!

CUT OUT A DECORATION AT THE CIRCUMFERENCE. MAKE EACH ONE ABOUT 1"-2" APART.

5. BAKE FOR 25 MINUTES. PUT ON A WIRE RACK UNTIL ALMOST COOL (30 MINUTES)

6. CAREFULLY REMOVE METAL BOWL. CAREFULLY REMOVE THE FOIL.

PLACE THE BOWL ON A WIRE RACK TO FINISH COOLING...

Figure 14-1: A peppar-kakor — gingerbread — bowl.

Pastillage Containers

Pastillage Containers look and feel so much like porcelain that nobody will believe you made them — let alone want to eat them. It's delightful deception and impishly fun to watch people's reaction when they find out that the container is edible. And even better is that they're fun to make. There's no end to the shapes that you can make.

Special equipment: Four 5½-x-3¼-inch mini loaf pans

Preparation time: 25 minutes, plus 24 to 36 hours drying time

Cooking time: 30 seconds

Yield: 4 open boxes (5½ inches x 3¼ inches)

¼ cup cold water

1 envelope unflavored gelatin

3⅓ to 3½ cups confectioners' sugar

3 tablespoons cornstarch

¼ teaspoon cream of tartar

Cornstarch for dusting

1 Pour the water into a small saucepan. Add the gelatin and let it sit for 5 minutes to soften.

2 Meanwhile, sift together the smaller amount of confectioners' sugar, cornstarch, and cream of tartar into a medium bowl. Set aside.

3 Heat the gelatin over low heat until just barely dissolved. (It will still be cloudy and about 100 degrees.) Remove from the heat. Cool slightly.

4 Stir the gelatin into the confectioners' sugar mixture. Incorporate as much as possible and then turn out onto a surface and knead until smooth. It will be sticky for a while but should become like dense modeling clay, not sticky but very pliable. If it's still sticky, add more confectioners' sugar, a little at a time. If it gets too dry, you can add a teaspoon of water (no more!) at a time. It will be very slimy at first, but keep kneading; the water will work into the mixture.

5 Divide the dough into four pieces. Cover tightly with plastic wrap or a plastic bag, being sure to work out any air pockets. Keep the unused portions well covered.

6 Invert a loaf pan and lightly dust outside with cornstarch. Shake off any extra. Set aside.

7 Roll out one piece of the dough to a rectangle a little bigger than 10 inches x 7 inches. (Sprinkle the surface with cornstarch only if the dough is sticking.) If the rolled-out dough starts to dry, moisten (don't wet) a paper towel and rub it over the dough. Trim to 9½ inches x 6½ inches with a sharp knife. Carefully place the dough on the inverted loaf pan and let it drape down the outside of the pan. Gently ease and smooth the piece to fit the shape of the pan. Gently pinch the overhanging sides together at the corners. If you want, make a hole with a skewer through the pinched-together sides about 1 inch from the point. A thin ribbon can be tied through the holes when the box is dry.

8 Repeat with the remaining pieces of dough. Let dry for 24 to 36 hours. Store at room temperature. Place in an airtight container if the humidity increases. These containers keep 3 months.

Tip: *Smooth out any rough edges after it's dry by gently sanding with a clean emery board or fine sandpaper.*

Use this technique with an 8-x-8-inch baking pan to make a bento (or obento) box for the Candy Sushi recipe in Chapter 6.

Beyond basic pastillage

You can make all kinds of interesting variations on the basic pastillage container, and you don't have to let on to the kids that you're really messing around with adult play dough. Here are some ideas to get you started:

✔ Cut the edges with a fluted pastry wheel or clean pinking shears.

✔ Explore your kitchen cabinets for other shapes to use as molds. For example, consider 4¾-inch tartlet pans with removable bottoms. Make sure that they're clean and grease free. New ones are best. Dust the inside of these with cornstarch and shape as you would a pie crust. You can also mold the pastillage over the bottom of a tortilla bowl maker, or a shallow bowl. Or simply drape the dough in a free-form shape over the bottom of a glass.

✔ Sprinkle colored sugar on the surface. Give the dough one more roll to make sure the sugar adheres before shaping.

✔ Sprinkle colored nonpareils on the surface of the dough. Then roll them in.

✔ Tint the dough with food paste coloring.

✔ Try decorating finished pieces with food-safe markers. (See the list of resources in Chapter 18.)

✔ Roll the dough ¼ inch thick and cut with cookie cutters. Pierce a hole for the string at the top of each cookie with a skewer and use for an ornament or gift tag.

Chocolate Nest

Oooh, more chocolate. Just fill this nest (see Figure 14-2) with truffles, and everyone will be ecstatic. Even when the truffles are gone, there's no empty nest syndrome here. Just eat it!

Special equipment: *1½-quart metal bowl (about 8 inches x 3 inches), pastry bag fitted with ½-inch tip*

Preparation time: *40 minutes, plus 2 hours setting time*

Cooking time: *10 minutes*

Yield: *One 8-inch nest*

10 ounces good-quality bittersweet, semisweet, or milk chocolate

1 Invert the bowl and cover the outside with aluminum foil. (Don't use heavy-duty foil.) Use the back of a spoon to smooth out as many of the crinkles as possible because the chocolate can stick to them and crack. Grease lightly with nonstick cooking spray. Set aside.

2 Quick temper the chocolate. Start by finely chopping good-quality dark (bittersweet or semisweet) chocolate. Place about three-fourths of it in the top of a double boiler or bowl over, but not touching, water that's just simmering. Make sure that there isn't any moisture on the spatula and that no steam escapes around the pot. Melt the chocolate to a temperature of 115 degrees for dark chocolate or 110 degrees for milk chocolate. (Use an instant or digital candy thermometer to measure the temperature.) Remove the top of the double boiler or bowl from the heat. Gradually add the remaining chocolate until the temperature reaches 84 degrees for dark chocolate or 82 degrees for milk chocolate. Return the chocolate to the heat and stir until it just reaches 90 degrees for dark chocolate or 88 degrees for milk chocolate. Cool until it starts to thicken but has not set up yet.

3 Pour the chocolate into the pastry bag. Start by squeezing a line of chocolate around the circumference of the bowl about an inch from the lip of the bowl. This gives you a guide to aim for. Now just go to town — zigzag the chocolate all over the bowl. The lines should be a little thick to make it sturdy. The only rule here is the lines have to connect one way or another to hold together. When you're done, smooth and flatten the section on top of the bowl. (This will be the bottom of the chocolate nest when reinverted.) Let the chocolate set about 2 hours.

4 Gently separate the metal bowl from the chocolate nest. Then carefully peel the aluminum foil away from the chocolate nest. Store in a cool, dry place. The bowl will keep for 2 weeks.

Tip: *You can use a resealable plastic bag instead of a pastry bag. Make a small cut across the corner. (You can always make it bigger, but you can't make it smaller.) Drizzle the chocolate back and forth as you would if you were using the pastry bag.*

Vary It! *Before the chocolate has set, sprinkle with nonpareils or colored sugar. Tilt the bowl when sprinkling so that some of the decorations get in the gaps and show on the inside when finished.*

For a truly decadent presentation, apply gold leaf — a microscopically thin sheet of gold (for the source, see the listing for Sweet Celebrations in Chapter 18). You don't have to use much; just apply little touches of gold to the interior of the bowl after the foil has been peeled away.

BUILDING A CHOCOLATE NEST

1. INVERT THE BOWL. COVER THE OUTSIDE WITH ALUMINUM FOIL. USE THE BACK OF A SPOON TO SMOOTH OUT WRINKLES. GREASE LIGHTLY WITH SPRAY SHORTENING.

2. AFTER THE CHOCOLATE HAS BEEN QUICK-TEMPERED AND COOLED, POUR INTO A PASTRY BAG GO TO TOWN! (IT HELPS IF YOU START BY SQUEEZING A LINE AT THE CIRCUMFERENCE, 1" FROM THE BOTTOM. THIS GIVES YOU A GUIDE.) ALL THE LINES SHOULD CONNECT TO HOLD IT TOGETHER!

3. WHEN YOU ARE DONE, SMOOTH AND FLATTEN THE BOTTOM OF THE BOWL. (WHICH WILL BE AT THE BOTTOM WHEN YOU RE-INVERT. SMOOTH AND FLATTEN

4. LET SET 2 HOURS. GENTLY REMOVE THE METAL BOWL, THEN CAREFULLY PEEL OFF THE FOIL.

STORE IT IN A COOL, DRY PLACE.

Figure 14-2: Chocolate Nest.

Shopping for a Few of Your Favorite Things

All right, I confess. I'm a hoarder. I see cute little shopping bags. I buy them — just in case. I see unusual ribbon. I buy it — just in case. And oh, yes, hand-made wrapping paper, remarkable boxes, and odd-colored tissue paper — just in case. Help! Mine is a tough addiction to bring home to a city apartment — but rewarding when people tell me how memorable my packages are.

So here's the point. Having a few containers, bags, or wraps on hand isn't a bad thing. They're convenient for spontaneous gift giving, so try to get in the habit of looking for these things when you're shopping. This section is a guided tour of places to look. You never know what unusual things you may be the first to discover.

Just remember that everything food comes in contact with should be food safe. If you're not sure, wrap the gift in food wrap first.

Craft stores

A really good craft store can be one-stop shopping. Many craft stores now even carry cookie cutters and cake-decorating supplies. Roam the aisles and have fun. You're sure to discover all sorts of boxes, ribbon, baskets, papers, pipe cleaners, crepe paper, twine, raffia, twisties, and doodads. Consider buttons and beads for finishing touches at the end of ribbon. Small silk flowers can be a nice touch. Cruise the frame aisle and look for a small shadow box frame. It can improvise for a "bento" box for Candy Sushi (Chapter 6). Let your imagination do the walking.

Look for little gadgets like ribbon shredders and deckle scissors (scissors like pinking shears that cut interesting edges) to add interesting touches to paper and ribbon.

Don't let your kids have all the fun. Head for the rubber stamps to make special labels or to customize wrapping paper.

Super discount stores

Super discount stores are another place to have fun. Check out the toy department and see what's available in the way of buckets and such. The card departments carry cute little shopping bags. Housewares departments have napkins, mugs, and canisters. If you keep looking, you're bound to come across other ideas.

Gourmet food shops

These shops probably have the "real" food containers. Usually they carry the fancier decorative bottles and French canning jars. These items are great if they fit within your budget.

These stores are great places to shop for ideas. See how the fancy food companies package their stuff. Be inspired by it and then do your own version.

Party goods stores

Seasonal ideas are usually available in party goods stores. Wrapping paper, ribbon, tissue paper, and colorful napkins are standard items. Larger stores have individual cellophane bags, doilies, and gift boxes.

Flea markets and related places

Those immortal words, "One man's junk is another man's food container," should tell you that flea markets are ideal hunting grounds for food containers. Antique stores, garage sales, and tag sales are great sources for potential containers and wrapping items. Beautiful old glass, baskets, advertising containers, linens, bowls, teacups, wine glasses, molds, and crockery are all there for the creating. Try finding old postcards or stickers for labels. Old buttons, odd pieces of crystal, and bits of lace make interesting add-ons.

Make sure that all items are thoroughly cleaned before adding a food gift. Line old baskets with napkins or doilies before placing food in them. Check for any chips or cracks in old glass before putting your food gift in the container.

Your own house

Home is where the heart is, and the starting point for finding recyclables. Reuse unusual glass water bottles (some water companies use colored bottles) by adding a cork and sealing it with paraffin (see Figure 14-3). Reuse pretty tins left over from commercial cookies. You can cut up old greeting cards and use them for tags or appliqués.

Recycle a clean, unrumpled brown bag as a gift bag. Fold over the top. Punch two holes a few inches apart. Insert a ribbon from the back through both holes and tie a bow in front.

Fabric and notions stores

Check out fabric and notions stores if you want to wrap your gift in cloth. Choose a fabric to suit your gift. Whether it's topping a jam jar with a square of gingham or wrapping the whole present in a fabric bundle, consider more than color or pattern. Think about texture, too. Burlap cloth is rustic, chintzes are country, and moirés are elegant. Felt is a good choice if you want to cut out designs and glue on other squares of felt. Don't overlook yarn for tying your gifts. Try twisting a few strands of yarn of different colors together. Consider buttons, tassels, and beads as decorative touches. Larger stores often have a craft section with unfinished boxes. Go wild.

Use pinking shears to notch the edges of fabric used to cover tops of jelly jars.

Stationery and card stores

Paper goods galore are available in stationery and card stores. They always have the usual wrapping paper, tissue, and cards, but more and more stores are expanding their lines to carry little tote bags and tins. The holidays bring new choices for packaging ideas.

If you have a little box that's just the right size but a bit shopworn, you can use it as a pattern to make a new box. Carefully break open the glued seams and unfold the box flat. Trace the edges onto colored poster board or "oak tag" paperboard. Fold and glue the new box with hot glue.

Garden centers and florists

Garden shops stock a lot more than the basic clay pot. They carry all sorts of containers in varying shapes nowadays. Many garden stores also carry patio tableware in all shapes, colors, and sizes. They're also a good source of baskets. Don't overlook dried flowers as a playful touch to a package. If the shop has a floral section or you have a floral supply store in the area, such places can be a good resource for wide rolls of colored foils.

Florist foil is not usually recommended as food safe. Always wrap food in plastic wrap or parchment paper first.

Hardware stores

Look in the paint department for disposable cardboard paint buckets — they're usually white, so you can have free rein to decorate them at will. Empty reusable metal paint buckets are another option. In the plumbing department, buy a short section of PVC pipe. (That's polyvinyl chloride for those of you who have never renovated a house.) Common sizes are 3 inches and 4 inches in diameter. Fill with individually wrapped candies or cookies. Wrap stiff fabric or paper around the pipe and tie the ends like a gigantic party popper. You can achieve the same effect with a large-diameter cardboard tube.

Putting Thought into Your Gifts

Here are a few random thoughts to keep in mind about giving gifts.

✔ Keep the recipient's tastes and preferences in mind, especially if you're including a reusable container. For example, remember that even if you don't really like contemporary decor, the recipient does, so choose a container appropriate for her tastes, not yours.

- ✔ The container in which you give the gift isn't always the best container in which to store the food. Don't forget to mention this fact to the recipient.

- ✔ Date and label food gifts. Tell the recipient how long a gift will last. If you suspect that anyone has a food allergy or if you want to be on the safe side, give a list of ingredients. At the very least, identify whether the gift contains nuts.

- ✔ Keep perishable gifts refrigerated until the last minute before giving. Make sure that the recipient knows that the gift is perishable.

Waxing Poetic

Finishing touches make a gift even more special than it already is. Topping off a bottle of flavored vinegar (Chapter 9) with paraffin serves a double purpose. To the recipient, the bottle will just look beautiful and will probably elicit the comment "It's too pretty to open!" But you'll know the wax also protects the flavor. Dipping a bottle in wax isn't hard, but you do need to exercise caution because paraffin is highly flammable. Take a look at Figure 14-3, and follow these steps:

1. **Place a piece of paraffin, about 1½ to 2 inches, in a clean, dry tin can.** (Remember that you have to dip a bottleneck in the can, so don't use a can that's too small or narrow.) Take crayon in a color that your kids no longer think is cool, remove the paper, and add the crayon to the paraffin. The amount of crayon you need to add will vary depending on the intensity of color you want to achieve and the number of bottles dipped.

2. **Place the can in a small saucepan. Partially fill the saucepan with water.** You may have to hold the can with a potholder or tongs to keep it from floating. Bring the water to a simmer and stir the paraffin with a disposable spoon or a wooden stick from a frozen treat. Remove from the heat when almost melted.

3. **Carefully remove the can from the water. Hold the can with a potholder or tongs and invert the bottle into the paraffin, tipping the can if necessary. Cover the cork and about ½ inch of the neck. Allow to cool.** Redip to ensure a total seal.

Here are a couple of words of caution about using paraffin: Don't allow the paraffin to smoke and don't use your microwave to heat the paraffin.

DIPPING BOTTLES IN PARAFFIN

1. PLACE A PIECE OF PARAFFIN IN A CLEAN, DRY TIN CAN. ADD A COLORED CRAYON TO THE PARAFFIN.

2. PLACE THE CAN IN A SMALL SAUCEPAN. FILL THE SAUCEPAN WITH WATER, PARTWAY, UP THE CAN & BRING TO A SIMMER. STIR WITH A DISPOSABLE SPOON OR POPSICLE STICK.

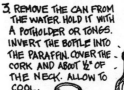

3. REMOVE THE CAN FROM THE WATER. HOLD IT WITH A POTHOLDER OR TONGS. INVERT THE BOTTLE INTO THE PARAFFIN. COVER THE CORK AND ABOUT ½" OF THE NECK. ALLOW TO COOL.

REDIP TO ENSURE A PROPER SEAL.

Figure 14-3:
Waxing a
bottle top.

Chapter 15

Over the River and Through the Woods: Delivering the Goods

● ●

In This Chapter

▶ Deciding what to carry and what to send

▶ Packing smart

▶ Mailing your gift

● ●

Grandmas are a lot cooler now than they used to be. Come Christmas, yours may be in the Bahamas sitting under a festooned palm tree. So, obviously, hand carrying a bag of goodies to her is out of the question.

Delivering gifts to your offspring is equally challenging. Kids go to camp in one direction, to college in another direction, and across the country to find a job. Even though we all stay in touch through cyberspace, you know from reading *Gifts from the Kitchen For Dummies* that there is a better way. A home-made present of food doesn't simply reach out and touch someone; it gives them a great big hug.

Okay, you've gone to a lot of trouble shopping, schlepping, chopping, beating, cleaning, measuring, and baking. All that's left is the packing and . . . waiting in line at the post office. You are, indeed, a truly wonderful person.

Some Gifts Travel Easily and Some Don't

The fragile and frail are not good travelers. They would prefer to go next door to a neighbor. But the bold and the brave will go anywhere. The lists in this chapter will give you an idea about the shipability of recipes in this book.

Cream puffs — they like to be hand carried

The following gifts don't ship well. Some need to be kept refrigerated, and some would never arrive in one piece via commercial delivery.

- Chocolate Truffles (Chapter 5)
- White Chocolate Coeur à la Crème (Chapter 5)
- Alive-and-Kicking Chocolate Gateau (Chapter 5)
- Triumvirate of Chocolate Sauces (Chapter 5)
- Toast-of-the-Town Big Apples on a Stick (Chapter 6)
- Crispy Cappuccino Froths (Chapter 7)
- Lemon-Cardamom Shortbread (Chapter 7)
- Fortune Cookies (Chapter 7)
- Frico Cheese Crisps (Chapter 7)
- Happy Hubby Steak Sauce (Chapter 8)
- Blissful Blueberry Citrus Syrup (Chapter 8)
- Pear-Cranberry Compote (Chapter 8)
- Scallion Butter (Chapter 8)
- Hot Diggity Dog Relish (Chapter 9)
- Grainy Apricot Mustard (Chapter 9)
- Banana-Mango Chutney (Chapter 9)
- Strawberry-Pineapple Jam (Chapter 9)
- Rhubarb-Fig Conserve (Chapter 9)
- Sweet Onion Marmalade (Chapter 9)
- Scarborough Fair Herb Jelly (Chapter 9)
- Orange Cannoli Pie (Chapter 10)
- Lemon-Lime Icebox Pie (Chapter 10)
- Plum-Almond Tart (Chapter 10)
- Pineapple-Ginger Scones (Chapter 11)
- Prosciutto-Fig Quick Bread (Chapter 11)

✔ Jumbo Pretzels (Chapter 11)

✔ Red Pepper Hummus (Chapter 12)

✔ South-of-Somewhere Salsa (Chapter 12)

✔ Shrimp in Green-Sauce Dip (Chapter 12)

✔ Downtown Lox Spread (Chapter 12)

✔ Uptown Smoked Salmon Spread (Chapter 12)

✔ Pâté 101 (Chapter 12)

✔ Marinated Olives (Chapter 12)

✔ Provençal Cheese and Olive Bites (Chapter 12)

✔ Layered Goat Cheese Mold (Chapter 12)

✔ Pastillage Containers (Chapter 14)

✔ Chocolate Nest (Chapter 14)

Good sports — they do their best to arrive intact

All these items are okay to ship even though physical size or freshness may be concerns.

✔ Not-So-Basic Brownies (Chapter 5)

✔ Peanut Butter and Chocolate Dimple Cupcakes (Chapter 5)

✔ Eggnog Cookies (Chapter 7)

✔ Flavored Oils (Chapter 9)

✔ Flavored Vinegars (Chapter 9)

✔ Pecan-Cream Cheese Pound Cake (Chapter 10)

✔ Buttermilk-Streusel Coffee Cake (Chapter 10)

✔ Banana-Blueberry Bread (Chapter 11)

✔ Chili-Cheese Muffin Loaf (Chapter 11)

✔ Cranberry-Walnut Monkey Bread (Chapter 11)

✔ Oat and Ale Bread (Chapter 11)

✔ Pepparkakor Bowl (Chapter 14)

MVPs — they deliver consistently

- 1-2-3 Milk Chocolate Chunky Clusters (Chapter 5)
- O.M.G. Fudge (Chapter 5)
- Freckled Chocolate, Cinnamon, and Hazelnut Biscotti (Chapter 5)
- No-Bake Black Forest Bites (Chapter 5)
- Easy Alabaster Mints (Chapter 6)
- Benne Seed Candy (Chapter 6)
- Microwave Kaffee Klatsch Nut Candy (Chapter 6)
- Candy Sushi (Chapter 6)
- Balsamic Vinegar Candy (Chapter 6)
- Piña Colada Candies (Chapter 6)
- Tea Party Sugar Cubes (Chapter 6)
- Anzac Granola Bars (Chapter 7)
- Almond and Date Mandelbrot (Chapter 7)
- Savory Walnut-Pepper Digestives (Chapter 7)
- Fido's Fetching Bones (Chapter 7)
- Vanilla-Flavored Sugar (Chapter 8)
- Bountiful Fruitcake with Almond Paste "Wrapping Paper" (Chapter 10)
- Curried Cashews (Chapter 12)
- Barbecue Almonds (Chapter 12)
- All the mixes in Chapter 13

Packing the Gift

Listen to insurance agents and they'll lead you to believe that you can never have too much protection. Keep that in mind when you pack your food gifts. Remember these general pointers:

✔ The first layer of wrapping should be around the food itself. Make sure that it is sealed for freshness, particularly if you aren't using an airtight container. Individually wrap brownies in plastic wrap before layering them in a box. Doing so helps keep them fresh and serves as added insurance against crumbling.

✔ Place sheets of wax paper between layers of cookies or candies. You can also help prevent shifting in the box by placing one final layer of wax paper on top of the food. Then loosely wad tissue paper and place it on top. Use just enough to assert a little pressure, not enough to mash down the food. Close the lid gently.

✔ Decorative tins are good choices for shipping because, in addition to being air tight, they're rigid.

✔ Double up on boxes. After you place your gift in a sturdy gift box, fit that into a bigger, rigid, corrugated shipping box. Leave plenty of room on all four sides, as well as the top and bottom of the box to add protective buffers. Use material that's available — crumpled newspaper, recycled packing peanuts — but don't skimp.

Use plenty of filler in between the two boxes. Yours will not be the only box on the plane. Your Peanut Butter and Chocolate Dimple Cupcakes could wind up under the Encyclopedia Britannica.

✔ If you choose to send a jar or bottle, wrap a few extra layers of bubble wrap around it before you proceed with the packing. The U.S. Postal Service doesn't want everyone's packages soaked with your homemade flavored oil.

✔ Put a card with the recipient's address on the inside of the box . . . just in case.

✔ Enclose a little note with the name of the gift and, if appropriate, how to enjoy it.

✔ Seal the package with a strong packing tape, not regular adhesive tape.

✔ Put a strip of clear packing tape over the address on the outside of the box to keep the address from smearing. There's always a chance it could wind up sitting on a runway while Hurricane Brunhilda blows through.

✔ Clearly mark it "Fragile" or "Handle with Care."

Up, Up, and Away

Here are a few more hints about sending food gifts:

- ✔ Invest in overnight shipping if you can. You made the gift. It cost you ingredients and time. So try to get it there as fresh as possible.

- ✔ Consider sending something other than chocolate in the warmer months. Even if you send chocolates overnight, your package still sits over hot runways and roadways some of the time.

- ✔ If you're considering sending a gift overseas, first find out about delivery schedules to the destination country. Then decide what to make. If you're mailing at the holidays, be sure to find out what the last mailing day is to ensure arrival by the holiday.

Even if something happens along the way and your food gift needs a facelift at the arrival end, it will still taste great and be totally appreciated by the recipient. And, as everyone knows, broken food contains no calories, or at least it shouldn't.

Part VI
The Part of Tens

The 5th Wave By Rich Tennant

"Look, Brother Dom Perignon, the nuns really enjoy your sparkling mayonnaise and blanc de turnip soup. But is there anything else you can think off to do with these grapes."

In this part . . .

Every *For Dummies* book contains this part, the Part of Tens — quick takes on a variety of topics that complement the other chapters. Chapter 16, for example, suggests ten ideas for theme baskets you can put together as creative settings for your food gifts. Chapters 17 and 18 invite you to surf the Web for cooking supplies, wrappings, and equipment that's not available locally. To borrow a slogan, let your fingers do the walking!

Chapter 16

Ten Great Gift Baskets

● ●

In This Chapter

▶ Wrapping your food gifts with personality

▶ Coming up with themes for special times and special people

● ●

Good for you — you took time away from a busy schedule to do something really nice for someone. You made a gift from the kitchen, which is always a winning recipe. But maybe you want to be a little more grandiose. Consider the possibilities of a gift basket — a one-of-a-kind present that speaks louder than words. Be serious. Be silly. Be inventive. But above all, have fun. This chapter contains ideas for ten great gift baskets that will get your creative juices flowing.

Guys' Night

Know a sports fan suffering from those cruel symptoms of post-season withdrawal? Make a batch of Barbecue Almonds (Chapter 12) and bag them up with a video of football's greatest bloopers. That should ease the pain a little.

Midnight Icebox Raid

Have a friend who insists on staying up to watch the late-night talk shows? Bake a pan of Anzac Granola Bars (Chapter 7) or Crispy Cappucino Froths (Chapter 7) and stash them in an old cookie jar from a flea market or garage sale. Then the commercials won't seem quite so long.

Visit a City Friend

Someone trapped in the hot city in August? No problem. For starters, fill a bottle with Berry Berry Vinegar (Chapter 9). Grab a head of lettuce and some crispy fresh vegetables from your garden. Toss in a salad spinner to round out the offering, and you're ready to bring a little country cool to a friend living in a world of concrete and steel.

Sunday Brunch

Did the first beautiful weekend of summer finally arrive? Deliver a crock of Uptown Smoked Salmon Spread (Chapter 12), a packet of Bloody Mary Mix (Chapter 13), and the Sunday paper. The recipient will be pampered with a delicious, lazy day in the hammock.

Young at Heart

Is someone approaching an "older than they'd like to admit" birthday? Give a blowout gift of Triumvirate of Chocolate Sauces (Chapter 5), a set of ice cream dishes, an ice-cream scoop, and an ice cream maker. Rekindle the indulgence of youth.

Dashing thru the Snow

Do you know an avid cross-country skier, a snow bunny, a parent who watches ice-skating practice, or anyone else who may need his or her internal temperature raised a few notches? Give your cold comrade some Thai Bean Soup Mix (Chapter 13) Mix along with a thermos and a lap robe. That will warm body and soul.

Gay Paree

You say a friend is about to leave for a life-long dream vacation to the City of Lights? Start the excitement with a ramekin of Pâté 101 (Chapter 12), a French-translation dictionary, and an Edith Piaff CD. Au revoir!

Right-O

Has a friend just returned from a life-long dream vacation to the other side of the pond? Prolong the happy memory with a batch of Pineapple-Ginger Scones (Chapter 11). Pair the scones with a teapot, a selection of teas, and a book of Keats's odes. Settle in and listen to tales of the adventurer's travels.

Home on the Range

Looking for a little something for your resident grill master? Everyone seems to be an expert when it comes to grilling, but even if your intended recipient can't roast a hotdog, try giving a bottle of Happy Hubby Steak Sauce (Chapter 8), a flameproof barbecue mitt, and a set of steak knives. But remember: Superstition says that if you give someone a knife, he or she has to give you a coin so as not to "cut" the friendship.

Girls' Night Out

Everyone needs a good cry once in awhile, don't they? Roll some Chocolate Truffles (Chapter 5) in cocoa and deliver them with a video of *Love Story*. Of course, include a box of tissues.

Chapter 17

Ten-Plus Web Sites to Shop for Food and Inspiration

- -

In This Chapter

▶ Finding mail-order sources for hard-to-find ingredients
▶ Surfing around the culinary world

- -

*I*f your supermarket is big on charm but short on choices, the wide-wide epicurean world is just a few clicks away. Here are some catalog stores to call or shop on the Web. The market will come to your doorstep.

Penzeys Spices

P.O. Box 933
Muskego, Wisconsin 53150
Phone: 800-741-7787; 414-679-7207
Web site: www.penzeys.com
Fax: 414-679-7878

This catalog and Web site contains a mind-boggling selection of high-quality spices and herbs. Wide arrays of seasoning mixes are also available as well as items like double-strength vanilla extract. Penzeys is a trip around the world without leaving your favorite armchair or your computer desk. Just sit back and read the spice descriptions.

The Baker's Catalog

P.O. Box 876
Norwich, Vermont 05055
Phone: 800-827-6836
Web site: www.bakerscatalogue.com

The King Arthur's Flours catalog of baking equipment, ingredients, and tools is a treasure. You can find dried fruits, nuts, chocolates, and flavorings as well as pans, thermometers, and measuring utensils. And, of course, virtually any flour. Check out their catalog or Web site for a schedule of free two-hour baking classes. (They carry Lyle's Golden Syrup, used in Deep Dark Chocolate Sauce in Chapter 5.)

EthnicGrocer.com

162 W. Hubbard Street
Chicago, Illinois 60610
Phone: 877-611-3846
Web site: www.ethnicgrocer.com

Visit this site, and you can shop by product or by nation. A whole universe of delightful culinary choices opens up to you. The folks at EthnicGrocer.com carry ingredients from the Middle East, Japan, Germany, and Mexico — just to name a few locations. One highlight is an interesting selection of stuffed olives, vinegars, and condiments. The site also features some ethnic, specialty cookware. (They carry Lyle's Golden Syrup.)

Chef Shop.com

Phone: 877-337-2491
Web site: www.chefshop.com

An interesting selection of honey, pastas, and baking ingredients are just the beginning of the goods carried by this diverse purveyor. Happily roam the e-aisles and be inspired by the array of ingredients.

Ideal Cheese Shop

942 1st Avenue (at 52nd Street)
New York, New York 10022
Phone: 800-382-0109
Web site: www.idealcheese.com

One of New York's most respected cheese stores will deliver an amazing array of cheeses to your home. The Ideal Cheese shop features, you guessed it, cheese from 17 different countries (including Cyprus). The store also has specialty meats and a good selection of olives. Ed (the owner) has a message board where he will happily answer all your questions.

Murray's Cheese Shop

257 Bleeker Street
New York, New York 10014
Phone: 888-692-4339
Web site: www.murrayscheese.com

This highly regarded shop has been established for 61 years and carries over 250 cheeses, including some from Australia. Located in Greenwich Village, Murray's has a number of cheese samplers in a range of prices. The Web site includes a question section and a lot of information about cheese.

Kalustyan's

123 Lexington Avenue
New York, New York 10016
Phone: 212-685-3451
Web site: www.kalustyans.com

This site is a veritable treasure trove of goodies. Choose from categories that include beans, flours, coconuts, olives, nuts, spices, and oils. And if you're totally stressed out in the kitchen, Kalustyan's carries a few dozen varieties of incense.

Dean & Deluca

560 Broadway
New York, New York 10012
Phone: 800-221-7714
Web site: www.deandeluca.com

This culinary standard-bearer in New York City's Soho district offers a first-rate selection of oils, vinegars, cheeses, pâtés, exotic teas, coffees, and on, and on, and on. Dean & Deluca also has some cooking equipment and knives. This shop is definitely worth a visit if you're traveling that way. (They sell quince paste, which is also known as membrillo.)

Skinner's Nuts

Phone: 800-233-5856
Web site: www.skinnersnuts.com

Nuts, nuts, and more nuts. This company has just about every nut in every shape and size. This is the place to find raw or roasted hazelnuts, pepitas, or pignoli. Skinner's Nuts also has a huge assortment of dried fruits, including cantaloupe and mango.

Chocosphere

Phone: 877-992-4626
Web site: www.chocosphere.com

Oh yum — a grown-up candy store! Chocosphere carries lots and lots of fine, imported chocolates and some domestic chocolates too. Brands like Valrhona, Callebaut, Schokinag, El Rey, and Scharffen-Berger mark a few of the offerings. Gel packs are available at an extra charge for warm-weather delivery.

Wellcat.com

Web site: www.wellcat.com

I list this site under food resources because, well, it's food for thought. Anybody out there besides me remember this inscription from grade-school autograph books? (Do they still have autograph books?) "Can't think, brains dumb. Inspiration won't come. Rotten ink, bad pen. Good luck, Amen." If you feel that way, here's the site for you. When you visit it, click on Wellcat Quirky Holidays, which contains lots of made-up holidays as the rationale for a food gift.

Chapter 18

Ten-Plus Places to Buy Cooking Gear and Wrapping Supplies

"**S**urfing the Net" is the common phrase. But to me, "casting a Net" seems more appropriate. A wealth of resources is swimming around out there. All you have to do is toss out a line and make your catch of essential baking, cooking, wrapping, and shipping items.

Bridge Kitchenware

214 East 52nd Street
New York, New York 10022
Phone: 212-688-4220; 800-274-3435 (orders only)
Web site: www.bridgekitchenware.com

One of the venerable establishments for high-quality baking and cooking equipment, Bridge Kitchenware was selling to professional kitchens long before celebrity chefs became a household term. Now anyone can have a field day checking out all the supplies these folks offer. Visit the Web site or send for a catalog. And if you come to the Big Apple, the storefront is worth a visit.

Surfas

8825 National Boulevard
Culver City, California 90232
Phone: 310-559-4770
Web site: www.surfasonline.com

The motto at Surfas is "a chef's paradise," and from what I can see, the description is pretty accurate. Surfas carries a full line of baking equipment and a nice selection of ingredients. The company doesn't have a catalog, but its Web site promises a new, fully stocked site later in 2002. If you e-mail them, the customer-service folks will gladly help you find any item not listed yet on the site.

Sweet Celebrations

P.O. Box 39426
Edina, Minnesota 55439
Phone: 800-328-6722; 952-943-1508
Web site: www.sweetc.com

And how. Sweet Celebrations has just about everything you could possibly want to decorate a cake — sprinkles, dragées, sugar, and glitter in every shape and color imaginable, plus pans, tools, pastry bags, and tips. And did I mention the really great assortment of bags, boxes, cups, and colored foils to wrap your goodies in? Candy molds and cookie cutters abound as well as a nice selection of chocolate and flavorings. (For things recommended in this book, Sweet Celebrations carries the #100 scoop, Chapters 5, 6, and 7; caramel-apple bags, Chapter 6; digital thermometers, Chapters 6 and 11; and edible gold leaf for Chocolate Nest, Chapter 14.)

Kitchen Krafts

P.O. Box 442
Waukon, Iowa 52172
Phone: 800-776-0575
Web site: www.kitchenkrafts.com

Kitchen Krafts is another gem of a catalog full of hard-to-find ingredients, supplies, and tools. The catalog and Web site has a good selection of candy-making equipment including lollipop and candy molds and thermometers.

The baking equipment and pastry tips are sure to provide inspiration. The catalog and site also include a very good supply of canning equipment and jars as well as spice jars, vinegar bottles, and candy boxes. (For things recommended in this book, Kitchen Krafts carries digital thermometers, Chapters 6 and 11; pastry cloths, Chapter 10; food-safe magic markers, Chapter 14; and tart pans, Chapters 10 and 11.)

Cooking.com

2850 Ocean Park Boulevard
Suite 310
Santa Monica, California 90405
Phone: 800-663-8810
Web site: www.cooking.com

Just a wonderful Web site — what else can I say? It's chock full of every imaginable gadget, tool, and thingamajig. The site also features lots of useful information and buying guides. A catalog is due out soon. (It carries an olive pitter, useful in Chapter 12.)

GM Cake and Candy Supplies

824 Cincinnati Avenue
Xenia, Ohio 45385
Phone: 937-372-3205; 937-372-5272
Fax: 877-372-5720
Web site: www.cybercakes.com

Bingo! Another great site. It's loaded with supplies for making and wrapping candies and baked goods. (For things recommended in this book, these folks have florist colored-foil wrap, which isn't approved by the U.S. Food and Drug Administration.)

Sur La Table

1765 Sixth Avenue South
Seattle, Washington 98134
Phone: 800-243-0852
Web site: www.surlatable.com

From kitchen to table, this catalog has fine equipment with which to cook, as well as beautiful dishes to accentuate your handiwork. The catalog includes everything from kitchen aids to knives and baking pans in addition to interesting ethnic utensils. Sur La Table carries two different sizes of paper loaf pans that are great for "bake and give" goodies. The canning jars and glass flasks are nice, and the company's textured napkins make nice liners for gift packages. (Sur La Table carries microplane graters, mentioned in Chapters 3 and 8.)

Williams-Sonoma

P.O. Box 7456
San Francisco, California 94120
Phone: 800-541-2233
Web site: www.williams-sonoma.com

One of the original cooking catalogs, Williams-Sonoma maintains its high quality. Frequently published catalogs always have something new and exciting as well as the basic kitchen equipment. The catalogs often have some choice ingredients and appealing containers for wrapping.

Cookie Cutter Collectibles

P.O. Box 1021
Dover, Arkansas 72837
Phone: 800-711-8544
Web site: www.coppercutters.com

This site has 400 copper cookie cutters to contemplate. These cookie-cutter enthusiasts will even make up custom cutters — including one of your child's hand.

The Container Store

2000 Valwood Parkway
Dallas, Texas 75234
Phone: 800-733-3532
Web site: www.containerstore.com

The Container Store is the place to find delightful containers of all shapes, sizes, and materials. Use your imagination and think outside of the box by looking in other sections of the catalog and Web site (besides food) for small containers to give. The selection of glass jars is extensive, and The Container Store is a good source for heavy-duty shipping boxes.

Buygiftbox.com

Phone: 800-644-5678, Ext. 111
Web site: www.buygiftbox.com

You can find some good, basic, wrapping supplies here. The site includes ribbons and tissue paper with holiday themes and patterns for almost any occasion. A selection of assorted boxes in various sizes comes in red, white, or kraft (natural). They also have shopping bags and sturdy "gabled" boxes with handles, which are great for cookies and quick breads.

RibbonShop.com

Phone: 877-742-5142
Web site: www.ribbonshop.com

Ribbons in every size, texture, and width are what you can find at this site. Just for starters, it has sheer, holiday, metallic, and wire-edged ribbons as well as netting. You can ask for up to three samples to verify color. The company also has a catalog.

Bags & Bows

Phone: 800-225-8155
Web site: www.bagsandbowsonline.com

The bad news is this is a wholesale catalog. The good news is that if you can get a few people together, friends or a church group maybe, you can get some great wrapping stuff at good prices. You can also have the bags or boxes customized for your group. And the catalog does contain a few things that are affordable by one person — like the organdy bags.

Gift Box of America

405 North 75th Avenue
Building 3, Suite 184
Phoenix, AZ 85043
Phone: 800-GIFTBOX
Web site: www.800giftbox.com

This is another wholesale company that requires a minimum purchase. The people here couldn't be more delightful, and they have an amazing selection. Maybe this is the time you want to invest in your own "signature" tote bag.

Index

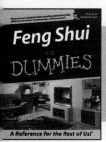

FOR

DUMMIES®

Plain-English solutions for everyday challenges

OME & BUSINESS COMPUTER BASICS

0-7645-0838-5

0-7645-1663-9

0-7645-1548-9

Also available:

Excel 2002 All-in-One Desk
Reference For Dummies
(0-7645-1794-5)

Office XP 9-in-1 Desk
Reference For Dummies
(0-7645-0819-9)

PCs All-in-One Desk
Reference For Dummies
(0-7645-0791-5)

Troubleshooting Your PC
For Dummies
(0-7645-1669-8)

Upgrading & Fixing PCs For
Dummies
(0-7645-1665-5)

Windows XP For Dummies
(0-7645-0893-8)

Windows XP For Dummies
Quick Reference
(0-7645-0897-0)

Word 2002 For Dummies
(0-7645-0839-3)

TERNET & DIGITAL MEDIA

0-7645-0894-6

0-7645-1642-6

0-7645-1664-7

Also available:

CD and DVD Recording
For Dummies
(0-7645-1627-2)

Digital Photography
All-in-One Desk Reference
For Dummies
(0-7645-1800-3)

eBay For Dummies
(0-7645-1642-6)

Genealogy Online For
Dummies
(0-7645-0807-5)

Internet All-in-One Desk
Reference For Dummies
(0-7645-1659-0)

Internet For Dummies
Quick Reference
(0-7645-1645-0)

Internet Privacy For Dummies
(0-7645-0846-6)

Paint Shop Pro For Dummies
(0-7645-2440-2)

Photo Retouching &
Restoration For Dummies
(0-7645-1662-0)

Photoshop Elements For
Dummies
(0-7645-1675-2)

Scanners For Dummies
(0-7645-0783-4)

Get smart! Visit www.dummies.com

- **Find listings of even more Dummies titles**

- **Browse online articles, excerpts, and how-to's**

- **Sign up for daily or weekly e-mail tips**

- **Check out Dummies fitness videos and other products**

- **Order from our online bookstore**

FOR DUMMIES®

Helping you expand your horizons and realize your potential